Praise for *The Financial Times Guide to Saving and Investing for Retirement*

'A complex set of vital concepts written in an easy to follow and comprehensive way. Really useful.'

Richard Butcher, Managing Director, PTL, award-winning professional pension trustee

'Yoram Lustig's work provides a comprehensive framework for savings, investment and consumption in the real world during different phases of one's life-cycle. A must-read for every individual.'

Professor Narayan Y. Naik, Professor of Finance and Co-Head of Finance Department, London Business School

'An invaluable and very comprehensive guide to help in making such a crucial lifestyle decision.'

Nigel Stapleton, Chair of Trustees, National Grid UK Pension Scheme

'Clear, concise and erudite. Yoram Lustig cuts through the noise to give you the practitioner's insight on developing and implementing a robust financial plan.'

Nick Bartlett, CFA, Director of Education, CFA UK

'It seems that the investment and savings' landscape gets more complex by the day, so there is a clear need for Yoram's excellent book. Anyone that is serious about their financial health should read this guide.'

Professor Andrew Clare, Chair in Asset Management, Cass Business School

'Millions of savers look forward to retireme⟩ prospect of planning for their retirement. Th⟩ of all the key elements anyone who takes t⟩ consider. It covers them with great balance ⟩ making the challenge one which ordinary p⟩ anyone whether they are 20, 60 or 80 to read this book. It will make their retirement much more financially enjoyable.'

Lawrence Gosling, ⟩roup Editorial *Dire* ⟩nal Pensions

525 343 98 7

THE FINANCIAL TIMES GUIDE TO SAVING AND INVESTING FOR RETIREMENT

••

THE DEFINITIVE HANDBOOK TO SECURING YOUR FINANCIAL FUTURE

YORAM LUSTIG

PEARSON

Harlow, England • London • New York • Boston • San Francisco • Toronto • Sydney
Auckland • Singapore • Hong Kong • Tokyo • Seoul • Taipei • New Delhi
Cape Town • São Paulo • Mexico City • Madrid • Amsterdam • Munich • Paris • Milan

PEARSON EDUCATION LIMITED
Edinburgh Gate
Harlow CM20 2JE
United Kingdom
Tel: +44 (0)1279 623623
Web: www.pearson.com/uk

First published 2016 (print and electronic)

© Yoram Lustig 2016 (print and electronic)

Contains public sector information licensed under the Open Government Licence (OGL) v3.0. http://www.nationalarchives.gov.uk/doc/open-government-licence/version/3/.

Pearson Education is not responsible for the content of third-party internet sites.

ISBN: 978-1-292-12929-7 (print)
     978-1-292-12931-0 (PDF)
     978-1-292-12932-7 (ePub)

British Library Cataloguing-in-Publication Data
A catalogue record for the print edition is available from the British Library

Library of Congress Cataloging-in-Publication Data
A catalog record for the print edition is available from the Library of Congress

10 9 8 7 6 5 4 3 2 1
20 19 18 17 16

Cover image: © Peter Dazeley/Getty Images

Print edition typeset in 9/13pt Stone Serif ITC Pro by SPi Global
Printed in Great Britain by Henry Ling Ltd, at the Dorset Press, Dorchester, Dorset

NOTE THAT ANY PAGE CROSS REFERENCES REFER TO THE PRINT EDITION

CONTENTS

ABOUT THE AUTHOR

Yoram Lustig is a multi-asset portfolio manager and author. He has been professionally managing assets since 2002 and writing since 2012.

In 2013 he joined AXA Investment Managers as Head of Multi-Asset Investments UK, experiencing innovative investment techniques, such as outcome-oriented, risk premia, smart beta and factor investing. From 2009 to 2012 he was Head of Multi-Asset Funds at Aviva Investors, managing over £60 billion, focusing on institutional investors. From 2002 to 2009 he was Head of Portfolio Construction at Merrill Lynch, managing multi-asset discretionary portfolios for wealthy individuals. He began his career in 1998 as a lawyer.

Yoram's previous books, *Multi-Asset Investing: A Practical Guide to Modern Portfolio Management* and the award-winning *The Investment Assets Handbook: A Definitive Practical Guide to Asset Classes*, were published by Harriman House in 2013 and 2014. His first book was translated to simplified Chinese in 2015 and translation of his second book is a work-in-progress.

He was awarded the Chartered Advisor in Philanthropy (CAP) designation in 2007; the Professional Risk Manager (PRM) certification in 2005; the Chartered Financial Analyst (CFA) designation in 2004; an MBA from London Business School in 2002; and a law degree from Tel Aviv University in 1997. He is admitted to both the Israel and New York State Bars. When younger, he studied Electrical Engineering for two years in the Technion – Israel Institute of Technology.

Yoram lives in London; he's married and is a father of two young children.

PREFACE

'An investment in knowledge pays the best interest.'

Benjamin Franklin

Why did I write this book?

One of the biggest risks many of us face in modern society is running out of money after retirement. This might be nothing less than a personal tragedy. People may work their entire life, accumulating wealth for a comfortable retirement, just to discover it is insufficient. And they realise it when it is too late to do anything about it. Minimising this risk is this book's foremost objective.

The meeting of a long-term trend and a recent development in the UK was my motivation for writing this book. The long-term trend is the diminishing defined benefit (DB or final salary) pensions and growing defined contribution (DC or money purchase) pensions. The scales are shifting. For the first time, the number of members in DC schemes surpassed that in DB schemes in the UK. Consequently, most long-term savers must assume responsibility for saving for their retirement.

The saying, 'If I am not for myself, then who will be for me?' reflects the current pension situation. If you do not take care of yourself, nobody will do it for you. It is up to you now. You are responsible.

The recent development in the UK was **pension freedom** day in April 2015. Savers are no longer obliged to buy an **annuity** when retiring; they have freedom to do as they see fit with their savings. With freedom comes responsibility.

It is your choice to buy a Ferrari with your savings when retiring. Nobody will stop you. But will you have enough assets left to support you for the rest of your life?

In the current low-yield world, cash deposits and bonds are inadequate to generate sufficient returns to assure financial security for you and your loved ones. You must invest. You need your money to work hard, making more money. Putting your money under a mattress is not enough.

This book fills a gap. Many savers in the UK lack professional advice and understanding of saving and investing – the two activities you must diligently do. This book aims to help.

Another, more privileged group of savers does have access to professional advice. But this group's members do not have time or resources to learn about saving and investing to challenge the advice.

Saving for retirement is too important to leave unchallenged. This book offers the tools to comprehend the advice. It does so in a concise, non-technical and simple way.

I have summarised in this book everything I wished I knew on saving and investing 15 years ago. It aims to cover all you need to know about saving and investing, but did not know which questions to ask and how to find the answers.

Why should you read this book?

Typically, if you are employed, your employer and, perhaps, you contribute regularly into a pension. If self-employed, you need to make your own pension arrangements.

If you are a member of a DC pension, you need to choose how to invest your contributions. This can be a demanding, even daunting task. However, whether you like it or not, financial security post-retirement might depend on the amount you have managed to save during your working life.

You may be actively managing your pension or oblivious to how it is invested. If the former, you are probably interested in investing. If the latter, you should start taking interest in investing. The reason is simple: without growing your savings through appropriate investing, you are unlikely to achieve your financial goals.

Some savers could not care less about their pension. Whenever a letter or an email concerning their pension arrives, they do not even bother opening it. This is especially true for young people. When you are young, retirement is such a distant affair. When you are 25, the age of 65 seems like a million years away. But it arrives sooner than expected. And, when it arrives, you had better be prepared.

Not having sufficient money in your pension pot when retiring might be a grievous problem. That is, unless you have a time machine to go back and start saving early. Who knows, perhaps by the time we retire that would be possible. But, until then, we need to save.

If you do not mind surviving cold winters without heating or buying value ranges in supermarkets, budgeting every penny you spend, then do not worry about saving for retirement. If I have succeeded in frightening you, I have accomplished my first mission: generating a sense of urgency about saving for retirement. To enjoy comfortable golden years, read on. It is probably not too late.

This book guides you on what you really need know about saving and investing for your pension. It covers the essential information to make informed saving and investment decisions.

My aim is to keep it as simple as possible. It is intended for non-investment professionals. I tried to source all the information from free internet websites for easy access. Whenever jargon is used, it is explained to build your vocabulary, allowing you to grasp the cryptic professional mumbo-jumbo.

The book includes numerous notes, covering sources, calculations and adding extra curriculum material, for those who are interested. Skip them and the technical stuff, if you want.

If I convince you to take action, start saving as early as possible and help you to make some good decisions, one day you will be glad to have read this book.

Planning for your financial future is a paramount assignment. I cannot stress it enough. I recommend you take professional advice; this book is not replacing it. Do-it-yourself books are not the answer for everything. When you are sick, you go and see a doctor. Generally, you do not read a book or Wikipedia or try to treat yourself.

Nevertheless, no doctor knows better than you how you feel. Similarly, this book should equip you with the basic knowledge about saving and investing.

Finally, this book's goal is not to show you how to get rich from investing. This rarely happens in real life. I would take books claiming to hold the secret for finding riches through DIY investing with a big pinch of salt.

The aim here is to save and invest prudently towards genuine financial goals following a structured and disciplined investment process. The ambition is teaching you to do it like a pro. We will try to make some extra money along the way. But that is not the top priority. It requires skill and luck. *'An ounce of luck is worth more than a stone of wisdom.'*

Good luck!

ACKNOWLEDGEMENTS

I thank those who have supported and inspired me over the years – my dear colleagues, friends and family, especially my lovely wife Mika, my wonderful children Yoav and Yael, as well as my mother-in-law Eliya and my father-in-law Shuki Weinstein, whose fascination with pensions was infectious.

I thank the endorsers and really appreciate their kind words. I would also like to thank the team at Pearson including Lisa Robinson, Natasha Whelan, Sarah Owens, Sue Gard and, in particular, Christopher Cudmore. Chris patiently helped with simplifying, which is much harder than complicating.

Writing a book on pensions during ever changing regulations and financial markets is challenging. Keep yourself educated since some stuff in the book will become outdated soon.

Last, but certainly not least, I thank you, my reader. An author without readers is a body without a soul.

Publisher's acknowledgements

We are grateful to the following for permission to reproduce copyright material:

'Factor in the changing investment cycles', *Financial Times*, 14/05/2014 (Stevenson, D), © The Financial Times Limited. All Rights Reserved; 'Retirement savings: how much is enough?', *Financial Times*, 19/08/2015 (Evans, J.), © The Financial Times Limited. All Rights Reserved; 'Saving for retirement is the new cool, *Financial Times*, 18/05/2014 (Grene, S.), © The Financial Times Limited. All Rights Reserved; 'Wealthy investors' alternative decision, *Financial Times*, 25/03/2014 (Suter, C.), © The Financial Times Limited. All Rights Reserved.

I dedicate this book to my beloved father, Haim Lustig (1933–2014), and mother, Esther Lustig, may she live long. Not because I need, not because I want, but because I feel.

CHAPTER 1
WHY SHOULD YOU SAVE FOR RETIREMENT?

Act today for a better future

'You can be young without money, but you can't be old without it.'

Tennessee Williams

Introduction

Why should you save for your pension? If you are reading this, you probably know the answer; it is obvious. When you work, earning an income, you have a regular source of money. You spend it on essentials, such as food, housing and education. You spend it on recreational activities, such as holidays, hobbies and entertainment.

After retiring, you still need a source of income to maintain a decent standard of living. You want to enjoy your retirement. If you have your health and wealth, being a pensioner can be sweet. You can take a long trip, pick up a new hobby and enjoy the dividends on your children – your grandchildren. Having enough money allows you to be a cool grandparent. This is the reason to save all your working life. Simply put, act today to secure your financial future.

In the past, most workers were members of **defined benefit** (DB) pensions. A DB pension (**final salary**) pays its pensioners a monthly income for the rest of their lives. The income is determined through either a formula considering some average of their salaries whilst they were working or the amounts they and their employer paid into the plan during their career.

Pensioners do not need to worry about how to invest the amount saved in their pension. The company or employer offering the DB pension (**sponsor**) assumes the risks. If the pensioner lives longer than expected (**longevity risk**), the sponsor pays more. The sponsor guarantees the income. If assets in the pension are not enough, it is the sponsor's liability. The sponsor needs to top up the shortfall. This is **sponsor risk**.

The pensioner's risk is the sponsor's insolvency – the sponsor can go bust, unable to make pension payments. The word *guaranteed* in financial services always comes with small print.

Since sponsors could not or did not want to take the liabilities and risks of DB pensions, many schemes closed to new members. This means the DB scheme continues to pay to its pensioners and will pay to existing members when they retire. But it does not accept new members and, in some cases, existing members stop accumulating benefits. Instead of DB pensions, employers now often offer **defined contribution** (DC) pensions.

Typically, in DC pensions, the employer and, perhaps, the employee contribute a percentage of the employee's salary into the plan every month.[1] Contributions are exempt from income tax as they come out of gross salary. If the member makes additional contributions or is self-employed and contributes to a pension, a **tax relief** ensures the contributions are tax-free. Whilst within the pension, interest and capital gains are tax-exempt.

DC pensions incentivise saving with truly valuable tax benefits.

But there is a catch. Once the money is in the DC pension, your responsibility is how to invest it. If you do not choose how to invest, in some cases the money may be invested in a **default fund**. If your investment choices or the default fund perform poorly, when you retire the pension pot might be insufficient to sustain your desired standard of living. You are accountable; neither a sponsor nor the Government. There are no safety nets.

Another catch is that only when retired, normally at least at the age of 55, you can access the money in the pension. In effect, pensions force long-term saving in a tax-efficient way. That is not bad – you cannot blow the money on a red Ferrari when having a midlife crisis.

When retiring and starting to draw retirement benefits, you can take a quarter (25%) of the money immediately as a tax-free **lump sum**. As for the remainder, take it when you wish. However, it is taxed at your marginal tax rate every tax year, so you should pace the drawings, minimising your tax bill.

Since you can live long and prosper after retirement, you must decide what to do with your pension in order to have enough to support you for the rest of your life.

And that is it.

Your employer does not need to pay you any income, unless you are a member of a DB pension. You bear all the risks of how much money is in your DC pension and whether it is adequate for the rest of your life. Do not expect anyone to save you, neither your employer nor the Government. Currently, **State Pension** is probably less than £119.30 a week, which is hardly sufficient. It is entirely up to you.

New UK legislation makes it mandatory for every employer with at least one member of staff to **automatically enrol** all eligible employees to a **workplace pension scheme**, unless they opt out, and to contribute towards it. Often, employees are not even aware they are members of a pension and their savings are invested in a default fund.

A default investment strategy may be appropriate.[2] However, it is designed to meet the common objectives of most savers. You may have different financial needs and often it does not adapt to your changing circumstances. Therefore, you should and can make your own saving and investment decisions.

Pensions are a crucial issue on a global proportion. In many developed countries, such as the UK, the USA, Germany and Japan, the population is aging. People live longer and low fertility rates mean families are now smaller than in the past. The workforce is shrinking whilst the retired populace is growing. State pensions are running into bigger deficits. The burden of paying into pensions is becoming heavier.

Maintaining DB plans is more difficult and rare. Too many people are not saving enough or at all in their DC pensions. If people do not start taking saving seriously, the world will head towards a global pension crisis. Only by increasing the awareness of pensions and taking action can we all alleviate this crisis.[3]

Article 1.1

1.4m risk inadequate retirement income, says report

By Josephine Cumbo, Pensions Correspondent

Financial Times, 16 March 2015

Up to 1.4m people are at risk of not having enough income in retirement as they are given the freedom to spend their savings as they wish, warns a new report.

The study, published just weeks before radical pension reforms are due to come into force, examined how the policy change will affect retirement income levels for pensioners over the next three decades.

The new freedoms will allow people aged 55 and over new flexibility to take savings in a defined contributions (DC) pension as a cash lump sum, with no requirement to turn the pot into an annuity.

Due to low savings levels, 1.1m people in England risk not having an adequate income in retirement, even if they bought an annuity with a DC pension pot, the report warns – that is, unless they claim additional pensioner benefits, or use their non-pension assets, such as savings or investments.

Up to 1.4m in total run the risk of inadequate retirement income, if they "blow" their pension pot on big ticket items such as a car or a holiday.

"Evidence from abroad suggests that consumers in countries that have liberalised retirement income markets often squander their hard earned savings, favouring consumption today rather than smoothing it over their lifetime," said Baroness Sally Greengross, chief executive of the International Longevity Centre-UK, which prepared the report.

"And while recent UK consumer research has shown that those approaching retirement would favour a guaranteed income for life, many consumers are confused about what their options are and have low levels of financial capability.

"The potential for a mismatch between what people might want and the products and services they ultimately access with their money is high."

The report assessed retirement income adequacy using the "replacement rate", which is a ratio of income before and after retirement.

The report found average projected replacement rates would be almost 70% if savings were annuitised, or less than 40% if the savings were blown on big ticket items.

"While we do not advocate that everyone should take a particular course of action, our analysis clearly highlights the benefits of annuitising for those individuals who have a high concentration of wealth in DC savings," said Ben Franklin, senior research fellow with the ILC-UK.

"Annuities are generally misunderstood and the group who stand to lose the most from spending everything too early also score relatively poorly on financial capability, making them particularly susceptible to poor decision making. Without the appropriate support including a new default strategy, these individuals could end up significantly worse off in retirement."

Saving and investing

This book covers two topics: saving and investing.

On saving, we will review throughout the book how you can tax-efficiently save for your retirement. The focus is on pensions, Individual Saving Accounts (ISAs) and residential property.

The three main points on saving are:

- Start saving early and regularly.
- Maximise tax-efficient savings.
- Buying property with a mortgage is a type of saving as well as investing. Paying off your mortgage forces disciplined saving.

Chapter 2 introduces the background for savings, including taxes, ISAs and pensions, and Chapter 11 is dedicated to residential property.

On investing, we will review what you should know to design and manage your investment portfolio. When managing investments it is helpful to follow an **investment management process**. It is a framework of all the steps and considerations at each step. By following a process, you will know what to do now, what to do next and what your endgame is. It adds structure and discipline, aiming to minimise emotions and poor investor behaviour.

The process spans four steps:

- Establishing objectives.
- Setting an investment strategy.
- Implementing a solution.
- Reviewing.

The book's chapters on investing follow the order of this four-step process, which forms a roadmap for the book.

Always start with **establishing objectives**. Investment objectives represent your financial goals and needs. Think what outcome you want to achieve from investing, what risks you can take and what the constraints are. The desired outcome must be aligned with the risk level and fit the constraints; otherwise, it is not achievable.

For example, you want an average return of 8% per year with a risk of not losing more than 5% in any year and a constraint that your time horizon is two years. Alas, this does not work.

Unless you are lucky, to generate an 8% average return you need to accept higher risk over a longer time horizon. A more realistic set of objectives is an annual 5% average return with a risk of not losing more than 10% in 19 out of 20 years over a 10-year time horizon.

One of this book's aims is to help you formulate your realistic investment objectives and decide which expectations are reasonable and which are not. Saving and investing require trade-offs. The target value of your portfolio at retirement, the income you plan to draw from it after retirement and your life expectancy all compel trade-offs to minimise the risk of running out of money.

Your investment objectives are personal – they fit your unique financial needs, tailored to your specific circumstances. As your circumstances change during life, so do your objectives – they are not static.

When young you may seek high returns and accept high risk. As you get older and approach retirement your objectives change. You may accept lower risk since you cannot afford large losses just before stopping work. When retired your objectives may switch to seeking regular income from your portfolio with modest growth, emphasising capital preservation and keeping pace with inflation.

The minimum is reviewing your objectives at important milestones in life.

Chapters 3, 4 and 5 cover how to establish return and risk objectives and investment constraints.

The second step in the investment management process is **setting an investment strategy**. Investment strategy is the plan of what you are going to do to maximise the chances of meeting your investment objectives. The strategy must be aligned with objectives.

Formulating a strategy needs an understanding of the characteristics of the investments available to you and how to blend them at different phases of your life. The strategy is dynamic. It should change with your objectives and market conditions.

Chapters 6 to 15 review how to formulate an investment strategy, the characteristics of major asset classes and how to mix them to form an asset allocation matching your objectives.

The third step in the investment management process is **implementing a solution**. Here, you translate your strategy into a portfolio of actual investments. You select and buy securities or funds.

The implementation step also includes portfolio maintenance. For example, periodically rebalancing your portfolio to keep it aligned with your strategy and managing cash flows.

Chapters 16 to 22 go over how to implement your solution, including active asset allocation, selecting investments and managing your portfolio.

The fourth and final step of the investment management process is **reviewing**. In this step you review everything. You monitor the performance of your portfolio and funds. You assess whether it is on the right track towards achieving your objectives. You think whether your objectives and strategy are still valid or need updating. And you follow financial market conditions, deciding whether the characteristics of investments have changed.

The key is to be dynamic and adapt to the changing environment, including both your personal circumstances and general market and economic conditions. The entire process is a never-ending loop. You need to follow all the steps cyclically, ensuring everything is up to date.

Chapter 23 covers reviewing.

Investing is probabilistic, not deterministic. Nothing is guaranteed or certain. All you can do is make the best decisions with the information available to you at the time of making them. Doing so increases the probability of success. Tax-efficient saving and a disciplined investing approach can prevail despite adversity.

Summary

- The shift from DB to DC pensions means more people assume responsibility for saving and investing for retirement.
- The three main points on saving are: (1) start early and save regularly; (2) take advantage of tax-efficient saving in your pension and ISAs; and (3) buy property with a mortgage if it is appropriate for you to do so.
- On investing, follow a four-step investment management process of: (1) establishing objectives; (2) setting an investment strategy; (3) implementing a solution; and (4) reviewing.
- The process is never-ending, as everything needs reviewing and updating as and when necessary.

Notes

1 According to the 2014 'Occupational Pension Schemes Survey' run by the Office for National Statistics, for private sector DC schemes, the average contribution rate was 2.9% for members (employees) and 6.1% for employers.

2 Default funds normally aim to offer a diversified investment strategy with a minimum charge. This usually means static asset allocation and using passive index trackers. This might be inappropriate for all investors, missing opportunities to enhance returns through active management.

3 For free and impartial guidance on workplace and personal pensions contact The Pensions Advisory Service (TPAS) at **www.pensionsadvisoryservice.org.uk**. Pension Wise at **www.pensionwise.gov.uk** provides guidance on DC pensions. The Government plans to merge TPAS and Pension Wise to create a new pension guidance body.

CHAPTER 2
SAVING FOR YOUR RETIREMENT
Savings in the UK

'Twenty years from now you will be more disappointed by the things that you didn't do than the ones you did do.'

Mark Twain

Saving for retirement is central to your financial plan. It means avoiding spending a portion of your income today, accumulating it and spending it in the future after retiring. In other words, it is giving up consumption today for future consumption.

Saving is not easy. It requires discipline, self-control and long-term vision. It involves taking some of your disposable income and, instead of enjoying it, putting it away for many years. When retired, your quality of life probably depends on your savings. It is as simple and as important as that.

Psychologist Walter Mischel conducted a series of studies over 50 years ago called the **marshmallow experiment**. Children sat in a room alone and were offered one marshmallow immediately or two marshmallows if they waited 15 minutes. About 25% of children passed the test, resisting immediate satisfaction. They had self-control and ability to delay gratification.

Later, studies found that those who passed the test were more likely to do well academically and socially than those who did not. They did better at overcoming problems in life; they were more successful in their career and were less likely to suffer from obesity, alcoholism and drug abuse.

Not only do you need to delay some satisfaction all your life, by saving for retirement, but also pension freedom means a possibility of instant gratification when you retire – you can take your savings and spend them. This calls for extra discipline and self-control.

The objective of saving for retirement is for your money's value to grow as much as possible over the long term. However, you cannot just forget about it. Rather, you need to take good care of it so it grows well.

First, think about the income you will need to live on in retirement. Next, consider how long you will need that income to keep coming in. Finally, calculate how much you need to save to generate that income for the expected period.

The amount of money you accumulate is a function of four variables:

1 **Contributions.** When saving, you make contributions into your saving pot. For example, regular contributions from your income or lump sums if you get a bonus. It is a balance between consumption today and contributions.[1]

2 **Growth.** Savings earn interest or generate income and capital gains through investing. Growth is measured in real terms, above the rate of inflation. The trade-off between growth rate and investment risk is one of this book's main focuses.

3 **Time.** More time enables more contributions and allows interest and investments to work longer. Start saving and investing as early as possible and delay retirement for as long as possible.

4 **Costs and charges.** Expenses, including taxes and fees, reduce savings. Be as stingy as possible with costs and charges without compromising the quality of your savings and investments. We will review some practical ways to do this.

We will explore three main saving channels: ISAs, pensions and paying off mortgages on residential property. This chapter details ISAs and pensions. Chapter 11 focuses on residential property.

Admittedly, this chapter includes some boring material, such as taxes. If you wish, skip it and come back to it later. The reason to start with it is not to put you off reading the rest of the book, but rather to first understand tax fundamentals. Taxes have a huge impact on savings and wealth. Understanding how taxes work helps minimise them.

Consider getting professional advice on taxes. This book does not replace such advice. It scratches the surface of the delightful world of taxes. It does not include, for example, any creative tax-avoidance schemes or estate planning.

Tax-efficient investment schemes

Tax-efficient investment schemes include the Enterprise Investment Scheme (EIS) and the Seed Enterprise Investment Scheme (SEIS). They are designed to help small companies to raise capital by offering a range of tax reliefs to investors who purchase shares in those companies, such as an income tax relief equal to 30% of the sum invested. A guide on EIS and SEIS is available at **www.gov.uk**. Another scheme is Venture Capital Trusts (VCTs).

The Venture Capital Schemes Manual (VCM) is available at **www.hmrc.gov.uk**. It contains guidance on a group of schemes and reliefs aiming to encourage investment in small companies.

These schemes may be valuable for tax-efficient investing for high earners, in particular after ISA and pension allowances have been used. However, they are a high-risk investment. Discuss with your adviser and ensure everything you do is legal.

A free, impartial, clear and concise information source on savings, pensions, taxes and much more is available at **www.gov.uk**.

Income tax and Capital Gains Tax

'The hardest thing to understand in the world is the income tax.'

Albert Einstein

We begin with a review of income, dividend and capital gains tax. The reason to start with taxes is that to appreciate the tax benefits of tax-efficient saving wrappers, such as ISAs and pensions, first we need to understand taxes. Before finding a solution, understand the problem.

Income tax

You can put savings in your bank savings account. However, its major disadvantage is tax. When earning interest on savings in the UK, you pay income tax.

The standard tax-free **Personal Allowance** is £11,000 for each tax year (£11,500 from April 2017).[2] Income, interest on savings and rental profits above the Personal Allowance are taxed, depending on how much of them fall within each tax band.[3,4] The UK follows a **progressive tax system**, taking a larger percentage from the income of high-income earners than it does from low-income individuals.

For income, including interest and rental profits, up to £32,000 above the Personal Allowance (£33,500 from April 2017), the **basic rate** is 20%. For income between

£32,001 (£33,501 from April 2017) above the Personal Allowance and £150,000, the **higher rate** is 40%. And for income over £150,000 the **additional rate** is 45%.

If you are a basic-rate taxpayer with up to £1,000 interest on savings, your bank or building society will pay it tax-free. If you are a basic- or higher-rate tax payer with interest on savings above the **Personal Savings Allowance** (see endnote 3) HMRC will collect the tax due by changing your tax code. If you fill in **Self Assessment**, carry on doing so to calculate and confirm your taxes on savings.

If you are a higher-rate taxpayer, for example, every additional £1 you earn as interest on savings above £500 falls under the higher rate. So, 40 pence goes to the taxperson, leaving you 60 pence. Now, wouldn't it be nice to keep the whole £1 to yourself?

Paying 45%, 40% or even 20% on interest and income is significant. When saving for multiple years, this really bites into your savings.

For example, you have saved £100,000, you earn 5% annual interest and you are on the higher tax band (40%). In 10 years' time, you earn *gross* interest of £62,900.[5] Your *net* after tax interest is £40,124.[6] You 'lost' £22,766. Isn't that a shame?

Dividend tax

Since April 2016 tax on dividends from stocks (shares) has changed. The first £5,000 of dividend income in each tax year is tax-free (**Dividend Allowance**). Above it, basic-rate taxpayers pay tax at a 7.5% rate, higher-rate taxpayers at 32.5% and additional-rate taxpayers at 38.1%.

No tax is deducted at source. You must use Self Assessment to pay the tax due. Dividend income is still eligible for Personal Allowance. For example, if you receive £17,000 dividend income, Personal Allowance covers the first £11,000 and Dividend Allowance another £5,000. You will pay dividend tax only on £1,000. Dividends earned in ISAs and pensions are not taxed.

Capital Gains Tax (CGT)

CGT is levied on profits you make when disposing of assets that have increased in value.

You do not pay CGT if your profits in the tax year are below your tax-free CGT allowance, called **Annual Exempt Amount** (different from Personal Allowance). The Annual Exempt Amount is £11,100 or £5,550 for assets held in a trust.[7]

Disposing of an asset includes selling it, gifting it (except to your spouse, civil partner or charity), swapping it or getting compensation for it, such as insurance if it was lost or destroyed.

CGT is levied on **chargeable assets**. These include personal possessions worth over £6,000 apart from your car; property that is not your main home; your main home if you let it, use it for business or it is very large; investments (stocks, units in unit trusts, and certain bonds but excluding UK Government gilts, **Premium Bonds** and Qualifying Corporate Bonds); and business assets.

Premium Bonds

Premium Bonds are a savings account with an interest rate decided by a monthly tax-free prize draw. They are offered by the National Savings & Investments (NS&I), a UK state-owned savings bank.

Winnings on lottery and gambling prizes (such as football pools, horse racing and proceeds of spread betting) are also tax-free.

When holding assets overseas you may need to pay CGT when disposing of them. There are special rules for UK residents who are **non-domiciled** (non-dom status).

CGT rate is 20% for higher or additional-rate taxpayers. It is 10% or 20% for basic-rate taxpayers, depending on their capital gains and income. An additional 8% surcharge applies to residential property, so the rates are 18% and 28%.

You can reduce your total taxable gains by deducting certain costs of buying, selling or improving chargeable assets. Also, if you make a loss in a tax year (**allowable losses**) you can reduce gains and carry forward unused losses to a future tax year.[8]

Report capital gains, cost deductions and losses in your Self Assessment.

For example, you bought a Van Gogh painting for £200,000 and sold it for £250,000. Your gain is £50,000. You incurred costs of £6,000 when buying and selling the painting, such as the auction house's fees. Your net gain (**chargeable gain**) is £44,000.[9] Your *taxable gain* is £32,900, which is the chargeable gain minus the Annual Exempt Amount of £11,100.

If your total income (including salary, interest and rental profits) is more than £43,001 (£45,001 from April 2017) you are a higher-rate taxpayer.[10] Your entire taxable gain is taxed at 20% and your CGT is £6,580.[11]

If your total income is below £43,001 (£45,001 from April 2017) you are a basic-rate taxpayer. Some or all of your taxable gain is taxed at 10%.

For example, your total income is £30,000 meaning £13,001 of your basic-rate band is available.[12] The first £13,001 of your taxable gain is taxed at 10% and the rest at 20%. You pay total CGT of £5,280.[13]

This is not as complicated as it seems. When completing Self Assessment online, HM Revenue & Customs (HMRC) calculates your taxes, as long as you input the correct figures. Keep records of all your gains and expenses to make Self Assessment quick and easy. Keep records of your Self Assessments for at least six years.

Tax-efficient savings

Taxes are a hefty charge on savings and investments. Minimising them can save a fortune.

It does make sense to keep some cash in your current and savings bank accounts. You need cash for everyday life and a cash reserve for emergencies.

How much cash do you need as a reserve?

The old rule of thumb calls for easy-to-access cash covering three to six months of expenses. However, it depends on two considerations. First, how long it would take you to land a job if you lost your current one. If it would take about six months, keep cash on hand for at least six months of expenses. Second, it depends on how financially secure you feel. Build your stash to your comfort level.

If you are saving for the long term, shelter as much as you possibly can from tax. The British Government gives two simple and quite generous ways to do so: ISAs and pensions.

ISAs

An ISA is a tax-efficient account.[14] It is not a deposit or an investment. Rather, it holds or wraps within it savings or investments – it is a wrapper.

ISAs allow tax-free saving. At present you can save up to £15,240 each tax year in ISAs (£20,000 from April 2017), choosing between two types: **cash ISAs** and **stocks and shares ISAs**. As long as your savings are in ISAs you pay no taxes on interest, income and capital gains. You do not declare any interest or profits on your ISAs in your tax return. It is all completely tax-free.

You can save the entire £15,240 (£20,000 from April 2017) in one ISA or split it between a cash ISA and a stocks and shares ISA, however you want. You can save in your ISAs any time during the tax year.

Cash ISAs enable you to save with banks, building societies and some National Savings & Investments products. Stocks and shares ISAs enable you to invest in stocks, unit trusts, investment funds, corporate bonds and government bonds.[15]

ISAs are flexible, giving easy access to your money. You can make a withdrawal from your ISAs at any time without losing your tax benefits. You do not pay any taxes when withdrawing money.

Since April 2016 ISAs have become more flexible. Savers are now able to withdraw cash from cash ISAs and stocks and shares ISAs and put it back in in the same tax year without losing their tax entitlement. This enables savers to hold emergency cash in ISAs.

ISAs are transferable. You can transfer them from one provider to another or a cash ISA to a stocks and shares ISA and vice versa.

Like every other financial product, shop around for the best ISA deal. For cash ISAs consider interest rates, whether it is a fixed (check notice or term) or variable rate and what the charges are. For stocks and shares ISAs consider available investments and charges.

If you are unhappy with your ISA provider, switch. Your provider and you are in a business relationship, not a friendship. It is nothing personal. However, mind the potential costs of transferring ISAs.

Transferring cash ISAs normally should not cost you anything, but there could be penalties, in particular on fixed rate ISAs. Also, your money can spend up to 15 working days moving between providers, not earning interest during this time.

Transferring stocks and shares ISAs might incur costs of closing an account and transaction costs of selling and buying investments. Your investments could be sold or bought at the wrong time and spend time out of the market.

ISAs are great to save and invest within a tax shelter. Use your entire ISA allowance every tax year, do not lose it. Even if you do not want to invest, park the money in cash ISAs, transferring it to stocks and shares ISAs when deciding to invest.

Here is an example to demonstrate ISAs' benefits. Assume you are a higher-rate tax-payer, saving £10,000 every year. You can choose between a taxable savings account, offering an annual 3% gross interest rate, or a cash ISA, offering a 3% tax-free annual interest rate. After 20 years you save £242,481 in your savings account and £276,765 in your cash ISA. That is an extra £34,284 in the ISA because you did not pay income tax.[16]

A new **Lifetime ISA** (Lisa) will be available from April 2017, allowing savers under 40 to save up to £4,000 a year until the age of 50 and receive a government bonus of 25% on their savings, up to £1,000 a year. You can use the savings to buy a first home (worth up to £450,000) at any time from 12 months after opening the account or withdraw them tax-free from the age of 60 (withdrawal under other circumstances will lose the government bonus and incur a 5% charge on the remainder).

Pensions

Pension choices in the UK are plentiful. Understanding the different types of schemes, each with its advantages and disadvantages, will help you choose one suitable for your circumstances, investment style and needs.

Pension savings focus on efficient tax planning, minimising charges and enhancing investment returns. When drawing from your pension also plan to minimise taxes. To do so, know your legal rights and obligations.

The Pensions Advisory Service (TPAS) at **www.pensionsadvisoryservice.org.uk** provides free, independent and impartial information and guidance on pensions.

Defined benefit (DB) pensions

Are you a member of a DB pension?

A DB scheme is normally a valuable and increasingly exceptional benefit.

Calculate the income you are expected to receive from your DB pension. Normally, income is calculated using a formula, considering three variables:

1 **Pensionable service.** The number of years you have been a member of the scheme.
2 **Pensionable earnings.** This could be your **final salary**, an average of some of your salaries over your career (**career average**) or another formula.
3 **Accrual rate.** The percentage of the pensionable earnings you receive as a pension for each year of pensionable service. Typically, it is 1/60 or 1/80.

For example, if your pensionable service was 20 years, your pensionable earnings are £40,000 and the accrual rate is 1.67%, your annual pension income is £13,333.[17] That is gross £1,111 per month and £1,072 net of income tax (£1,081 from April 2017).[18]

Your benefits may be linked to inflation or increase by a set amount. Often, benefits increase by Limited Price Indexation (LPI): usually annual inflation rate, capped at 2.5% or 5%, with a floor of 0%. However, this is not mandatory. If benefits are not linked to inflation, their *real* value diminishes over time, in particular when inflation is high.

Normally, you can take benefits from the age of 65. Some schemes allow you to start taking benefits from 55, but this usually reduces your pension income. You may take benefits without retiring. You may be able to defer taking benefits, possibly increasing them. When you die, your spouse, civil partner and dependents typically get paid a fixed percentage from your benefits (commonly 50%).

Taking your pension as a lump sum may be possible when reaching 55. Up to 25% of the sum is tax-free; the rest is taxed.

The **Pension Protection Fund** protects DB schemes. This should cover cases where the sponsor becomes insolvent or the scheme does not have enough assets to pay benefits. However, the protection might not cover the full amount.

Boosting DB pensions

You can boost your expected benefits through **additional voluntary contribution** (AVC) and **free-standing additional voluntary contribution** (FSAVC) schemes.

AVC schemes may be offered by employers, letting employees on DB schemes contribute to DC schemes or buy additional pensionable service in their DB scheme.[19] FSAVC schemes are not connected to any employer. They are DC schemes offered by insurance companies.

The sum of your employer's contributions into your DB and your additional contribution into AVC/FSAVC schemes need to fall under your **annual allowance** to enjoy a **tax-relief**. These concepts are explained later.

If you are in a private-sector DB pension or a funded public-sector scheme you can transfer to a DC scheme if you are not already taking benefits.[20] This is rarely a good idea. It could be a good idea if: you want to retire early and avoid your DB scheme's penalties; you want to retire late and wish to invest your money in a DC pension; you have ill health and do not expect benefits for long from your DB pension; you are single so no spouse will benefit from your DB pension; or, based on your lifestyle, you do not want income.

Defined Contribution (DC) pensions

If you are not a member of a DB pension, save in a DC pension, which is a 'wrapper' to hold your investments until you retire and start drawing income.

Are you employed or self-employed? If you are employed, your employer should arrange a **workplace pension** for you. If you are self-employed, arrange a **stakeholder** or **personal pension** for yourself.

In the next sections we will review different DC schemes, clarifying the terminology.

Workplace pension

A workplace pension (**occupational** or **company pension**) typically is arranged and provided by large employers.[21] Often, they make contributions into the pension. You can also contribute into it.

Multi-employer pension

Since October 2012, a new system of **automatic enrolment** for workplace pensions has been phased in.[22] By 2018 most workers will automatically be made members of a workplace pension and employers will pay in contributions on the employees' behalf. Currently, contributions are relatively modest, but it is planned to ratchet them up over coming years. The employer chooses the scheme, which must meet minimum standards. In many cases, employers use a multi-employer pension (**master trust**).

Some employers offer their own workplace pension. A **multi-employer pension** works like a workplace pension but it is provided by an organisation that is not the employer (**pension provider** or **pension administrator**).

NEST pension

NEST (National Employment Savings Trust) is a low-cost pension you can join through your workplace or if you are self-employed. NEST is a DC workplace pension master trust set up by the Government. Many employers are likely to choose NEST for auto enrolment. Check **www.nestpensions.org.uk.**

Personal pension

In a personal pension you choose the administrator and arrange for your contributions to be paid into the pension. You can choose investments from a range of funds offered by the provider. If you do not have a workplace pension, use a personal pension.

Personal pensions may be offered through your employer. These are called **group personal pensions** (GPP). The employer selects the pension administrator, but the pension is an individual contract between you and the provider.

If you change jobs, your GPP usually is converted automatically into a personal pension and you can continue paying into it independently. Check whether your new employer offers a pension and compare it with your GPP. Focus on charges and available investments. You can stop paying into the GPP, paying into your new pension instead, or transfer your old GPP into the new pension.

Stakeholder pensions

Stakeholder pensions are a type of a personal pension. They must meet minimum standards set by the Government, including low and flexible minimum contributions, capped charges, charge-free transfers among investments and a default investment strategy if you do not select your investments.

Employers offering a stakeholder pension select the pension administrator and may arrange for contributions to be paid out of your wages or salary. Employers may contribute to the scheme. You can set up a stakeholder pension for yourself. It is suitable if you are self-employed or on a low income.

SIPP

A **self-invested personal pension** (SIPP) is suitable for experienced investors. SIPPs are designed for people choosing and managing their investments. SIPPs allow freedom to deal with your investments and switch among them when you want.

SIPP is the preferred pension to manage your own investments. When choosing a SIPP, always shop around.[23] Different providers offer different investment choices and charges. You want the widest choice for the lowest charge.

If you have a number of DC pensions, consider consolidating them. It can make it easier to manage and charges could be lower when having more money invested with a single provider. However, consider any transfer charges and exit penalties.

If you have changed jobs over the years and lost track of your DC and DB pensions, the following steps can help:

1   List all the companies for which you worked.

2   Check correspondence on pensions.

3   Contact their human resources (HR), asking for info on your pensions.

4   Use the Government's free **Pension Tracing Service** at www.gov.uk/find-lost-pension.

Retirement age and drawing income

The retirement age in the UK is 55 – that is pretty young.[24] You can access your DC pension in any way you wish from that age.

You can take your whole pension pot as a **lump sum**. A quarter (25%) is tax-free (called **pension commencement lump sum** – PCLS) whilst the rest is subject to tax at your income tax rate. A large lump sum can move you into a high tax bracket for the tax year, meaning it is an inefficient tax plan.[25]

You can take the tax-free lump sum whenever you want after the age of 55. You can use it for a well-deserved holiday or pay off debt. Keeping the money in the pension, however, allows it to continue growing, sheltered from tax. You can choose to take either the first 25% of your pension tax-free or 25% of each withdrawal tax-free. The latter option is more tax-efficient, especially if your pension portfolio grows over time.

Consider taking up to a quarter as a tax-free lump sum, using the rest to withdraw lump sums as and when you need, drawing regular taxable income (**income drawdown**) and/or buying a taxable retirement guaranteed income, known as **annuity**. They are subject to tax at your normal marginal tax rate during each tax year.

When you want to start drawing income, you can transfer your pot into **Flexible-Access Drawdown** (FAD). You can choose to delay taking money out – you do not have to buy an annuity or transfer to FAD. The untouched pot is called uncrystallised funds. You can make one-off cash withdrawals from your uncrystallised funds, known as **uncrystallised funds pension lump sum** (UFPLS, pronounced 'ufplus').

Drawdown describes accounts where, typically, most of the money remains invested but savers can take cash out regularly or as needed. **Phased retirement** is a process of taking your pension assets in stages. By using only part of the accumulated pension savings each year, you create a tax-efficient income stream.

National Insurance Contributions (NICs) are not levied on pension income, including the tax-free lump sum.

Advice

Pension Wise (www.pensionwise.gov.uk), a service offered by the Pensions Advisory Service and Citizens Advice, offers free and impartial guidance. Pension Wise cannot advise which option is best for you or how to invest your pension savings.

Consult a regulated financial adviser. Use the website **www.unbiased.co.uk** to find one. Financial advisers charge a fee for their services. However, there are more details and subtleties to pensions than what is covered briefly here. They may be pertinent to your specific circumstances. Seek advice but use your own common sense.

Self-employed and State Pension

Being self-employed, you need to arrange your own pension. No employer arranges it for you. There are no employer's contributions. And irregular income patterns can make regular saving difficult.

Whether self-employed or employed, you may be eligible for basic **State Pension**. Currently, the full basic State Pension is set at £119.30 a week (£6,204 a year). Getting the full amount requires 30 years of NICs.

People retiring on or after 6 April 2016 (men who were born on or after 6 April 1951 and women who were born on or after 6 April 1953), can be eligible for the **new State Pension**. Its full amount is £155.65 a week (£8,094 a year).

The simplified new State Pension replaces the current system that includes top-ups, such as pension credit for people on a low income. In theory, everyone can eventually get the same amount. However, in reality, there will be wide variations in payments since you need 35 years of NICs to qualify for the full amount.

Calculate your expected State Pension based on current law at **www.gov.uk/calculate-state-pension**. **State Pension age** is not the same as retirement age. Check your State Pension age at **www.gov.uk/state-pension-age**.

And that is it. That is what you get from State Pension, unless for example you had periods of unemployment during your working life or you are eligible for **Pension Credit** if retired on a low income. State Pension is unlikely to be sufficient to maintain your current standard of living. So it is crucial you save for retirement.

Tax relief, annual and lifetime allowance

Your employer's contributions into your pension are tax-free since they are deducted from your pre-tax pay. HMRC tops up your contributions into a pension as part of income **tax relief**. If you are a basic-rate taxpayer, for every £100 you contribute into your pension, HMRC adds an extra £25.[26] This is the advantage of pensions over ISAs.

However, tax on pensions might transform in the future. Instead of the current tax-exempt contributions and investment roll up and tax when withdrawing (EET), it might change to tax on contributions and exempt investing and withdrawing (TEE, like an ISA). This is dubbed pension ISA.

Pension administrators typically claim tax relief at the basic rate, add it to your pension and invest it within two to six weeks. If you are a higher-rate or additional-rate taxpayer, claim the additional rebate through your tax return. You will get the rebate directly; it will not be added to your pension. After reaching the age of 75, no tax relief is granted on contributions. Tax relief may change in the future, moving to a flat rate for everyone, instead of a rate equal to your marginal tax rate.

Starting as early as possible to save in your pension allows you to benefit more from contributions, tax relief, growth through investing and compounding.

For example, you contribute £100 per month for 40 years from the age of 25 to 65. You are a basic-rate taxpayer (HMRC tops up each £100 contribution by £25). Assuming 5% average annual investment return and an annual charge of 0.75%, your pension pot will grow to £154,693. Without tax relief, the pension pot would grow to £123,754, so that's an extra £30,938 due to tax relief.

Starting 20 years later and contributing £200 per month, your pension pot will grow to only £93,784 with the tax relief. By starting 20 years later, you saved nearly £30,000 less, even when doubling your contributions.

You can contribute into your pension as much as you want each year. However, there is a limit on the amount for which you get a tax relief. The maximum yearly amount benefiting from a tax relief is called **annual allowance**. Currently, it is £40,000 (including your and your employer's contributions). From April 2016, your **lifetime allowance** (LTA) is £1 million, including contributions and investment growth (if you are a high earner read endnote 27).[27] If the value of your pension pot tops the LTA, you could be hit with a tax penalty when accessing the pot or when reaching age 75.

No tax relief is awarded on higher amounts. However, you can **carry forward unused allowance** from three previous years.

If your income varies from year to year, use unused allowances to maximise your pension savings in years when your income is high.[28] Even with unused annual allowance carried forward, tax relief is limited to your annual income for the specific year. If you save more than your annual allowance, you may have to pay a **tax charge**, which is added to your taxable income through your Self Assessment and taxed at your marginal tax rate.

Pension payments follow 12-month **input periods**. These do not follow the tax year and may differ if you pay into different schemes. The tax year in which an input period ends determines the annual allowance that is applied.

If you can, use your entire annual allowance. Carry forward any unused tax allowance from the previous three years. After three years, unused annual allowance is lost forever.

For example, in 2015 you contribute £20,000 to your pension, not using £20,000 of your £40,000 annual allowance. In 2016 your annual salary is raised to £45,000. You live like a hermit and want to contribute as much as possible to your pension. Although you carry forward £20,000 unused annual allowance from 2015, taking your annual allowance to £60,000 in 2016, you can contribute only up to your £45,000 annual salary.

In 2017, your annual salary jumps to £70,000 (living like a hermit paid off). You carry forward £15,000 from 2015 and 2016, taking your annual allowance to £55,000 in 2017. Since your annual salary is higher, you can contribute the entire £55,000 into your pension.

Once you withdraw money from your pension under certain conditions (trigger event) after the age of 55, your annual allowance drops to £10,000 (**money purchase annual allowance** – MPAA) for all your DC schemes. You cannot top it up with unused allowance from previous years.

Offshore pensions

Contributions to offshore pension schemes can fall outside your annual and life-time allowances. Offshore pensions, in the right circumstances, can be a valuable retirement, tax and estate-planning tool. However, UK and pertinent foreign laws must be carefully considered.

Offshore pensions include **Employer Financed Retirement Benefit Schemes** (EFRBSs), **Qualified Recognised Overseas Pension Schemes** (QROPSs), **Qualifying Non-UK Pension Schemes** (QNUPSs) and **International Pension Plans** (IPPs).

If you plan to spend your retirement living abroad, check the tax rules. Living in some countries and jurisdictions can come with significant tax benefits when drawing income from onshore UK pension schemes.

Seek professional advice.

Boosting DC pensions

If you are a member of a workplace pension, often employers offer **contribution matching**. They agree to contribute to your pension up to a certain limit if you increase your contributions. This is a valuable benefit – effectively a free salary increase. Take advantage of it to its maximum, if you can afford living with a lower current income.

Additional Voluntary Contributions (AVCs) are normally available for DC pensions. Use AVCs to top up contributions to your annual allowance.

A **salary sacrifice** is an arrangement where you, as an employee, reduce your cash income in return for some form of non-cash benefit, such as an additional contribution into your DC pension. The contribution can be exempt from both income tax and NICs.

Salary sacrifice can be beneficial for both you and your employer, who does not need to pay Employer's National Insurance on the sacrificed sum. Generous employers can pass some or all of these savings to you.

For example, you earn £28,000 a year and decide to sacrifice £1,500 of your salary in return for your employer paying an extra £1,500 into your pension. Your take-home pay, after tax, NIC and your own pension contributions, falls from £20,452 to £19,492. But the value of your total take-home package, including employer's pension contribution, increases from £20,452 to £20,992. You are better off by £540.

Inheritance tax (IHT)

IHT is due if your estate is currently worth more than £325,000 (**Inheritance Tax threshold**).[29] The IHT rate is 40% on anything above the threshold. Transfers of any assets between spouses upon death are IHT-free.[30]

There are two types of transfer for IHT purposes: a **chargeable lifetime transfer** and a **potentially exempt transfer**. A chargeable lifetime transfer creates an immediate 40% IHT charge if accumulated transfers within the past seven years exceed the £325,000 threshold. A potentially exempt transfer is not liable to IHT as long as the donor does not die within seven years of the gift.

In most cases, pensions are not counted as estate for IHT purposes since pensions are a legal trust. Fill in a **nomination form**, naming who should inherit your unused pension assets upon death.

Consider naming your children instead of your spouse to inherit your pension. The spouse gets all property IHT-free, whether it is a pension or not. Leaving your pension to your children is a way to mitigate IHT since they do pay IHT on other assets.

Unused pensions used to be subject to a 55% **pensions death tax**, which was applied from the first £1 without a tax-free band, as with IHT.[31] Luckily, this ruinous tax was abolished.

When someone dies before the age of 75, the recipients of unspent pension pay no tax. When someone dies after 75 (as in most cases), recipients (not just dependents) of unspent pensions are taxed at their marginal income tax rate. They can minimise tax by spreading drawdowns over different tax years. In effect, it puts the recipients in the same position as the deceased.

Pensions are a tool for minimising IHT, allowing for cross-generational estate planning. This is one reason residential property cannot be owned inside a pension; otherwise, it would have been used to avoid paying IHT on homes.

As for ISAs, surviving spouses inherit their spouses' ISAs tax-free without losing the tax shelter of assets in the ISAs. For other recipients, the tax sheltering is lost. ISAs form part of the estate and are subject to IHT.[32] Draft a will, leaving your ISAs to your spouse to avoid IHT. It is recommended to draft a will anyway, not only to mitigate taxes, but also to avoid long probates and ensure your estate reaches your intended beneficiaries.

Consider setting up a trust for estate planning. As opposed to common belief, trusts are not the exclusive privilege of the super-rich. Trusts can be instrumental in mitigating IHT, as well as controlling the ability of beneficiaries to spend assets. Take professional advice from a solicitor to design a trust fitting your needs and special circumstances.[33]

Savings for children

Cash ISAs are available for UK residents aged over 16. Stocks and shares ISAs are available for UK residents aged over 18.

Everyone in the UK under 65 earning up to £11,000 (including wages and interest, £11,500 from April 2017) per year does not pay income tax. Most children do not get anywhere near this, so they do not pay tax on their bank's savings account.[34] Some banks offer attractive interest rates on children's savings accounts up to a certain amount.

However, if money given to children by each parent generates interest above £100 per year it is taxed at the parent's marginal tax rate. Also, once the child earns more than the Personal Allowance, income tax kicks in.

Consider a **Junior ISA** for your children under 18. The annual saving limit for a Junior ISA is £4,080.[35] You can choose between a cash Junior ISA and a stocks and shares Junior ISA. Your child can have either one or both and can take control of it at the age of 16, starting withdrawing money at 18.[36]

The money is locked in until the child turns 18. This could be good (long-term disciplined savings) and bad (inflexibility). Then, the Junior ISA converts to a standard ISA. The child benefits from accumulation of the allowances used all the years in the Junior ISA. Otherwise, unused allowances are lost. The child has full control of the money at the age of 18 – not you.

Often, cash Junior ISAs offer higher interest rates than bank savings accounts. However, the choice in stocks and shares Junior ISAs is quite limited since it is a relatively new product.

Junior ISAs are great to save for your children's wedding, house deposit and first car. You are likely to end up helping them anyway, so start tax-efficiently saving for it.

University tuition fees is another reason to save. However, do not rush to pay your children's tuition fees. First-time undergraduates can get the fees paid by the **Student Loans Company**. They need to repay the loan only when earning enough (over £21,000) after graduation. Run the numbers to check whether paying the tuition upfront is better or worse than taking the loan and repaying it much later.

Student loans

The Government, through the Student Loans Company, primarily provides student loans in the UK. For information on student loans check **www.gov.uk** for student finance and the website of the Student Loans Company at **www.slc.co.uk**.

You can open a pension for your child. It sounds crazy, but it allows saving for your children's future. Children's pensions benefit from a tax relief at the basic rate, up to a maximum of £3,600. On every £2,880 you contribute per year, the Government adds £720.

Children can take control of the pension when they are 18, but they can access it only at the age of 55. They will not be able to spend it like they could do with a Junior ISA when reaching 18.

Start saving for your children's retirement. They will thank you one day.

Maximising pension contributions for a couple

If you do not pay tax, you can still pay into a personal pension, benefiting from a tax relief at the basic rate up to a maximum of £3,600. You can contribute into someone else's personal pension, like your spouse, civil partner, child and grandchild.

If your spouse does not work, consider contributing to your spouse's personal pension to benefit from tax-efficient saving and tax-relief at the basic rate. If your spouse works and on a higher tax band than you, gift money to your spouse to contribute to your spouse's pension to enjoy a tax relief at a higher tax rate. Together, you and your spouse can maximise pension contributions up to your combined annual allowance. Annual allowance is personal so you have one and your spouse has another one.

Insurance

Insurance is an important part of your financial plan. Different kinds of insurance help protect you and your loved ones against the costs of risks such as accidents, illness, disability and death. Such risks cannot be left unmitigated.

Life insurance is crucial if you have dependents. It pays a lump sum or regular payments when you die to help your surviving dependents to maintain their standard of living, repay debt (such as mortgage) and fund education tuition costs.[37] If you are employed, your employment package can include **death in service** benefits, covering you for a multiple of your annual salary.

Income protection insurance pays an income stream if you are unable to work. It is especially critical if you are your household's main provider.

And this was the most boring and technical chapter in the book – guaranteed. However, it includes important information and tips about how to maximise your tax-efficient savings. I am glad we have got it out of the way.

Article 2.1

Retirement savings: how much is enough?

By Judith Evans

Financial Times, 19 August 2015

Sweeping reforms to retirement savings rules this year have put pensions in the spotlight, but half of UK workers still have no idea how much they have saved into a pension scheme, according to Aegon, the Dutch life assurer.

And the affluent are not immune to a lack of interest: among those earning above £50,000 a year, people with more opportunity than most to save for the future, almost four in 10 are still not saving enough for a comfortable retirement, according to a Scottish Widows report.

➡

For many, part of the problem is knowing where to start. Does saving begin with imagining the retirement you would like, even if it is 30 or 40 years away, and setting your target accordingly? Or is it better to start with how much you can afford to set aside now? Here, we talk to experts about how best to start, plan and grow retirement savings at every stage of working life.

1. Make a start

"For most people, it's probably sensible to start from your current income and look forwards," says Patrick Connolly, a chartered financial planner at Chase de Vere, who warns against frightening younger savers into inertia with daunting and big numbers. "It can be very difficult to judge how much you will need in retirement and for younger people there's a risk they will overestimate that and be terrified by the amount they would need to save in order to reach it."

While savings depend on circumstances, Mr Connolly says that 15 per cent of a salary, including employer contributions, is an "ideal" starting amount for earners at any age.

Scottish Widows, meanwhile, puts "adequate" at 12 per cent. These proportions assume savers are members of a defined contribution pension scheme, in which retirees buy an annuity or take income drawdown based on the total sum they have saved during their working years, rather than of a defined benefit scheme, which guarantees a retirement income based on factors such as final salary and years worked.

How might workers adjust those proportions as they reach mid-career? "Effectively in your 20s and 30s you can focus on what you can afford to put away, in your 40s and beyond, look the other way around – what is this going to get me on target to hit?" says Mr Connolly.

Richard Parkin, head of retirement at Fidelity Worldwide Investment, says a useful trick is to increase the percentage you save each time you receive a pay rise, an option now offered to some US workers under a formal "auto-escalation" system.

2. Keep track

The next hurdle is calculating the lump sum you are on track to save. Online calculators from pension providers such as Standard Life can offer an estimate if you enter in variables, such as the value of your current pension pot, your age and your present salary. But the results are guesses because the real outcome will depend on how investments will fare in future.

Research by Altus, a consultancy, found that predicted pension pots under the same savings scenario varied between such calculators from £115,000 to £370,000 because their results were based on assumptions.

However, online calculators become more useful as a saver approaches retirement, when there are fewer variables left to affect the outcome, Mr Connolly says.

3. A professional action plan

How does a lump sum become income? That has become a more complex question since April's rule change gave savers more freedom over their pension pots. Those over 55 are now allowed to withdraw cash lump sums from defined contribution funds or opt to keep their savings invested, rather than being forced to buy annuities, which have plummeted in popularity since.

Mr Parkin says his company starts by outlining annuity rates, which are often dauntingly low, when meeting clients for the first time.

"With annuity rates as they are at the moment, we are effectively giving a worst-case scenario without making assumptions about someone's appetite for risk or their capacity to take loss. We are erring on the side of caution," he says.

For example, £100,000 will currently buy a 60-year-old an annual income of £5,131, according to figures from Hargreaves Lansdown.

However, actual rates depend on the type of deal buyers choose, for example they can buy annuities that will pay out to a spouse after death, and annuity rates change over time.

While annuities are still a useful reference point, retirees can now choose between options that include living off investment income and gradually drawing down capital. Each option affects what income level is achieved from a lump sum, but choosing what strategy to adopt requires professional advice.

4. Consider tax

For wealthier savers with substantial pension pots, there is another consideration: the lifetime allowance, which limits pensions tax relief and has been cut from £1.8m to £1.25m over five years. It will fall again to £1m from April 2016.

Current savers have a limited opportunity, therefore, to protect existing pensions from taxation above this limit. For those further from retirement, the lifetime allowance may indicate a point at which it might be worth switching to wrappers, savings formats other than a pension such as individual savings accounts, or ISAs, rather than a pension. Investment growth can push your pension pot towards the limit.

"Anyone with more than about £500,000 in a fund and a few years to go runs the risk that they are going to exceed a million and it becomes almost worthless saving into a pension beyond that amount," says Jamie Jenkins, head of pensions strategy at Standard Life.

Many savers opt for a combination of pensions and Individual Savings Accounts (ISAs), he says.

5. Near the time

As retirement approaches, savers can think more specifically about the post-work life they want and the amount of money required to live it.

About two-thirds of pre-retirement income is a good starting point, according to Standard Life. The fall in income is often made up in savings on costs associated with working life, such as commuting. Many workers have paid off their mortgages by this point, too, saving on housing costs.

Like other pension providers, Standard Life offers a calculator, where savers can input the lifestyle they want such as cars, holidays and so on and receive an estimate of the income they need.

Savers should remember to take into account the state pension, which is this year being revamped to a flat-rate system, under which retirees with 35 years of national insurance contributions will be paid at least £151.25 per week, which may be liable for tax.

For those disappointed with the income they are expected to receive, there are still options. Workers are advised to start saving in their 20s, but those who begin at 30 could add more than 40 per cent to their eventual savings by continuing to work until the age of 65 or 70, Scottish Widows says.

And many people choose to increase pension contributions steeply shortly before retirement, says Mr Parkin.

"The new pension freedoms give the ability to be a bit more positive about making contributions to pensions as they get closer to retirement," he says.

Summary

- Saving for retirement is part of your financial plan.

- The amount you save is a function of: (1) contributions; (2) growth; (3) time; and (4) costs and charges. Maximise contributions, growth and time, whilst minimising costs and charges, including taxes.

- Progressive income tax is levied on your personal income, interest on savings and rental profits. Tax rates on dividends from stocks are different, but the bands are the same. CGT is levied on capital gains. Minimise taxes using ISAs and pensions.

- Shop around for the best interest rates and lowest charges for cash ISAs and consider available investments and charges for stocks and shares ISAs.

- If you have a DB pension, boost it through AVC/FSAVC schemes. DB schemes are normally rare and valuable. If you have one, do not give it up lightly.

- SIPP is the most flexible DC pension to manage your own investments.

- If you have a number of DC pensions, consider consolidating them. You may reduce charges when investing more with a single provider.

- Use your entire annual allowance or carry forward unused allowance from three previous years. Aim to use your entire lifetime allowance.

- Insurance is a critical part of your financial plan. Life insurance protects your dependents after you are gone.

Notes

1 Personal savings or **household saving ratio** in the UK averaged 6.4% from 1955 to 2015, according to the Office for National Statistics. As of the third quarter of 2015 it was 4.4%. Household saving ratio is the percentage of disposable income that is saved. Total savings = disposable income – household consumption.

2 The Personal Allowance may be bigger for people who were born before 6 April 1938 and for those who get Marriage Allowance or Blind Person's Allowance, or smaller if your income is above £100,000 (it is reduced by £1 for every £2 income in excess of £100,000).

3 From April 2016 no tax is deducted on the first £1,000 on interest earned every year on savings (Personal Savings Allowance). The allowance is £500 for earners on higher tax rate and nil for earners on additional tax rate. This may make cash ISAs redundant for some savers.

4 Rental profits are rental income minus allowable expenses or allowances.

5 $£62,900 = £100,000 (1+5\%)^{10} - £100,000$.

6 Net interest is after reducing 40% of interest above the £500 Personal Savings Allowance every year.

7 In common law a trust is a relationship whereby one party holds property for the benefit of another. The settlor transfers property to the trustee. The trustee holds the property for the trust's beneficiaries.

8 When you report a loss, the amount is deducted from your capital gain in the same tax year. If your total taxable gains are still above the tax-free allowance, you can deduct unused losses from previous tax years. If they reduce your gain to the tax-free allowance, you can carry forward the remaining losses to a future tax year.

9 $£44,000 = £250,000 - £200,000 - £6,000$.

10 $£43,001 = £11,000 + £32,001$.

11 $£6,580 = 20\% \times £32,900$.

12 $£13,001 = £43,001 - £30,000$. From April 2017 the threshold for paying the high-rate 40% tax will increase from £42,385 to £45,000. So instead of £13,001 it will be $£15,001 = £45,001 - £30,000$.

13 $£5,280 = 10\% \times £13,001 + 20\% \times (£32,900 - £13,001)$.

14 In 1999 ISAs replaced both Personal Equity Plans (PEPs) and Tax-Exempt Special Savings Accounts (TESSAs).

15 Self-select ISAs allow you to select individual securities and Exchange Traded Funds (ETFs). You can use online brokers who operate on an execution-only basis whereby they offer no advice, only a security dealing service for low charges.

16 Calculations assume annual compounding, a constant interest rate, without considering inflation. You can easily find free online ISA calculators.

17 £13,333 = 20 × £40,000 × 1.67%.

18 £13,333 − £11,000 = £2,333 taxed at base rate of 20%, which is £467 per year or £39 income tax per month. £1,072 = £1,111 − £39. From April 2017 use £11,500 instead of £11,000 in the calculation.

19 Benefits from additional pensionable services can be taken only when those from the main scheme are taken.

20 The value of the assets of a funded DB scheme exceeds that of its liabilities. The scheme is in surplus. An unfunded scheme is in a deficit.

21 The Pensions and Lifetime Savings Association (PLSA) offers ample information and guides focusing on workplace pensions at **www.plsa.co.uk**. A Small Self-Administered Scheme (SASS) is a trust-based occupational DC pension with relatively wide investment flexibility. It generally has less than 12 members and mostly appropriate for the company's directors and senior and key staff.

22 The Pensions Regulator at **www.pensionsregulator.gov.uk** offers information on automatic enrolment and other topics on work-based pension schemes.

23 Thorough analysis of costs and providers of SIPPs is available at **www.telegraph.co.uk/sipps**.

24 The retirement age is expected to increase to 57 by 2028. State Pension age is expected to increase as well and to continue doing so in the future as life expectancy increases.

25 If you are under 75 and your life expectancy is less than one year due to serious illness, you may be able to take your whole pension pot as a tax-free lump sum. If you are over 75, you will pay 45% tax on the lump sum.

26 £100 = £125 × (1 − 20%). After deducting the 20% basic tax rate from £125 you are left with £100.

27 Since April 2016, the size of annual allowance is reduced gradually from £40,000 to £10,000 for those earning between £150,000 and £210,000 a year (including their employer's pension contributions). You can carry forward unused annual allowance of £40,000 from previous years even when you are subject to a reduced annual allowance. From 2016 onwards the amount of carry forward will be based on the unused tapered annual allowance. Lifetime allowance was £1.25 million until April 2016. The lifetime allowance applies to an individual's entire pension savings (excluding State Pension). If pension benefits may exceed lifetime allowance, consider applying for one of several forms of **lifetime allowance protection** (check **www.gov.uk** for details).

28 You must be a member of a pension scheme during the years you want to carry forward.

29 The inheritance tax threshold is £650,000 for a couple. The Government plans to increase the threshold for a couple from April 2017 with an additional £100,000 (rising over the following three years to £175,000) allowance for each partner when passing on their primary residence.

30 There is no IHT on gifts that married couples or civil partners give each other (as long as they live permanently in the UK). Otherwise, the original owner needs to live seven years after gifting the gift. If they do not, their estate or the person receiving it must pay IHT. The amount due is reduced on a sliding scale if it was given between three and seven years before the person died.

31 If the pension has not been touched and the person died before the age of 75, unspent pension was inherited tax-free.

32 ISAs are exempt of IHT on stocks traded on AIM (the London Stock Exchange's market for smaller companies) held for at least two years.

33 Check **www.gov.uk** for ways to reduce IHT. Explore **www.advicenow.org.uk** for information on rights and the law.

34 You may need to fill an R85 form and give it to your bank to get interest without tax taken off. Ask your bank.

35 Before the introduction of Junior ISAs, **Child Trust Funds** were available. You cannot open a Junior ISA for a child with a Child Trust Fund. But you can transfer the Child Trust Fund into a Junior ISA and start saving in a Junior ISA.

36 You can open one cash Junior ISA and one stocks and shares Junior ISA per tax year, splitting the £4,080 allowance between them as you wish.

37 **Whole-of-life insurance** is designed to give a specified amount of cover for the whole of the customer's life. It pays a lump sum on death. **Term assurance** policy is designed to pay a lump sum if the customer dies within the plan's term. The customer chooses the lump sum amount and period of cover. Terminal Illness Cover and Critical Illness Cover can be included.

CHAPTER 3
INVESTMENT OUTCOMES
Why invest?

'In the long run, it's not just how much money you make that will determine your future prosperity. It's how much of that money you put to work by saving it and investing it.'

Peter Lynch

Whilst in the previous chapter we covered savings, in this chapter we move to investing. Saving means putting your money in cash products, like deposit accounts. Investing means buying things that may increase in value, such as stocks and property. Generally, investing is riskier than saving, but we will see how to control risk and what risk level is appropriate for you. Following the four-step investment management process, Chapters 3, 4 and 5 will help you to establish your investing objectives.

When beginning saving for retirement, the amount you save is by far the most important aspect. Good or bad, early investment returns have a relatively small impact on the amount of money with which you end up.

For example, compare the decision whether to save £500 or £1,000 in the first year and whether you make 10% or lose 10%. The saving decision has an impact of £500 on your savings. The investment return has an impact of between a £100 loss and a £100 gain on your savings.[1]

Spend the first decade of your saving and investing life focusing on maximising savings. Experiment with investing, comfortingly knowing that whether you make good or bad investment decisions, this is, primarily, a learning experience.

Over the long term, however, investment returns have a big influence on the final outcome – the amount you save and the income it can generate. When having £100,000 in your savings, a 10% return is meaningful.

Why should you invest and not just save?

You can earn an annual interest rate of about 1.5% on cash ISAs (variable, easy-access, not fixed) in the current low-yield environment. The **base rate** of the Bank of England (BOE) is 0.5%. Most cash deposits pay a higher rate than that, but not much more.[2]

The BOE targets a 2% annual inflation rate. With cash deposits you are unlikely to beat inflation. UK Government bonds with a 10-year maturity currently yield below 2%. When taking into account inflation, it is nil growth (although current inflation rate is far below 2%). That is one reason to invest.

Another reason is that with investing you can generate a return of cash plus 4% or even more. That could be considerable when investing over many years.

You invest to make money. You want your money to work hard for you, generating more money. You participate in capital markets to win.

Investors typically care about nothing else but the return or outcome of investing. The results you desire to achieve are your **return objective**.

The first step of planning your investments is thinking about why you are investing and what you are trying to accomplish. Before planning a trip, know your destination (unless you are after an aimless wander).

This is the same as investing and most other things in life. First, figure out where you want to reach. Then figure out how to get there. There are no guarantees you will reach your destination, but at least you have a general direction.

Investment outcomes are divided into four groups:

1 Growth.
2 Beat inflation.
3 Income.
4 Hedge liabilities.

Growth

The most commonly sought investment outcome is growing the portfolio's value. This outcome should be expressed as a return in percentage over a specified time period, usually a year.

For example, savers for a retirement nest egg should, typically, aim to generate 5% or 6% *on average* every year. With such a return, £100,000 will grow on average by £5,000 or £6,000 annually.

The nature of investing is that, in some years, returns are high whilst in others they are low – this is investment risk. The important point is to aim, on average, over time, for an annual return that is broadly in line with the return objective.

This is one reason to invest for as many years as possible. The larger the number of years, the higher the chances are of hitting the average yearly return. The other reason is that *time is money.*

With 5% average return per year, a £100,000 pension pot grows to £265,330 in 20 years.[3] It will reach £432,194 in 30 years' time.[4] More time is more money.

These calculations assume no cash inflows or outflows. Typically, up to retirement your employer and you contribute every month to your pension, helping it grow. If you are self-employed, you need to contribute.

After retirement, cash flows go in the opposite direction as you draw pension income. If cash outflows outpace growth, the pension pot gradually depletes. Investment returns can prolong its life.

It is perfectly fine not having a precise target growth rate, especially when you are far away from the finishing line. Aiming to grow your portfolio as much as possible, given some constraints, such as a risk level, is a reasonable return objective. As retirement is getting closer, however, and you know roughly how much you want to save, you should formulate a more accurate target return.

Table 3.1 demonstrates how a pension pot would grow over different time horizons with three different annual growth rates of 1.5% (cash or deposit rate), 5% and 6%. It assumes annual contributions of £20,000.[5] A decent growth rate working for many years is the winning formula for long-term savings.

Table 3.1

Pension growth over different horizons and growth rates	10 years	20 years	30 years	40 years
1.5% return pa	£217,265	£469,410	£762,035	£1,101,638
5% return pa	£264,136	£694,385	£1,395,216	£2,536,795
6% return pa	£279,433	£779,855	£1,676,034	£3,280,954

Note: Assuming £20,000 annual contributions, including tax relief, with annual compounding
pa = per annum.

Beat inflation

Inflation reflects changes in the amount of money needed to buy a basket of goods and services. For example, today you buy weekly groceries for £100. If the annual inflation rate is 2%, next year you will need £102 to buy the same groceries. The **purchasing power** of £100 is 2% less than it was a year ago. You need more money to buy the same basket; your money is worth less.

Now, 2% does not seem a lot. But inflation is insidious. If you are a long-term saver, and the average annual inflation rate is 2%, in 20 years' time £100 will be worth only £67.3.[6] That is 32.7% less – a third of your money's value has evaporated. That is a lot.

Losing a third of your money seems unfair. You did not do anything reckless or risky. But that is exactly the problem. You did not do anything with your money. Doing nothing is reckless and risky.

Therefore, an important outcome of investing, in particular over the long term, is keeping pace with inflation.

Inflation is actually one of the motivations to invest. The least you should expect your investments to earn is the inflation rate. Otherwise, you will lose money just because of the passage of time and the ravages of inflation. Do not put your money under a mattress or leave it idle in a current account. Make it work.

Here is a good point to introduce two terms: **nominal return** is return including inflation; **real return** is return above the inflation rate. Real return represents growth in purchasing power.

Nominal return = real return + inflation[7]

For example, a 5% nominal return when the inflation rate is 2% means a real return of about 3%.[8] If nominal return is 3% and realised inflation turned out to be 4% real return is −1%. You lost money in real terms. This is **inflation risk**.

Income

Some investors design their portfolio to generate regular payments or income. When expressed as a percentage of a portfolio's value it is called **yield**. If you retire without other regular sources of income (such as salary, annuity, DB pension payments or rent) or want to top them up, you may desire to earn a yield on your investments.

For example, with a 4% yield a £100,000 pension pot pays a £4,000 annual income. That is not much. You cannot live off £4,000 per year. With the same yield £1 million provides an annual income of £40,000. That is more like it.

Table 3.2 Annual income for different yields and portfolio sizes

Portfolio size/yield	3%	4%	5%
£100,000	£3,000	£4,000	£5,000
£250,000	£7,500	£10,000	£12,500
£500,000	£15,000	£20,000	£25,000
£1,000,000	£30,000	£40,000	£50,000

A general rule of thumb is that to maintain your current standard of living after retirement you need at least half of your current income, depending on the way you want to live.[9] Table 3.2 shows annual income for different yields and portfolio sizes.

Replacement rate (replacement income) is pension as a percentage of earnings. Another general rule of thumb (there are many rules of thumb, some contradicting) says that an adequate replacement rate is two-thirds of salary. Achieving this replacement rate needs a contribution rate of about 15% (depending on time and growth rate of savings).

The Joseph Rowntree Foundation, a British social policy research and development charity, publishes an annual **minimum income standard** (MIS) for the UK. In 2015 the MIS for a single pensioner without mortgage or dependents is £9,515 a year and for a couple it is £13,730 a year. Use the minimum income calculator at **www.minimumincome.org.uk** to check your MIS.

To accumulate a pension pot of £500,000 to £1 million, start saving early, contribute regularly to your pension and aim to grow your savings through investing. Nobody said it was going to be easy.

Some investments pay regular cash flows. For example, bank deposits and bonds pay interest, stocks pay dividends. However, even if investments do not generate regular payments, you can do it yourself by selling some, raising cash when needed.[10] Drawing investment income (**taking natural yield**) is more sustainable than drawing capital (selling investments), in particular during volatile markets. It allows markets to recover.

Selling investments is possible as long as they are **liquid**, meaning you can sell them at a reasonable cost and time, turning them into cash (liquidating them). Property, for example, is illiquid. Selling it can take a long time and a substantial amount of money. You also cannot sell small parts of it to raise your monthly cash needs. It is normally all or nothing.

If your investments are liquid, generating income is possible even if they do not pay out regular cash flows. For example, you hold a £500,000 portfolio invested in stocks. Every month you can sell stocks worth £5,000 to generate income. But there are caveats.

The two main differences between income-generating investments and the DIY method are costs and taxes. Selling investments incurs transaction costs.[11] The tax treatment on capital gains is different from that on income. CGT is typically lower than income tax, so the DIY method can be tax advantageous (although taxes do not matter when assets are in tax-exempt wrappers).

When considering income avoid depleting the value of your portfolio so much that it cannot continue generating income for as long as you live.

For example, spending £50,000 or 10% of your £500,000 pension pot, next year its value will be £450,000. The same 10% will generate only £45,000. The income-generating capacity of your portfolio diminishes unless you preserve its capital. Drawing the same percentage every year, instead of a fixed amount, is a strategy to mitigate depleting your portfolio. However, income will decrease over time.

When thinking about income, think about preserving your portfolio's value, as well as keeping pace with inflation. In other words, retain your portfolio's real value. If you target a 4% yield and the inflation rate is 2% your portfolio needs to grow by 6% just to pay the annual income and keep pace with inflation.

The ultimate desired outcome of a pension is accumulating and growing assets over your working lifetime so assets provide income in retirement and this income maintains its real value.

Annuities

In 2014 UK pension regulations dramatically changed. No longer must you purchase an annuity with the bulk of your DC pension when retiring. Nevertheless, consider using an annuity as part of your pension solution.

An annuity is a financial product, usually sold by an insurance company, promising to pay a guaranteed retirement income until death. Essentially, annuities are like insurance in reverse. You pay a lump sum (from your pension) to an annuity provider and, in return, receive regular monthly payments for the rest of your life. It is like buying a DB pension (with some differences).

Payments are based on the **annuity rate**. For example, on a £100,000 lump sum with a 5.3% annuity rate (current rate for a 65-year-old non-smoker in good health), you receive £5,300 a year. It does not matter how long you live; payments are guaranteed.

Annuity rates depend on several factors, such as bond yields, the annuity's terms (such as **guarantee**, which continues to pay for at least the guarantee period, even if you should die before that time, or linking with inflation) and your condition (age, marital status and health).[12] **Standard annuities** are available to all. **Enhanced annuities** are available for people with a lower life expectancy, generally smokers or those with a medical condition.[13]

Rates of enhanced annuities are more generous since the insurance company estimates that the payments are not going to last for a long time. Smoking eventually kills you, but you can get a higher annuity rate.

When buying an annuity, shop around. Before reaching retirement, you will receive a letter from your pension provider with the value of your pension and an annuity quotation. You do not need to accept this offer.

Different insurance companies offer different annuity rates. Annuities have been criticised for the fat profit margins some providers make. Choosing a provider makes a difference.

Currently, you have one chance to buy your annuity. Then, it is with you for life. Annuity switching is a controversial topic and is not available yet in the UK.[14] Make the best choice you can when you can.[15] You also need luck with the timing of your retirement since annuity rates vary.

Annuities' main advantage is certainty and peace of mind; knowing how much income you are going to get, however long you live (longevity insurance). The main disadvantages are inflexibility (no switching, no access to the lump sum); most annuities are not linked to inflation; and annuity rates have decreased over the years.

A 5% annuity rate requires living 20 years to break even – the time it takes to receive back the lump sum (income/life expectancy calculation). The rate of an inflation-linked annuity is currently about 60% lower than that of standard annuity – it will take much longer to break even.

With a 5.3% annuity rate, £5,300 per year for every £100,000 is not likely to be enough for achieving your financial goals post-retirement (unless you are off to live on a beach in Thailand). You will want to have a decent quality of life, to travel, to spoil your grandchildren – you want to enjoy a pleasant retirement.

Because of the low rates of annuities and their rigidness, more pensioners look for other ways to generate income, such as high-yielding investments. The main downside of such investments is that they risk capital to generate satisfactory returns. It is a trade-off between annuities' low risk/low yield and these investments' high risk/high yield.

One way to benefit from both worlds is blending an annuity with higher yielding investments.

Another disadvantage of annuities is their inheritance rules. When someone with an annuity dies, the deceased's spouse can continue receiving annuity pension payments, as long as the deceased asked for it to happen and paid extra (**joint life annuity** or **death-depended annuity**).[16] When the spouse dies, or if the deceased did not sign up for this deal, the insurance company offering the annuity takes the remaining pot. Children get nothing (they typically do not inherit DB payments, either).

This means that another advantage of income drawdown pensions is the ability to pass them to children.

Deferred annuities

Deferred annuity is purchased but its income payments start at a later date. A possible scenario to use it could be if you take a 25% tax-free lump sum from your pension but do not need income. Another scenario is blending flexible drawdown and a deferred annuity. The annuity payments will kick in when you are older and less likely to be able to manage your finances, perhaps due to dementia, or when other assets are exhausted.

By deferring annuity payments, when you start taking them their level will be higher as the period for which they are paid is shorter.

Variable annuities

Variable annuities (**investment-linked annuity**) are a relatively recent innovation in the UK. Popular in the USA, variable annuities are financial products where, in exchange for a lump sum, the insurance company guarantees a minimum income for a fixed term, usually not for life like standard lifetime annuities.

The product allows you to invest in a portfolio of stocks, bonds and, perhaps, other assets with a prospective upside. Any income and gains above the guaranteed minimum payments vary, depending on the portfolio's performance.

The objectives of variable annuity are providing an element of a secured income, with some flexibility of accessing part of the lump sum used to purchase the product and potential gains. Some variable annuities guarantee a certain level of value at the term's end to purchase a lifetime annuity.

Each variable annuity is different. Carefully read and understand the terms since there are risks. The guaranteed income is not for life. The portfolio's value can go down as well as up. Variable annuities are markedly different from lifetime annuities.

If you purchase an annuity to guarantee a minimum income level for your entire life to address longevity risk, variable annuities might be inappropriate. Instead of a variable annuity, blend a standard annuity with investments, giving you some minimum income with flexibility and potential upside. Do it yourself.

Hedge liabilities

We all have liabilities. We need to pay for food, utility bills, transportation, rent, mortgage, education and so on. Income should cover ongoing liabilities – if it does not, spend less or earn more; balance your budget. But for larger sums, such as a down payment on a house, replacing a car or tuition for kids' university, we need to prepare cash.

It is possible to design investments so they generate cash flows when large payments are due – if you know their timing and amount. For example, you plan to replace your car in five years. You put aside, in a five-year time deposit, the car's expected price. If the price is £10,000 and interest on the time deposit is 5% per year, put aside £7,835.[17] In five years you should have £10,000.

The 5% is a nominal return, including the expected inflation rate. If inflation exceeds expectations, you may fall short of your objective as the car's future price may be higher. In that case, you will need to take some cash from another source or settle for a cheaper car. Anyway, it is always good to have a contingency plan. If plan A does not work, have a plan B.

Portfolios can be divided into **growth assets** and **matching assets**. The role of growth assets is producing capital growth and income. The role of matching assets is maintaining a value in line with that of liabilities and generating cash flows matching those of liabilities.

Some DB pensions divide their assets in such a way. Matching assets are commonly called **Liability Driven Investment** (LDI).[18] DB pensions must pay a stream of payments to members. This is a DB scheme's liability. If it does not have enough assets to meet liabilities, it is the sponsor's liability – the sponsor will need to inject (contribute) money into the DB.

Since the money in your pension is effectively locked until you retire, you cannot use it to hedge liabilities before retirement. You can withdraw money from your ISAs at any time. However, if you withdraw money, you need to put it back in in the same tax year to enjoy the tax shelter. The best approach is using money outside your pensions and ISAs to hedge liabilities before retirement, if possible.

If you consider buying a buy-to-let property, for example, and you must access your ISA savings to do so, then it is down to a cost/benefit analysis.

Say you expect an annual 6% pre-tax rental profit on a property. You are on the 40% tax bracket. The net annual profit is 3.6%.[19] If you expect to generate a tax-free return of 8% per year on your stocks and shares ISA, then, based on these calculations, you might be better off keeping the ISA.

However, a property should appreciate in value. Its after-tax total return may surpass 8%. Also, consider the risks of the two alternatives. Stocks' returns may deviate substantially from the expected 8%, whilst property's rental profit may be closer to its expected 6%. A property may be safer than financial assets in a bank. Property rights protect your ownership. A property cannot go bankrupt, while a bank can. Additionally, estimated expected returns are not the sole consideration. Owning a property when retired can be the prevailing argument, tilting the balance in favour of buying it.

One advantage of ISAs is flexibility to make such decisions. You can access your ISA money whenever you want.

Blending outcomes

Often, investors target a combination of some of the four investment outcomes, not just a single one.

For example, when young and working, you cannot access your pension for a good number of years. Your focus is inflation-beating high growth. You are looking to increase your portfolio's purchasing power. This investment objective often is termed **long-term capital growth** or **aggressive growth**.

When retired, you want your pension not only to pay a steady income stream, but also to grow over time, at least keeping up with inflation. You are looking to preserve capital and your portfolio's income-generating power in real terms. This combined outcome often is called **income and growth** or income and capital preservation.

Alternatively, perhaps you do not need income yet from your pension since you work part time or earn rental income. You are seeking your pension to modestly grow and beat inflation, without incurring large losses. You are looking to retain your portfolio's purchasing power for later years when needing it. Such a combined outcome often is named **capital preservation**.

Maybe you wish your portfolio to grow and generate a big cash flow when you retire. You can then take a tax-free lump sum to buy that red Ferrari you have always wanted. This combination of outcomes is customised to your unique financial desires.

The outcomes and their combinations are personal. Form a set of investment objectives based on your individual circumstances and aspirations.

Total return

When defining return objectives, think in terms of **total return** (TR). It includes both change in market price (capital appreciation or price return) and income.

Income includes interest on cash deposits and fixed income investments, dividends on stocks and rent on property.

For example, you want your portfolio to produce 2% income and 3% growth per year. Your total return objective is 5%. You can choose either spending the 2% income or reinvesting it, putting it back to work. When spending the income, your portfolio grows by only 3%.

When comparing an investment's performance with that of a benchmark, compare like with like. Total return with total return or price return with price return. Do not mix the two. Total return can look deceivably good relative to price return.

For example, the FTSE 100 Index measures the performance of the 100 largest listed (exchange traded or quoted) companies in the UK. The index's return can be reported as **price return**, excluding dividends, or as total return, including reinvestment of dividends.

A big difference between the two is likely, especially over the long term.[20] Dividends can make up over 3% or 4% of total return every year.

Compound return

'The most powerful force in the universe is compound interest.'

Albert Einstein

Compound return is the return investments earn over a time period considering not only the original principal, but also the impact of gains and losses.

For example, your £1,000 deposit earns 5% per year. Each year you spend the earnings. After 10 years you will have £1,500.[21] Conversely, leaving the earnings in the deposit, you earn every year 5% on a growing amount (5% on £1,000 in the first year, 5% on £1,050 in the second year and so on). After 10 years you will have £1,629.[22]

You made an extra £129 or 12.9% by reinvesting earnings, letting compound return do its magic. The longer the time horizon, the higher the effect of compound returns. That is one reason it is recommended you start saving as early as possible. Time is an invaluable force.

Figure 3.1 shows the accumulated savings of three savers. Each saver contributes £10,000 each year to a pension. The first saver started at the age of 25, investing in a portfolio returning 5% per year. The second saver started 10 years later, at the age of 35, investing in the same 5% return portfolio. The third saver started also at the age of 35, but invested in a more conservative portfolio, returning 3% per year.

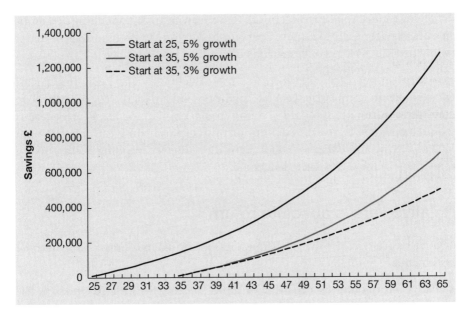

Figure 3.1 Accumulated savings

The first saver managed to save over £1.2 million by the age of 65. This is over the lifetime allowance. Well done.

The second saver, who started later, managed to accumulate about £700,000 by the age of 65. That is £500,000 short of the first saver. Starting early is beneficial, letting compound return to work on the savings for longer, as well as to contribute more. However, the first saver's excess contributions account for only £100,000 of the £500,000 difference. It is mostly due to compound return.

The third saver started late and invested in a portfolio generating 2% less than that of the second saver. The third saver managed to save only £500,000. An annual lower compound return of 2% over 10 years made a difference of £200,000. That is a lot of money.

The conclusions are straightforward – start early and aim to increase your **compound annual growth rate** (CAGR).

Required versus desired outcomes

Some financial goals are required (essential). Others are desired (non-essential).

For example, generating regular income after retirement to maintain a reasonable standard of living is required. Beating inflation is required, especially over a long investment horizon. However, buying that red Ferrari when you retire is desired.

Achieving required objectives is critical. Failure can mean compromising a comfortable life. Plan carefully to achieve your required objectives, minimising the risk of failing to do so. As for your desired objectives, they would be nice to have, but you can risk not achieving them.

For example, an annuity can generate an income stream for the rest of your life to maintain a minimum standard of living. You are not taking risk to achieve this required outcome. A diversified portfolio of stocks and bonds can generate high returns and income to finance holidays and discretionary spending. You are taking some risk to achieve this desired outcome.

Relative versus absolute return

Relative return does not live in vacuum. It is measured in comparison with some benchmark.

A relative return objective can be, for instance, beating the FTSE 100 Index by 2% per year. One problem with this objective is that you do not know what the level of return is likely to be over the short term. Can you know whether the FTSE 100 Index is going to return +15%, 0% or −15% next year? All are plausible. The index's average return over the long term is more predictable.

Another problem is that the magnitude of a relative return objective is small compared to the potential benchmark return. The total return of the benchmark plus the relative return is determined largely by the equity market return, not the objective.

The final and most acute problem with such a relative return objective is that it is not linked to your financial goals. If next year the FTSE 100 Index falls by 20% and your investment returns −10%, is that good or bad? The investment exceeded its relative return objective fivefold – a 10% outperformance. However, you still lost 10%. That is not a great result. Surely, it is not what you hoped your investment to do.

Absolute return, in contrast, is not measured relative to any benchmark or index. It is benchmark agnostic. Some examples of absolute return objectives include 5% per year, cash (LIBOR) +4% and inflation +3%.[23] The advantage of an absolute return objective is that it is **outcome-oriented**. It focuses on a result linked to your financial goals.

If you are a long-term saver, targeting an average annual return of about 5% or 6%, such absolute return objectives match your financial needs. The return is not guaranteed. It is unlikely to achieve its return objective every year. However, at least it aims to achieve what you need, rather than what the general equity market happens to do.

Watch out for a return objective detached from inflation. The advantage of an objective expressed as cash or inflation plus a percentage is that it is linked to inflation. It is a real return, rather than nominal. If your return objective is just 5%, for example, whether inflation is 2%, 4% or 6% makes a big impact on results in real terms.

An 'inflation plus' objective is obviously linked to inflation. What is less obvious is that a 'cash plus' objective should also be linked to inflation. When inflation rises, short-term cash rates should rise with it as part of the central bank's efforts to control inflation.

The best way to express your return objective is linking it to your specific target outcome, including an element of inflation.

Gross versus net return

'In investing, you get what you don't pay for.'

John Bogle

Gross return is before and net return is after charges, costs and taxes. Net return represents your investing experience, your take-home money.

You cannot control many things in investing. But you can control expenses. Every penny you save on charges, costs and taxes is another penny added to your net return.

Estimating your target return

Estimating your portfolio's target return entails a number of assumptions and a calculator. Conveniently, the Citizens Advice offers a free savings calculator at **www.citizensadvice.org.uk** (as well as free, independent, confidential and impartial advice on a range of topics, including savings and pensions).

Begin with estimating the income you will need when retired. The following steps can help:

1   Add up all expected expenses (outgoings) in retirement for one year. Consider housing costs (mortgage, rent), dependents (spouse, children in education, as more people have children later in life, elderly relatives who might need support), transportation, holidays and hobbies. You are likely to spend more time at home, so expect higher heating costs and utility bills. You may have more free time to spend on social outings and activities. Private healthcare costs (not covered by NHS) might rise. Travel costs can decrease due to cheaper fares

on public transport for senior citizens and with no need to commute to work. Expenses can initially drop soon after retiring, but then rise again later in life when care costs kick in.

2 Subtract State Pension and other income (DB, rental income).

3 The result is the **annual shortfall**. You need your pension savings to generate the annual shortfall. Check the expected income in your annual **Pension Benefit Statement** from your pension administrator. Use the current annuity rate as benchmark for flexible drawdown. Are you on track to generate the annual shortfall?

A rule of thumb is that 20 times the annual shortfall is your savings goal.

Using the online calculator, input your savings goal (target portfolio size); date when you need your savings (target retirement date); how much you have saved already (current pension savings); and gross annual interest rate (target return). The calculator outputs the monthly contributions needed to achieve your target portfolio size.

Play with the calculator, entering different target returns until, through an iterative process of trial and error, the monthly contributions match those you and your employer pay into your pension.

For example, your target portfolio size is £1 million (with current annuity rates it is expected to generate the income you need), you are 35 and wish to retire at 65 (30 years from now), you have no pension savings and you assume a 5% return per annum. The calculator says you need to save £1,220 per month.

However, your annual salary is £40,000 and you and your employer contribute 10% each. That is £8,000 per year or £667 per month, way below £1,220.[24] Going back to the calculator, you change the target return, whilst keeping the other variables constant, until the output matches monthly contributions of £667.

The result is a total *real* net return of 8.3%. If you expect contributions to increase with inflation, you need 8.3% total *nominal* net return. Contributions are a fixed percentage of your salary. Salaries normally are not adjusted for inflation every year. However, promotions or changing jobs can bring salary increases.

Now, decide whether your objectives are reasonable and fit your financial plan. You can amend the target portfolio size (change lifestyle post retirement) and perhaps your retirement age or plan to continue working part-time. Maybe you can adjust the contributions, in particular yours if total contributions (including your employer's) are below the annual allowance.

Unfortunately, an 8.3% return, net of charges and transaction costs, is aspirational. Since January 1998 to December 2015 the FTSE 100 Index's average annual total return was 4.9%. And this is a gross return, before charges.

Being more realistic, given your contributions, time horizon and a reasonable 5% average annual return, your expected target portfolio size is £550,000. Judge whether it is enough. You can try maximising it within pragmatic constraints.

Split the target portfolio size into two buckets: one satisfying your required needs and a second satisfying your desired needs. Consider splitting your savings into two portfolios: one to generate the required return to reach the required bucket and a second to generate the desired return to reach the desired bucket. Make every effort to achieve the required return.

Importantly, evaluate whether your target return is achievable and whether the risk level you will need to tolerate it is too adventurous. The target return is a function of investment risk. Careful, the next chapter is risky.

Summary

- Investors seek four types of investment outcomes: (1) growth; (2) beat inflation; (3) income; and (4) hedge liabilities.
- Your pension pot's final value is a function of contributions, growth rate, time and charges and costs.
- The minimum to seek from your portfolio is keeping pace with inflation.
- Annuities are not compulsory any more. Annuity gives certainty of regular income for life. However, annuities are inflexible, normally they are not linked to inflation and their rates have decreased over recent years. Consider blending annuities with higher yielding investments.
- Hedge known liabilities (large cash outflows) with matching investments.
- Tailor your investing outcomes for your specific needs.
- Compound return is powerful. Let returns accumulate over a long time and reinvest income and profits so they work for you.
- Focus on achieving your required return. Not achieving it can adversely affect your quality of life. Desired return is nice to have, but you can live without it.
- Do not measure your return objective relative to some generic index. Rather, it should be absolute, linked to your personal investment needs and expressed in real terms (above inflation).
- Given your target portfolio size, expected retirement age, current pension savings and monthly contributions, you can easily calculate your target return using a free online savings calculator.

Notes

1   $-£100 = -10\% \times £1,000; £100 = 10\% \times £1,000$.

2   The base rate (official bank rate) is the interest rate set by the Bank of England for lending to other banks. It is used as a benchmark for interest rates generally in the UK. The Monetary Policy Committee (MPC) makes decisions regarding the level of interest rate. In July 2007 the base rate was 5.75%. In a series of MPC decisions, it was cut all the way down to 0.5% in March 2009 and has been at this level since.

3   $£265,330 = £100,000 (1 + 5\%)^{20}$.

4   $£432,194 = £100,000 (1 + 5\%)^{30}$.

5   For a basic-rate taxpayer on an annual contribution of £16,000 HMRC adds a tax relief of £4,000, making it £20,000. $£16,000 = (1 - 20\%) \times £20,000$.

6   $£67.3 = £100 \div (1 + 2\%)^{20}$.

7   The precise formula is $(1 + \text{nominal return}) = (1 + \text{real return})(1 + \text{inflation})$.

8   More precisely, the real return is 2.94%. $(1 + 5\%) = (1 + 2.94\%)(1 + 2\%)$.

9   Those earning between £32,000 and £51,000 a year should aim to retire with an income worth around 60% of their salary. Those earning more than £51,000 a year may need only 50% of their salary. Those earning less than £32,000 a year may need more than 60%. Check the paper 'Framework for the analysis of future pension incomes' at **www.gov.uk**.

10 Modigliani and Miller's irrelevance of dividend policy theorem claims that dividend policy does not matter since investors can generate income by selling stocks. This is true in a frictionless world. In the real world, frictions like taxes and transaction costs make a difference.

11 Transaction costs of selling securities include broker commissions and bid-ask spread.

12 Index-linked annuity payments are linked to the Retail Price Index (RPI). Young savers should consider index-linked annuities, although their initial payments are lower than those of standard annuities. Escalating annuities can have a fixed annual income increase (such as 3% per year). Level annuity's rate does not change over the annuity's life.

13 Innovative enhanced annuities can be based on postcode and lifestyle. Fixed-term annuities pay back a lump sum at the end of the term. U-shaped annuities' level of income increases over a time period until a set date and then decreases until death. Some planned modern annuities allow withdrawing lump sums.

14 The Government will soon allow people to sell their annuities if they can find a buyer. A secondary annuity market is planned from April 2017. Marginal income tax rate will apply.

15 You can find current annuity rates on the internet. For example, **www.ft.com/personal-finance/annuity-table** and **www.sharingpensions.co.uk**. The free website **moneyfacts.co.uk** compares annuity rates and provides useful information on a variety of topics.

16 Joint life annuities come with different percentages, indicating the amount that will be paid to the surviving spouse upon death of the annuity holder. For example, a 50% joint life annuity means that 50% of the income is paid to the surviving spouse.

17 $£7,835 = £10,000 \div (1 + 5\%)^5$.

18 The value of matching assets in LDI is designed to move in tandem with the value of liabilities. If interest rates fall, for example, the value of liabilities rises and the value of the matching assets should rise as well to minimise a mismatch between assets and liabilities.

19 $3.6\% = 6\% (1 - 40\%)$.

20 The average annualised *total* return of the FTSE 100 Index between January 1993 and December 2015 was 7.4%. The average annualised *price* return was 3.5% over the same period. That is a difference of 3.9% per year.

21 $£1,500 = £1,000 + 10 (5\% \times £1,000)$.

22 $£1,629 = £1,000 (1 + 5\%)^{10}$.

23 London Interbank Offered Rate (LIBOR) is a benchmark rate that banks charge each other for short-term loans. LIBOR is based on one of five different currencies (US dollar, euro, British pound, yen and Swiss franc) and one of seven different maturities (such as 1 month, 3 months). Often it is used as a benchmark rate for cash deposits and financial instruments.

24 $£667 = £8,000 \div 12; £8,000 = 20\% \times £40,000$.

CHAPTER 4
INVESTMENT RISK

The journey to your outcome

'Risk means more things can happen than will happen.'

Elroy Dimson

Investing is risk. Risk is the flipside of return; there is no return without risk. The journey to your desired outcome is more likely to be bumpy than smooth.

In this chapter we will define what investment risk is, assess your appetite for risk, show how to measure risk and introduce a number of concepts that we will use throughout the book. Crucially, we will emphasise that to generate investment returns you must take investment risk.

Investment risk means you might not achieve your target outcome, even when making all the right decisions along the way with the available information at the time of making them. Investing evolves around forecasting the future. Do not believe 'experts' saying they can predict it – it is likely to be different from what they predicted. Since the future is uncertain, investing is risky.

When depositing money in a savings account in a big bank – a relatively safe investment, you will earn a rather low interest rate. It is likely to relate to the BOE's base rate plus a spread. Say, for example, the base rate is 0.5% and the spread is 1.0%; the interest rate is 1.5%. Notwithstanding extreme circumstances, you will get the 1.5%.

BOE's target inflation rate is 2.0%. Earning 1.5% on a deposit lags inflation. Whilst nominal return is 1.5%, real return is negative −0.5%. In real terms, you might lose money. You did not take a high risk so you do not deserve a high return – there is no free lunch.

AER

An interest rate may be quoted as Annual Equivalent Rate (AER). AER assumes interest is compounded, depending on the number of times interest payments are made.

$$AER = (1 + r \div n)^n - 1$$

where n is the number of times per year interest is paid and r is the gross interest rate. AER allows for comparison across different interest rates. For example, the annual stated interest rate of your deposit is 5%, paid monthly. $AER = (1 + 5\% \div 12)^{12} - 1 = 5.12\%$.

A bank deposit or cash return is called **risk-free**. Well, it is not truly riskless. One risk is negative real return (**inflation risk**). Another risk is the bank going bust (**counterparty risk**), as Northern Rock or Lehman Brothers did in 2008. However, the British Government is unlikely to let any large, too-big-to-fail retail bank fail without protecting depositors.

Banks do not hold enough cash to repay all depositors in a bank run. The entire financial system can suffer a **systemic shock** due to loss of confidence when one large bank fails and all depositors want their money back. It can spread like waves after throwing a rock into a pond. To avoid this, the UK Government is likely to bail out any large financial institution on the brink of insolvency.[1]

In 2008, the British Government announced a bank rescue package totalling about £500 billion. You, I and the rest of the British taxpayers became bank owners. And the banks survived, as well as the financial system.

The **Financial Services Compensation Scheme** (FSCS) protects deposits and other financial products held with firms authorised by the UK regulator, the **Financial Conduct Authority** (FCA). The FSCS protects deposits up to £75,000.[2]

To mitigate the risk of your bank going bust, divide deposits, including ISAs, across several large banks, putting up to £75,000 in each. Diversifying deposits across several financial institutions avoids putting all your eggs in one basket.

Remember these basket and eggs; we will come back to them later.

Earning a return above the risk-free rate requires taking an investment risk. One of investing's fundamental principles is the higher the risk, the higher the *expected* return. The return is expected; not guaranteed. With higher risk come dangers, such as a chance of losing money. No pain, no gain; no guts, no glory.

What is investment risk?

The simplest definition of investment risk is the chance of not meeting your return objectives (**shortfall risk**).

For example, your target return is 5%. Alas, your portfolio returns 3%. It fell short of your objective. It does not matter that the return was positive; you did not lose money. What matters is the return was not what you targeted.

Frequently, people define risk as the chance of losing money. However, whilst this is clearly unpleasant and a true risk, a positive return can still miss your return objective. Also, what matters for long-term savers is average return over the entire time horizon. If you lose money in one year, but make it up later, then losing money is not detrimental.

Risk, like return, should be set against your individual financial goals and risk tolerance.

Risk tolerance

'If you have trouble imagining a 20% loss in the stock market, you shouldn't be in stocks.'

John Bogle

Risk tolerance is the risk level with which each person is comfortable. It consists of a subjective **willingness** to take risk and objective **ability** to take risk.

We are all different. Some people do not like taking risks. They work in a stable job, earning a stable salary. They enjoy relaxing holidays, nothing too extreme or challenging. And they like putting their money in a bank deposit without risking it. They are not willing to bear risk, they are **risk averse**.

For others, taking risks is normal, perhaps even exciting. They are entrepreneurs, running their own business. They enjoy the adrenaline rush of riding rollercoasters and extreme sports, such as parachuting out of aeroplanes and bungee jumping. They may enjoy gambling – try pulling them away from the roulette table in Las Vegas. And they are willing to bear risks when investing since they seek high returns.

Most people are somewhere in the middle of these two extremes. Rational investors are risk averse. Given two investments with the same expected return and different level of risks, rational investors will choose the less risky one. But we all have different degrees of risk aversion. Your personality and unique psyche determine your willingness to take risk. You should know your investor mentality and risk tolerance.

Questionnaires can help assessing your risk tolerance. One potential future development of asset management is **robo-advisor** – you will fill in an online risk questionnaire and a computer will automatically generate a portfolio matching your risk tolerance. However, before robo-advisors take over, whilst questionnaires can assist, they are generic. Think for yourself how you will feel when the stock market crashes or when the value of your portfolio fluctuates.

What are you going to do if the stock market falls by 20%? Does it make you anxious? Do you spend the night awake, thinking about how much money you lost today? Or do you keep calm and carry on?

You check your portfolio and it is down by 10% this month. How bad does it make you feel? Do you agonisingly regret investing in the stock market? What will you do?

The immediate instinct might be to sell all your stocks and rush to cash. But that could be a mistake. The stock market tends to rebound. By selling your stocks, you lose out when they fall and miss the rebound. Ouch and ouch.

The best way to know your investor-self is through first-hand experience. If you cannot stand the heat, get out of the kitchen. But first get into the kitchen to feel the heat.

A good rule of thumb is taking a risk level with which you can sleep well at night. You cannot live with worrying all day and all night about your portfolio. Saving for retirement is a multi-year project. Being concerned about your investments all the time is unhealthy. And you need health to accumulate wealth.

Whilst willingness to take risk is subjective, your ability to take risk is an objective measure of how much risk you can actually take.

For example, if you are 25 and you have just started working, you can take investment risk. A long investment horizon lies ahead, you cannot access your pension for a long time anyway and you probably earn a regular income. Even when losing, you have enough time to recoup losses. They are only paper losses until you realise them by selling.

However, this is not as straightforward as it seems. When you are young, you probably lack investing experience. Your total wealth is not much and losing on your portfolio hurts. So, your willingness to take risk may be low.

When you are 60, five years before retirement, your ability to take risk is low. If you make a big loss in your pension, time might be insufficient to earn it back. It might reduce your amount of money when retired, adversely impacting your standard of living.

Conversely, whilst your ability to take risk appears low, you may be a seasoned investor. Perhaps you own assets elsewhere to support you after retirement, such as properties to let. Maybe you have finished paying the mortgage on your home and your children do not need financial support. So, your willingness to take risk is high, as well as, perhaps, your ability.

The bottom line is that risk tolerance is individual and depends on your specific circumstances. Define what your risk appetite is, considering your willingness and ability to take risk. When assessing your risk tolerance, take a holistic view, considering all factors, such as time horizon, total wealth, likely reaction to market crashes and emotional state.

Risk measurement and management

Dealing with investment risk is done at three levels. The first level is to understand investment risks. Each type of investment comes with a number of different risks. You should qualitatively understand them. We discuss different risks throughout the book.

The second level is to measure risks. **Risk measurement** quantifies risks. We will review a number of risk measurements in this chapter.

The third level is to manage risks. **Risk management** is deciding which risks to take, which risks to mitigate and what actions to take to do so. We will cover risk management techniques in a dedicated chapter.

How to measure risk

The most common risk measure is **volatility** or **standard deviation** of returns.[3] Standard deviation is a statistical measure of the dispersion of returns around the mean (average) return.

All you need to know about standard deviation is that when the return distribution is normal (symmetrical bell-shaped), two-thirds (68%) of returns fall within one standard deviation of the mean and 95% of returns fall within two standard deviations of the mean.[4]

For example, an investment's average return is 8% with 15% standard deviation. Two-thirds of times, the range of returns is between −7% and 23% and in 95% of times the range is between −22% and 38%.[5,6] Figure 4.1 graphically illustrates it.

This investment's returns are volatile. It can have very low (negative) and very high (positive) returns. You will be happy with the high returns, but can you tolerate the negative ones? Can you live with its **downside risk**?

If average return is what we would expect the investment to generate on average every year, we can transform standard deviation to downside risk.

When standard deviation is annualised (volatility per year) we can say that since 95% is 19 ÷ 20, in 19 in 20 years the return is *likely* to be above −22% (two standard deviations below the mean).[7] But in 1 in 20 years the return is *likely* to be worse than −22%. Can you endure this? This is a way to assess risk tolerance.

These calculations assume a normal distribution. However, in real life, financial markets are not normally distributed. A 1-in-20 very negative return might occur more often than expected. Do not be surprised if this investment has a return worse than −22% every 5 or 10 years, more often than every 20 years. One shortcoming of standard deviation is that it assumes normal distribution.

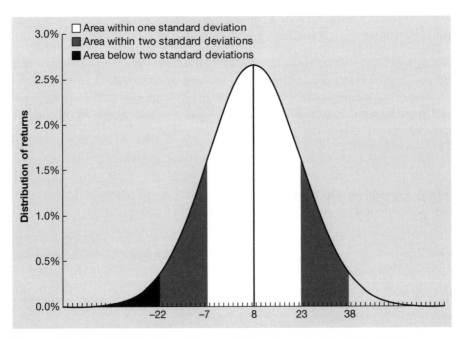

Figure 4.1 Normal distribution with mean 8% and standard deviation 15%

Normal distribution

A normal distribution is defined by its first two **moments** of mean and standard deviation. The third moment is **skewness**, measuring the distribution's symmetry. Skewness is zero for normal, symmetric distribution. Negative skewness means more observations to the left of the mean than to its right.

The fourth moment is **kurtosis**, measuring the distribution's peakedness. Kurtosis is three for normal distribution. Excess kurtosis measures kurtosis above three. Positive excess kurtosis means the distribution has more observations in its tails than does a normal distribution. A combination of negative skewness and positive kurtosis mean more frequent and more negative returns than are predicted by normal distribution.

Standard deviation does not say what the investment's worst return might be. The investment in the example might generate a return of −30% or −50%. Extreme negative returns are called **black swans** or **fat tails**.[8] These events do not occur often but when they do, it is painful.

Notably, standard deviation indicates the risk of missing your return objective. A wider spread of probable returns means the investment can deviate more from your expectations (target return) – its shortfall risk is higher.

Highly volatile investments can disappoint on the downside, as well as surprise on the upside with better returns than expected (**upside risk**). This is another short-coming of standard deviation: it panelises investments symmetrically for both bad, negative returns and good, positive returns. You are concerned only about bad returns (downside risk).

Volatility is not a risk by itself. Do not confuse volatility with risk. According to finance theory, higher volatility should be compensated by higher expected returns.[9] If you can sleep well at night with volatile investments, you may be rewarded with high returns over time. Volatility can be good.

For example, when investing in a volatile stock, it can generate high returns over time. The journey can be bouncy and stressful. But, even when down, the price can jump up. This is good volatility.

Bad risk that matters is **permanent loss**. That is the downside risk you cannot or do not have time to recoup.

For example, when investing in a stock or bond of a company with a volatile business and the company goes bust, your stock or bond can become worthless. Your investment is permanently impaired. This is bad volatility.

Bad volatility might also cause you to make bad investment decisions. When volatile markets fall, you might sell near the bottom because you do not know how further down they might drop. The volatility is not bad *per se,* but it results in bad investor behaviour.

In this sense, the timing of volatility is critical. Volatility could be fine if you have time. But if you are just approaching retirement, for example, you cannot afford a big loss since time is running out. You may need to cash in on the investment soon – this makes you a forced seller.

Risk tolerance and time horizon are strongly linked. Volatility can be good when time horizon is long, but bad when time horizon is short. Timing is everything.

The timing of returns also matters. Large negative returns have bigger impact closer to retirement, when the amount of savings is relatively large, than many years before retirement, when the amount of savings is relatively small. The timing of returns is called **sequential risk**. The final wealth outcome is a function of sequential risk and investment risk.

Different asset classes have different volatility levels. Equities are volatile. Their volatility is around 15% for developed market equity (such as UK stocks) and over 20% for emerging market equity (such as stocks in Brazil, Russia, India and China). Government bonds (such as UK gilts) have a volatility of about 5%. Cash has volatility below 1%.

Because equities are riskier than bonds and cash they offer higher *expected* returns. Why would any rational investor invest in a risky asset unless it offers higher *potential* returns? The higher returns are 'expected' and 'potential' since they are not certain. This higher equity return is called **equity risk premium**.

By blending different assets in different proportions you can tune your portfolio's volatility to match your risk tolerance. More stocks means higher volatility. Fewer stocks and more bonds and cash mean lower volatility. You can readily quantify your portfolio's risk level using volatility as a single metric.

It is not perfect. Volatilities change – they tend to spike up when markets are in stress and come down when markets are calm. And volatility has the shortcomings we mentioned (assuming normal distribution, undiscriminating between upside and downside). However, using volatility is a simple, pragmatic solution to measure risk and align your portfolio's risk with your risk tolerance.

Another reason to blend different imperfectly correlated investments, or investments that behave differently, is **diversification**. Through diversification volatility is reduced. Diversification is a proven way to mitigate risk.

Surely, you remember the basket and eggs. It is so important that, later, we dedicate a whole chapter to diversification.

Value-at-Risk and the VIX

Value-at-Risk (VaR) is a common downside risk measure, indicating how much a portfolio is likely to lose over a specific time horizon and confidence level. For example, a 1-month VaR of −8% at a 95% confidence level means the portfolio is expected to lose more than 8% over any one month in 5% of months or it is expected to gain more than −8% over any one month in 95% of months.

The VIX, a ticker symbol of the CBOE Volatility Index, measures **implied volatility** of index options on the S&P 500 Index. It is called the fear index because it tends to jump when equities fall and drop when equities rally. It reflects market expectations of stock market volatility over the short term (30 days). Implied volatility is the volatility that when used in an option-pricing model it gives the current option price.

Beta

Beta (Greek β) is another popular risk metric.[10] It measures volatility with respect of an index, reflecting an investment's tendency to respond to index movements.[11] Put differently, beta is the correlation between the investment and index times the ratio between the investment's volatility and the index's volatility.

A beta of 1 indicates the investment's price tends to move in the same direction and magnitude as the index. A beta below 1 indicates the investment tends to be less volatile than the index. A beta above 1 indicates the investment tends to be more volatile than the index.

A negative beta indicates the investment tends to move in the opposite direction of the index. A beta of zero indicates the investment is **market-neutral** – its returns tend to be independent of those of the index. A high positive beta (above 0.70) indicates the investment is **directional** – it tends to move in the index's direction and magnitude.

For example, investment A has a beta of 1.2. This directional investment tends to be 20% more volatile than the index. When the index moves up 10% or down 10%, investment A tends to move 12% or −12%, respectively.

Investment B has a beta of 0.2. When the index moves up 10% or down 10%, it tends to move only 2% or −2%, respectively. This is a **non-directional** investment. It is not completely market-neutral, but certainly not directional.

Since our focus is not on risk relative to a market or an index, we are not going to use beta as a risk measure. However, it is important to understand the concept of beta as a source of risk, and therefore return, due to exposure to the market.

A directional investment has **beta exposure**. Some of its risk and return come from market movements. A market-neutral investment has no beta exposure. Its risks and return come from other sources, rather than market movements.

Fixed income risks

Whilst for investments such as equities volatility is the common risk gauge, fixed income investments (bonds) have other risk measures, in addition to volatility.

Bonds pay investors a series of cash flows in the form of coupons (interest), typically twice a year, and then repay the loan's principal at maturity.

For example, you buy a 10-year gilt (UK Government bond) with a nominal face value (principal) of £1,000 and a 5% coupon. On 7 March you receive £25 (half of the annual 5% coupon). On 7 September you receive another £25. You keep receiving such coupons every six months until, upon the gilt's maturity date, you receive £1,025, which is capital repayment and final coupon.[12]

Fixed income investments are sensitive to three main types of risks:

1   Interest rate risk.

2   Inflation risk.

3   Credit risk.

Interest rate risk

The price of a bond, and that of most investments, reflects the **present value** of its future cash flows. Money today is worth more than money tomorrow. You have an opportunity to deposit it at a bank or invest it to enjoy a return – this is **time value of money**. By not having it today you incur an **opportunity cost**.

Calculating the present value of future cash flows requires discounting them to today's value by applying the expected rate of return you could have earned – the **discount rate**.

For example, you anticipate receiving £1,000 in five years. If you had the money today you could have invested it, expecting to earn 5% per year – this is the discount rate, which is the compound annual growth rate. In five years' time, your £1,000 would have reached an expected future value of £1,000 $\times$ $(1 + 5\%)^5$ = £1,276.3.

Using the same calculations, but in reverse, if the future value in five years is £1,000, the present value is £1,000 $\div$ $(1 + 5\%)^5$ = £783.5. The future value of £783.5 in five years is £1,000.[13]

One challenge with present value calculations is that the amounts and timing of cash flows are not always known in advance. Another challenge is that the appropriate discount rate typically is not certain. It should reflect the investment's risk level – the uncertainty of cash flows, or the **required rate of return** (RRR) that investors demand as compensation for holding the investment.

For example, for a low-risk bank deposit, RRR could be 2% – you know this is the return you will earn. But for a volatile stock the RRR could be 8% – you do not know the return you will realise. You should require a higher return or a risk premium for a riskier investment. Otherwise, why should anyone rational accept its risk?

Present value calculations demonstrate another important principle of investing: high price today means lower RRR, whilst low price today means higher RRR.

For example, two identical investments pay a single £100 cash flow in 12 months. The price of investment A is £95 whilst the price of investment B is £90. The RRR of expensive A is 5% and that of inexpensive B is 10%.[14]

When an asset's price is rich, expect lower future returns. When an asset's price is cheap, expect higher future returns, all else being equal. Pay careful attention to price when buying investments. High price means borrowing returns from the future.

Discount rate is made of the market's prevailing interest rate plus a spread, reflecting each particular investment's risk. In other words, it includes the risk-free rate of return for the appropriate horizon (such as BOE's base rate or 10-year gilt yield) plus a **risk premium** to compensate investors for risk.

As bonds produce a relatively foreseen stream of future cash flows, bond price closely reflects these cash flows' present value. Rising interest rates mean an increasing discount rate and decreasing bond price. Falling interest rates mean a decreasing discount rate and increasing bond price – an inverse relationship between interest rates and bond price.

Interest rate risk, therefore, is a potential fall in bond price, due to rising interest rates. For example, if the base rate is 0.5% and the BOE hikes it to 1%, bond prices may fall.

Interest rate risk is relevant to most assets that produce future cash flows, not only to bonds.[15] If the current price of an asset is the present value of its future cash flows, rising interest rates mean higher discount rate and potentially lower price.

Central banks, such as the BOE in the UK, set short-term rates. However, market forces of supply and demand set long-term rates. When more buyers than sellers buy government bonds with a maturity of 10 years, for instance, they push their price up. When price goes up, bonds' interest rate (yield) goes down. When more sellers than buyers sell 10-year bonds, they push their price down and yield up.

Another way to look at it is that when a bond is first issued, it offers a certain coupon rate. Demand sets its price and yield. This yield is appropriate for current market conditions. Say market rates rise. The bond is not attractive any more because its yield is not competitive now that rates elsewhere are higher. Supply surpasses demand until the price of the bond adjusts downward, increasing its yield so it is competitive again. This is interest rate risk.

Duration is a common interest rate risk measure. Modified duration measures the sensitivity of bond price to changes in interest rates.[16] Measured in years, duration reflects the weighted average maturity of cash flows.[17]

The longer the maturity, the longer is the duration. The smaller the coupons, the longer the duration, since the weight of capital repayment at maturity is larger. A longer duration means the bond price is more sensitive to changes in interest rates.

For example, a 10-year bond with a 5% coupon has a duration of 7.8 years. A similar bond with a 7% coupon has a duration of 7.4 years. Duration is shorter than maturity, unless it is a **zero-coupon bond**, which pays no coupons, so its duration equals its maturity.

Under certain assumptions (small, parallel shift of all interest rates across different maturities) change in bond price equals minus the change in interest rates times the bond's duration.[18]

For example, the duration of a 10-year gilt is 8 years. A 0.50% or 50 **basis points** (per cent of a per cent or $1 \div 10,000$) increase in interest rates means the bond price falls by about 4%.[19]

Because long-duration bonds are riskier than short-duration ones, long-maturity bonds must offer higher yields to compensate investors for risk. Otherwise, why would investors take the risk? This principle repeatedly pops up – higher risk requires higher return.

This is a similar logic to **time deposits** at banks and fixed rate cash ISAs. Banks pay a higher interest rate compared with regular deposits as you commit your money for a longer time. You are compensated for giving up some flexibility.

This is another principle: flexibility and optionality are valuable. Usually, you pay for flexibility and you can get paid for giving up flexibility. Here, you 'sell' the flexibility of your money to the bank. You give up the option of taking it whenever you want.

The compensation for long duration is called **term premium**. You should earn a higher return for investing for a longer term. Term premium reflects the higher uncertainty of future cash flows and the price of longer duration bonds (compensation for the risk of unexpected spike in rates).

Inflation risk

Inflation erodes the purchasing power of bonds' cash flows. Bond price incorporates *expected* inflation. Bonds' future cash flows are nominal, so expected inflation is part of the nominal discount rate when calculating their present value.[20] However, realised inflation might deviate from expected inflation. Therefore, bond yield and price are sensitive to inflation risk.

For example, to calculate the present value of a 10-year gilt paying a 5% semi-annual coupon with a £1,000 face value, you apply a 2% discount rate, reflecting expected future short-term rates of 1% and 1% inflation. The bond price is £1,272.

Due to an unexpected jump in oil price, inflation is now expected to rise to 3%. The new discount rate is 4%. The bond price drops to £1,085. You also expect interest rates to increase due to higher inflation, further increasing the discount rate and decreasing the bond price.

The longer the maturity, the higher is the risk of inflation deviating from expectations. Also, inflation's potential impact on cash flows is larger. Long-term bond rates reflect, among others, the market expectations of future short-term interest rates and inflation.[21]

When the economy is growing, inflation is expected to rise due to increased aggregate demand for goods and services. Central banks are likely to raise short-term rates to control inflation. So bond price should suffer when the economy grows due to both interest rate risk and inflation risk. The opposite should occur when the economy slows down.

Inflation risk is not exclusively relevant to bonds. It is a risk of most investments. However, the prices of some investments, such as inflation-linked bonds and property, are linked to changes in inflation. Such investments mitigate inflation risk.

Credit risk

Credit risk is the chance the bond's issuer will default on its obligations in accordance with agreed terms. A default includes not paying all payments – nothing at all or smaller amounts following a debt restructuring (haircut), or delaying the timing of payments.

When buying a bond you are the lender (creditor). You assume credit risk that you will not get fully paid or paid on time as you were promised.

Gilts issued by the British Government have negligible credit risk. The British Government will not default, or at least it is extremely improbable. It has a reputation to maintain. Otherwise, it will not be able to borrow at low interest rates. Its creditors will demand higher rates as compensation for higher risk. It can always increase taxes, borrow more or print money to pay off its debt.

Bonds issued by a corporation or a government of a country that runs into financial difficulties might default. A corporation can go bust and a country can run out of money. Argentina, Greece and Russia are examples of countries notoriously defaulting on their sovereign debt.

For assuming default risk you are compensated with a higher interest rate compared with gilts. This higher rate is **credit risk premium**.

Credit risk is pertinent not only to bonds, but also to other investments. When letting a flat, for example, your tenant can default on rent.[22] This is credit risk.

When taking out a mortgage to buy a house, the lending bank is your creditor. It undertakes a credit risk with respect of you. However, it minimises its risk since your house is the collateral for the loan. Because property is a full collateral for the entire loan, it is secured and mortgage rates are lower than other, more speculative loans. Mortgage rates reflect the price of risk.

One of the reasons for the 2008 credit crunch was sub-prime lending. Banks irresponsibly handed out mortgages to borrowers with a questionable ability to pay off their loans, without adequate collateral. They mispriced risk by not demanding appropriately high mortgage rates.

Liquidity risk

One of the riskiest, but often-ignored, investment risks is liquidity risk. It is the ability or inability to sell investments when you want at a reasonable price. It captures the time and costs associated with liquidating investments into cash.

Cash is the most liquid medium of exchange and store of value. You cannot go to the supermarket with stocks and bonds – you need cash. Therefore, it is important to be able to turn investments into cash.

Different types of investments generally have different degrees of liquidity. Cash, gilts and government bonds of countries such as the USA and Germany are the most liquid. Stocks of large companies traded in developed markets and highly rated corporate bonds are liquid. Stocks of small companies, stocks traded in emerging markets and lowly rated corporate bonds are less liquid. Property and ownership rights in private businesses (private equity) are illiquid.

Similar to other investment risks, the market must attract investors to accept risks by offering returns. The reward for liquidity risk is **liquidity premium**.

Investors with a truly long investment horizon, such as savers for retirement, can shoulder liquidity risk since they do not need cash quickly. This allows them to harvest the liquidity premium. For example, part of the return of property should reflect its illiquid nature.

Illiquidity means inflexibility. When buying an annuity, for example, you receive a guaranteed stream of income that can satisfy part of your financial needs. However, an annuity is illiquid – it is inflexible, you cannot sell it (although this may change when an annuity secondary market is introduced). This is its main trade-off.

Linking risk and return

As you can see, one of the basic philosophies of investing is that risks should be compensated by returns.

For example, investment A's expected return is 5% with 10% volatility. Investment B's expected return is also 5%, but with 15% volatility. Nobody will buy investment B since it has the same expected return as that of investment A, but with a higher risk.

Lack of demand for investment B pushes its price down, until its expected return increases to 7%. Now, investment B is interesting for investors seeking higher returns than that of investment A and willing to accept its higher risk.

Investing is all about taking risks. Risk is not necessarily a bad thing. Without risk you could not earn above risk-free returns. Risk is a scarce resource you should embrace as it generates returns.

For example, saving for retirement, you aim for a £550,000 target portfolio size. Given your income, contributions and time horizon, your portfolio needs to return 5% per year to reach your goal. The interest rate on cash deposits is 2%. The only way for your portfolio to generate a return above 2% is by taking investment risk. Without risk you could not reach your target.

By blending different **risk factors** you can benefit from different risk premiums. If one does not deliver – nothing is certain, it is a risk – others may do so. Once again, do not put all your eggs with a single risk.

Investing needs courage. However, it also needs patience. When taking risk you can go through rough times, seeing your risky investments disappointingly losing. Not everyone can easily undergo such bad patches. It depends on your risk tolerance.

The principle of high risk/high return works in practice. Empirically, riskier investments have generally generated higher returns than safer ones. However, it heavily depends on the specific time period. There are times when riskier investments do much poorer than safer ones. This is the reason it is called risk.

This all means you should take controlled risks in your portfolio. It is the only way to generate returns in excess of the risk-free rate. Harvest the equity, term, credit and liquidity risk premiums to benefit from different sources of returns.

Risk-adjusted performance

Since return and risk are linked, it is helpful to combine them into one ratio. **Sharpe ratio**, called after its developer Nobel laureate William Sharpe, is a common risk-adjusted return measure.

Sharpe ratio is the average return earned in excess of the risk-free rate per unit of volatility (absolute risk).[23] Higher Sharpe ratio means the investment generated higher reward per unit of risk.

For example, an investment generated a 10% return, the risk-free rate is 2% and the investment's volatility is 16%. The Sharpe ratio is 0.50.[24]

Sharpe ratio can vary substantially across different investments and times. However, a general rule of thumb for a diversified portfolio is assuming a Sharpe ratio of 0.50. This is useful to link the return objective to the risk objective.

For example, your return objective is 5% per year, and the risk-free rate is 1%. Assuming a Sharpe ratio of 0.50, you will need to tolerate a volatility level of 8%.[25]

Absolute versus relative risk

Absolute risk focuses on how much you might lose independent of any benchmark or reference. For instance, volatility and duration are absolute risk measures. When buying a stock or an equity fund, one concern is that it can lose money. When buying a bond, interest rates might shoot up and your bond price might drop. This is absolute risk.

Relative risk focuses on potential losses compared to a benchmark or your investment objectives. For example, when investing in an actively managed equity fund, its fund manager aims to outperform a benchmark. The manager's job is justifying the fee paid for the potential return in excess of the benchmark.

To outperform the benchmark, the manager needs to perform differently from it. To do so, the fund must hold different securities or in different weights from those in the benchmark; otherwise, the fund and benchmark's performance will be identical. The manager must take a tracking risk with respect of the benchmark. This relative risk is often measured as **tracking error**.

Tracking error is relative standard deviation. The difference between them is that standard deviation uses absolute returns whilst tracking error uses relative returns (the difference between the returns of the fund and benchmark).[26]

Tracking error is a function of the correlation between the fund and the index, as well as their volatilities.[27] Higher volatilities and lower correlation lead to higher tracking error. It is more difficult to perform in line with a volatile asset – it is like hitting shooting ducks in a funfair; a static bullseye is easier to hit.

Tracking error and standard deviation have the same statistical properties. For example, when tracking error is 2%, assuming a normal distribution of relative returns, in two-thirds (68%) of times relative return is between −2% and +2% (one tracking error) and in 95% of times relative return is between −4% and 4% (two tracking errors).

Passive index trackers aim to minimise tracking error relative to their benchmark. Do not expect passive trackers to underperform or outperform the index. They should track it!

For example, a FTSE 100 Index tracker should fall by about 10% when the index falls 10%. If the tracker falls by only 5% then it is good, since it outperformed, but really it is bad, since it does not do what it says on the tin. Good returns are not always good. Investments should do what they are supposed to do, not to surprise you.

Information ratio

Similar to Sharpe ratio in absolute return/risk space, in relative space a popular risk-adjusted return measure is **information ratio**. It is calculated by dividing relative return (fund's return minus benchmark's return) by tracking error.[28] Information ratio measures the value added by active management considering risk.

For example, a fund returned 10% whilst its benchmark returned 8%. If the tracking error was 2%, then the information ratio is 1.0.[29] An information ratio above 0.50 is considered good.

The need to take risk

When saving for retirement the risk level to bear is not only about your risk tolerance, but also about your need to take risk. Your goal is saving an amount of money by your retirement. This amount needs to support you financially for the rest of your life.

The amount is a function of three variables:

1 Time.
2 Contributions.
3 Net return.

Given time and contributions, you need a certain target net return. To achieve this return, you need to accept a certain risk level.

Whether you are happy with this risk or not, it is needed. The only other ways to achieve the target amount without taking investment risk are:

1 Save over a longer time period by either starting earlier (which is impossible from where you are now) or deferring retirement.
2 Increase contributions.
3 Settle for a lower standard of living post retirement by reducing the target saving amount.
4 Minimise costs and taxes (increase efficiency to reduce bleeding of money in pension).

For example, you are 40 and want to retire at 55 (time is 15 years). You and your employer contribute £40,000 per year (the annual allowance benefiting from a tax relief). You aim for £1 million when retiring. To reach your target, you need an annual average return of 6.4%.[30] Assuming a 0.50 Sharpe ratio and a 1% risk-free rate, you *need* to accept volatility of 10.8%.[31]

Your circumstances and objectives dictate the risk level you must tolerate. If risk is too high, you can postpone retirement to 65, for example. By extending time by 10 years, keeping contributions constant, you actually need nil return and nil investment risk (ignoring inflation risk). However, postponing retirement by 10 years is not a privilege or a desire of everyone.

Not taking sufficient risk is a risk.

Longevity risk

The average life expectancy continues to increase due to ongoing medical advancements, better healthcare and lifestyle education. Your life expectancy depends on your current health and heredity, among other factors (such as luck).

A man reaching age 65 in 2015 can expect to live, on average, for another 18 years, according to the Office for National Statistics (ONS). This is compared to six years for men reaching 65 in 1980. Women at 65 today can expect to live another 21 years, compared to 12 years in 1980.

Longevity risk means you might outlive your assets, as your time horizon may be longer than you realise. Be prepared to live a long time, ensuring you have enough money to maintain your lifestyle.

This is one of the most important risks when planning for retirement. Running out of money (financial ruin) could be dreadful.

Known unknowns and unknown unknowns

Risk means we do not know what is going to happen. But we know the distribution of potential outcomes. We can quantify risk, mitigate it and control it. Risk is known unknowns.

For example, when throwing a die, you do not know whether it is going to fall on 1, 2, 3, 4, 5 or 6. But you know it is going to be one of these outcomes with a probability of $1 \div 6$.

Uncertainty means we do not know what is going to happen. And we do not know the distribution of potential outcomes. We cannot quantify uncertainty; it is unknown unknowns.

Risk is a multi-faceted, multi-dimensional concept. When thinking about it, consider the range of potential results, how much you might lose, and the chance of a permanent loss. Reflect whether you can sell investments, if you want to do so. Contemplate whether the amount you have accumulated is sufficient, even if you live longer than expected. And ensure risk is in line with your risk tolerance and the returns you require to achieve your financial goals.

It is always more pleasant focusing on returns and the upside. However, focusing on the potential loss if things do not turn out as hoped for is more valuable.

Summary

- Earning a return above the risk-free rate needs taking investment risk, which is the chance of missing your return objective.
- The most important risk is shortfall risk – the chance of realised return falling short of your target return.

- Risk tolerance is your willingness and ability to take risk.

- Investing's true risk is permanent loss. Volatility is not bad, as long as your time horizon allows recouping losses. When time horizon is short, appetite for volatility should wane. Timing is everything – you cannot afford to lose a lot just before needing the money.

- Different assets have different volatilities. By blending them in different proportions construct a portfolio with a risk level matching your risk tolerance.

- Three main risks in fixed income are interest rate, inflation and credit risk. Liquidity risk is relevant to any illiquid asset.

- Higher risks should come with higher returns, but not always.

- You need to take risk. Calculate your target savings amount at retirement. Achieving this amount is a function of time, contributions and net return. Given time and contributions, target return dictates a certain risk level.

- Consider longevity risk when saving and investing for retirement. Avoid running out of money after retirement.

Notes

1 This can cause a **moral hazard**. Bankers can take excessive risks since they know that the government and the public bear the burden of these risks.

2 For compensation limits and other information on FSCS visit **www.fscs.org.uk**.

3 Standard deviation (σ, sigma) is the square root ($\sqrt{}$) of the sum (Σ) of the squared distances of each return i (r_i) from the mean return (μ, mu), divided by the number of returns (N). $\sigma = \sqrt{\Sigma[(r_i - \mu)^2 \div N]}$.

4 99.7% of returns fall within three standard deviations of the mean. Two-standard-deviation (2-sigma) event has a probability of 2.275% to occur or every 44 days. Three-sigma event is expected to occur once every 741 days, 4-sigma event every 31,560 days (126 years) and 5-sigma event every 13,932 years.

5 $-7\% = 8\% - 15\%$; $23\% = 8\% + 15\%$.

6 $-22\% = 8\% - 2 \times 15\%$; $38\% = 8\% + 2 \times 15\%$.

7 To annualise standard deviation based on daily returns, multiply it by the square root of 252 (number of business days in a year). If it is based on monthly returns, multiply it by the square root of 12 (number of months in a year).

8 They are called fat tail since there are more returns in the tails of the distribution than predicted by a normal distribution; the tails of the distribution are fatter than normal.

9 To be precise, according to the Capital Asset Pricing Model (CAPM) undiversifiable volatility, or market risk as measured by beta, should be compensated by higher returns.

10 $\beta = \text{Cov}(r_i, r_m) \div \text{Var}(r_m)$ where r_i is the returns of investment i, r_m is the returns of the market, Cov is covariance and Var is variance. Another way to define beta is $\beta = \rho_{i,m}(\sigma_i \div \sigma_m)$. Beta is the slope of a linear regression line when regressing investment's returns on index's returns.

11 The index could be an index representing an equity market, such as FTSE 100 Index, a bond market, other asset classes or a blend of asset classes.

12 The London Stock Exchange publishes on its website at **www.londonstockexchange .com** 'A Private Investor's Guide to Gilts', which includes detailed explanations on gilts.

13 $£1,000 = £783.5 (1 + 5\%)^5$. $PV = \Sigma[CF_t \div (1 + r)^t]$; where PV is present value, CF_t is cash flow at time t and r is the rate of return.

14 $£95 = £100 \div (1 + 5\%)$; $£90 = £100 \div (1 + 10\%)$.

15 Unless their cash flows change with interest rates, such as those of Floating Rate Notes (FRNs).

16 Duration measures how much time it will take the bond's cash flows to repay the bond's price to investors. Modified duration measures the sensitivity of bond price to changes in interest rates. $\Delta P = -D\Delta y$ where ΔP is change in price, D is modified duration and Δy is change in yield.

17 Check Investopedia at **www.investopedia.com** for a free duration calculator. One of the inputs of the calculator is yield (yield to maturity), which will be explained in Chapter 9 in the section 'Fixed income'.

18 Bond's duration changes when interest rates change. Convexity measures the sensitivity of duration to changes in rates. Using duration and convexity can improve estimating bond price sensitivity to changes in rates compared to using only duration. $\Delta P = -D\Delta y + 0.5C\Delta y^2$ where C is convexity.

19 $-4\% = -0.5\% \times 8$.

20 When cash flows are real the discount rate should be real and when cash flows are nominal the discount rate should be nominal.

21 The shape of the term structure of interest rates is explained by three theories. Long-term rates reflect expected future short-term rates (pure expectations hypothesis), liquidity premium (liquidity preference hypothesis) and supply and demand of different bond maturities (segmentation hypothesis).

22 Some ways landlords can protect rental stream include due diligence on tenants (credit checks and referencing), rent deposit, post-dated cheques, guarantees, guarantors and interest on late payments.

23 $SR = (r - r_f) \div \sigma$ where SR is Sharpe ratio, r is the asset's return, r_f is the risk-free rate and σ is the asset's volatility. SR can be based either on expected, future, *ex ante* return and risk or realised, historic, *ex post* return and risk.

24 $0.50 = (10\% - 2\%) \div 16\%$.

25 $8\% = (5\% - 1\%) \div 0.50$.

26 Tracking error = standard deviation $(r_i - r_b)$ where r_i is the series of investment returns and r_b is the series of benchmark returns. $TE = \sqrt{(\sigma_p^2 + \sigma_b^2 - 2\rho_{p,b}\sigma_p\sigma_b)}$ where σ_p and σ_b are the volatilities of the portfolio and benchmark and $\rho_{p,b}$ is the correlation between them.

27 Determinants of tracking error are number of securities in the portfolio (those in the benchmark and those not in the benchmark); size, style and sector deviations from those of the benchmark; beta and benchmark volatility.

28 $IR = (r_i - r_b) \div TE_{i,b}$ where IR is information ratio, r_i is investment's return, r_b is benchmark's return and $TE_{i,b}$ is tracking error of the investment with its benchmark.

29 $1.0 = (10\% - 8\%) \div 2\%$.

30 Using the savings calculator of the Citizens Advice at **www.citizensadvice.org.uk**, to reach £1 million in 15 years the monthly contributions are £3,333, which is £40,000 per year.

31 $10.8\% = (6.4\% - 1\%) \div 0.50$.

CHAPTER 5
INVESTMENT CONSTRAINTS

What else to consider beyond return and risk objectives?

'Nothing is more difficult, and therefore more precious, than to be able to decide.'

Napoleon Bonaparte

The two investment objectives are return and risk. Return objective defines what you want your investments to achieve – the outcome. Risk objective defines what risk level you should and can bear – the journey's volatility.

However, you may have other considerations and constraints influencing your portfolio. Beyond the two investment objectives, consider five groups of investment constraints:

1 Time horizon.
2 Liquidity.
3 Taxes.
4 Legal and regulatory.
5 Special circumstances.

Time horizon

Time horizon is the period over which you invest. It outlines when you will need the money.

For example, if you are 25 and save for expected retirement at 65, your time horizon is 40 years. If you are retired at 65 and your life expectancy is 90 years, the *expected* time horizon is 25 years. If you live longer, to the age of 100, your time horizon unexpectedly increases to 35 years. Hopefully, your portfolio was designed to survive 35 years, not only 25.

When planning and investing, expect the unexpected. Hope for the best but plan for the worst. Always have a margin of safety.

Your overall time horizon can be divided into separate phases. For example, 40 years until retirement, 40 years post retirement and perhaps perpetual after death, leaving an inheritance. The return and risk objectives for each phase are probably different.

Generally, the longer your time horizon, the higher the risk level you can assume. A rule of thumb says the proportion to invest in equities is 100% minus your age. When you are 20 invest 80% of your portfolio in equities. When you are 70 invest only 30% in equities. This is not accurate – do not follow this rule to its letter. But it does demonstrate the relationship between time and risk.

More time allows taking more risk. You have time to recoup losses so your ability to take risk is higher. You should have more appetite for volatility.

Markets tend to crash every number of years. If you panic and sell after the crash at the market's bottom or cannot stay invested, you crystallise the losses. But, if you wait patiently, markets rebound. It can take a long time, but they have always recovered eventually.

The markets have done so following the crashes of 1987 (Black Monday), 1998 (Russian default crisis), 2000 (high-tech bubble burst), 2008 (global financial crisis) and 2011 (European sovereign debt crisis). However, if you have no time and are forced to sell, then you cannot wait for a recovery. Had you retired in 2011, for instance, you would not have had time to recover from the 2008 and 2011 crises.

Lengthy time can justify investing in expensive investments. It allows generating returns to rationalise costs. For example, buying and selling a property could cost over 7%.[1] With a time horizon of only one or two years, stay away. The return might be insufficient to cover the expenses. However, with 10 years, investing may justify the costs since total return can comfortably surpass 7%.

Time justifies holding illiquid investments. Since you do not need to sell them any time soon, you can tolerate liquidity risk, which brings liquidity premium.

Back to the property example, if you must sell it after two years, you might lack enough time to wait for the right buyer or for supportive market conditions. With more time, you can be patient, selling when you want, not when you must.

A longer time horizon permits a higher risk appetite, flexibility and additional options. Critically, it enables accumulating money and returns, benefiting from compounding. That is why the sooner you start saving and investing the better.

If your time horizon is short, invest only in safe, conservative investments. For example, if you need your money next year, avoid equities. Their price can fall within a year and you cannot remain invested to make back losses. Instead, invest in cash deposits and short-term bonds without risking capital.

A long investment horizon is also emotionally reassuring. Checking your portfolio's performance every day, you will experience good days, when making money, as well as bad days, when losing money. This could be frustrating and psychologically draining. Do not do this to yourself. Anyway, unless you are a day trader, do not change your portfolio based on one-day movements.

With a really long time horizon, try refraining from high-frequency performance monitoring. Focus on the big picture over the long term. This can help to avoid making irrational, emotional investment decisions based on fear or greed.

Pension freedom means that no longer are you forced to sell your investments when retiring to buy an annuity. You can keep investing, extending your time horizon, at least with part of your portfolio.

Time is an invaluable luxury. The amount of time at your disposal shapes your portfolio – influencing its risk level, the types of investment it includes and how often you should review its performance.

Liquidity

Liquidity measures the marketability of investments – the cost and time to turn them into cash. Liquidity constraint determines the fraction of your portfolio holding liquid investments.

Some assets are liquid whilst others are illiquid. When selling a UK equity fund, for example, you can usually do so within two days, depending on its **settlement period** and **dealing frequency** – it does not take too much time.[2]

It involves some transaction costs. You will be charged for them, as they are reflected in the price you receive when selling your shares in the fund. However, UK equities are normally liquid so trading them does not involve high costs.

Selling property is a different story. It may take several months to hire an estate agent, publish your property, find a buyer, and go through the legal process of exchanging contracts. Transaction costs involve payments to estate agents, solicitors and perhaps CGT. Luckily for sellers, **stamp duty** (Stamp Duty Land Tax – SDLT) is levied on buyers. Selling property takes time and money. It is illiquid.

Cash is the most liquid asset. You can use it to buy and pay for whatever you require (as long as money can buy it). Liquidity constraints reflect your need for cash or assets that can be turned quickly and inexpensively into cash.

Settlement period

When buying or selling securities or funds, two important dates are: transaction date and settlement date. The settlement date usually occurs one, two or three days after the transaction date. The settlement period is indicated using the abbreviations T + 1, T + 2 or T + 3. Transaction date is when you put the trade order. Settlement date is when ownership is transferred and money is exchanged between buyer and seller. The standard settlement period in the UK is T + 2.

Liquidity needs are divided into **expected** and **unexpected**.

If you know when and how much cash you will need, plan to have it at hand. For example, your child's £10,000 university tuition fee is due in one year. The annual interest on 12-month term deposit is 2%. You put aside £9,804 in the deposit, letting it grow to £10,000 in one year. It is relatively easy to plan for expected liquidity needs.[3]

Unexpected liquidity needs include a cash reserve to cover unexpected payments. For example, your car might break down, requiring an urgent replacement. Keep some cash in your bank account to quickly pay for contingencies.

Some cash should be available to exploit emerging investment opportunities. For example, if you are looking to buy a property, having sufficient cash for a deposit or, better yet, to be a cash buyer, can give you an advantage. The trade-off is opportunity cost – the return the cash could have made had it been invested.

By blending different investments with different liquidity characteristics, design a portfolio meeting your liquidity needs. One challenge is that liquidity of some investments changes. Liquidity is ample when you do not need it, but it can dry up when you need it the most. It is also seasonal. During December, for instance, liquidity is low, due to the holiday season.

For example, you hold corporate bonds. In normal times you can readily find willing buyers. However, when financial conditions are stressed (like they were in 2008) and everyone looks to sell corporate bonds, it might be impossible to find buyers.

Liquidity is gone. You can either wait until it is back or drop the price of your bonds until someone is willing to buy them at a bargain price. You can sell almost everything; it is a question of price.

Illiquidity can come with a cost. If you need cash quickly, you might incur losses on assets you are forced to sell at fire-sale prices. This is liquidity risk.

Your DC pension before you are 55 and annuities are illiquid. ISAa can be liquid. Pension freedom means your pension can be liquid after retirement.

Liquidity constraint means keeping some assets in cash or close to cash (such as liquid gilts). Since you cannot access your pension before retirement and you should not raid your ISAs unless you must, keep some cash in a bank account.

Taxes

'In this world nothing can be said to be certain, except death and taxes.'

Benjamin Franklin

We have discussed taxes at length already; we will not do it again.

You pay income tax on your salary, interest and rental income. You pay tax on dividends. You pay CGT on capital gains. You pay stamp duty when buying UK equities or properties. You pay Value Added Tax (VAT) when buying some goods and services. And you pay IHT when you leave this world. Taxes are everywhere.

Taxes eat into returns. A basic investing principle is to minimise costs and taxes – this is one of the only ways to enhance returns without taking investment risks.

One of the major incentives to save within pensions and ISAs is favourable tax treatment. When hopefully earning interest and capital gains, they are sheltered from tax as long as you keep the investments in a pension or ISAs.

When withdrawing pension benefits after retirement, you have deferred income tax payments by many years. Time value of money plays in your favour. Instead of paying taxes today, paying them in the future is valuable.

This is an advantage of pensions over ISAs. You save money in ISAs after paying income tax, but you do not pay tax when taking money out (taxed, exempt, exempt – TEE). You put money in a pension without paying income tax, but you pay it later when drawing money (exempt, exempt, taxed – EET). The British Government is contemplating whether to switch pensions from an EET to a TEE regime.

Maximise contributions into your pension to the maximum permitted by law. Maximise yearly savings in ISAs. Tax savings can make a massive difference. Mitigate your tax bill as much as legally possible.

Tax constraint means you should invest in pensions and ISAs as much as possible rather than elsewhere. It limits your accessibility to your investments, encouraging long-term investing.

Legal and regulatory

Pensions and ISAs are heavily regulated. Regulations dictate the types of pensions and ISAs you can have, how much you can save, at what age you can retire and what you can and cannot do with your money when retired.

Regulations continuously change. Keep yourself informed and updated. The regulations seem complex and intimidating. However, they are meant to be understood by unprofessional savers outside of the pension or investment community.

Visit **www.gov.uk** often, familiarising yourself with your rights and obligations, as well as those of your employer, if relevant. Consider taking professional advice.

When the chancellor announces the budget, it includes key changes to regulations about savings and pensions. It would be all over the news.

Just as the rules governing pensions and ISAs have been changing during recent years, they might change again in the future. Build some flexibility into your planning to allow for this. While the main objective of pensions was income before pension freedom, now it is also the flexibility to access capital.

Legal and regulatory constraints shape the way you save and invest for retirement.

Special circumstances

Special circumstances are a residual category of constraints that are not covered by the other four groups. Unique to you, they cover any constraint you wish to impose.

For example, responsible investing (so-called **Socially Responsible Investing** – SRI, or **Environment, Social and Governance** – ESG) can include avoiding investing in companies in vice sectors, such as tobacco, alcohol, gambling, defence and porn (exclusions) or investing in companies with sustainable businesses (inclusions). You may buy such investments because of ethical reasons or since you believe they will generate superior returns.

Impact investing is investing in companies, organisations and projects with a positive impact on the environment or society, such as microfinance, green energy, clean drinking water and low-income housing.

Sharia law is a set of Islamic rules. It has restrictions on payment and collection of interest, investing in companies involved in prohibited businesses, using derivatives, since they might involve gambling, and day trading.

You are managing your portfolio for your future. You are the boss. Decide how to manage your assets. You are free to put whatever constraints you desire.

The caution is that you are limited by the available funds and investments in your pension and ISAs. For example, not all platforms offer choices of responsible investing. Your constraints are constrained by the available choices.

Free your manager

The more constraints you enforce on your portfolio or fund managers, the more difficult it is to generate returns. This stems from the philosophy of aspiring to have the widest **investment opportunity set**, which is the universe of investment choices. More choice means more freedom and flexibility.

Free your manager. A skilled manager can potentially turn choice into better results. If managers are unskilful constrain them. Better yet, if they are unskilful do not use them in the first place.

Constraints go against choice and freedom. Minimise investment constraints.

Establishing objectives

The return and risk objectives, complemented by investment constraints, form your investment objectives. We have completed the first step of the investment management process.

When planning for retirement, first form a realistic vision. How do you imagine your retirement? What kind of lifestyle do you wish to live? Where do you want to live? What financial resources do you need to make your vision a reality? This is the ultimate reason for saving and investing for retirement – your investment objectives.

Next, plan how you are going to achieve your vision. What actions will you take from now on for the rest of your life to progress you towards your vision? This plan is the investment strategy.

Summary

- Investment constraints complement the return and risk objectives to define how to design and manage your portfolio.

- Time horizon is critical to the ability to take risk and returns you should expect. Longer time means higher risk tolerance, higher potential returns, more time to accumulate money and letting compound return work.

- Liquidity constraint is the proportion of assets you keep in cash or to be able to quickly and inexpensively turn into cash to meet expected and unexpected liquidity needs. You cannot access your pension before retirement and you should not access your ISAs unless you must. Keep a cash reserve in your bank account, considering the opportunity cost.

- One advantage of pensions and ISAs is favourable tax treatment. Do everything that is legally permitted to minimise your taxes.

- Pensions and ISAs are heavily regulated. Keep yourself updated.

- Special circumstances include any other constraint you wish to impose on your investments.

- Avoid constraining yourself and your fund managers since it limits the choices that potentially can be turned into better results.

Notes

1 The costs of buying and selling property include stamp duty, mortgage fees, legal fees, estate agent fees, renovations and removals.

2 Daily dealing and daily pricing mean a fund can be traded every day and its price is published every day. Some funds have less frequent dealing and pricing, such as weekly or monthly.

3 £9,804 = £10,000 ÷ (1 + 2%).

CHAPTER 6
INVESTMENT STRATEGY
The plan

'If you don't know where you are going, you'll end up somewhere else'

Yogi Berra

Once you have formulated your investment objectives and constraints the next step in the investment management process is setting an investment strategy that has the highest likelihood of meeting your objectives whilst complying with the constraints.

Investment strategy (**investment policy**) is the plan of how you will position and manage your portfolio, aiming to achieve your desired outcomes given your risk tolerance. It is made up of a top-down asset allocation, deciding how much to invest in each asset class, and a bottom-up investment selection, deciding which investments to use under each asset class.

The future is unknown. But even if it is different from what you thought it would be, you must plan for it.

Investment strategy depends on two sets of factors. The first set is your particular internal objectives and constraints. It defines what you want to achieve. The second set is external factors of economic conditions. It determines whether and how you can achieve your objectives, depending on what financial markets are delivering.

For example, your goal is 8% annual average return over the next 10 years. Achieving this could have been possible during the 1980s and 1990s when both equities and bonds performed strongly. But it would have been unlikely to achieve during the 2000s when equity markets suffered two material bear markets in 2000 and 2008, taking off again only after 2011.

Planning appropriately is not always enough; you need financial markets to be supportive. There is a big element of luck in investing – it is better being lucky than smart. Adapt your plans and expectations based on market conditions.

Each combination of desired outcomes, risk tolerance and constraints necessitates a different plan. For example, long-term aggressive growth calls for an investment strategy focused mainly on risky assets, like equities. For income generation, a conservative strategy, focused on high-yielding investments, like bonds, may fit. When time horizon is short, the strategy should focus on preserving capital through low-risk investments.

As investment objectives and constraints change over time, so does the strategy – it is dynamic. Each phase of your overall time horizon may require a different strategy to address your needs and risks at the particular phase.

Formulating an investment strategy should begin at understanding the typical return and risk objectives during different phases of a typical saver's life. It demonstrates how to plan a strategy for each phase. Subsequent chapters will cover these strategies and characteristics of different investments.

Investment Policy Statement

An **Investment Policy Statement** (IPS) is a document listing your objectives, constraints, investment strategy and rules for managing the portfolio.

This document can aid in following a disciplined process. Sometimes, when markets crash, all you see is gloom and doom. Feeling punished, you want nothing more than getting out of the market. An IPS can remind you what the long-term plan is, helping you avoid acting recklessly and emotionally. Clear investment strategy and IPS can help make rational investment decisions.

Drafting an IPS is not mandatory. It guides some people, whilst others view it as an unnecessary burden. It is a common practice when institutional investors hire portfolio managers to outline in writing the portfolio management's rules.

You are an individual investor. You are managing your private portfolio. You may hire fund managers to manage portions of it, such as equities, bonds and cash. But you hire them through buying shares in publicly available funds they manage. You do not need to draft any documents or investment management agreements (IMAs).

It is entirely up to you. Draft an IPS only if you think it can assist. Use it to summarise all the information on your savings and investments. But do not do it if it is a nuisance.

For example, you should keep track of how much your employer and you contribute every year to your pension, where you are relative to your annual and lifetime allowances, and how much you have saved in ISAs. An IPS can help keep track of your actions and to-do-list.

Account aggregation views your entire assets. IPS can form one consolidated, holistic view of your wealth across different accounts.

For instance, if you own a house, you have large exposure to the property market. It may make no sense to invest in commercial property in your pension, doubling up your exposure. If you hold cash in your current and savings bank accounts, you should probably avoid it in your pension and ISAs. If you hold stocks in your ISA, consider holding fewer in your pension. And so on.

Summarising everything in an IPS can support considering the big picture, whilst not forgetting the small details.

Table 6.1 shows a basic IPS for illustration.

Table 6.1 Illustrative IPS

Investment Policy Statement (IPS)	
Investing purpose	Accumulate a pension pot of £550,000 for retirement at 65.
	When retired, use 50% to buy an annuity and keep 50% invested.
	Take £2,000 tax-free cash lump sum at retirement. Wait with the rest.
Return objectives	Long-term capital growth. At least LIBOR + 5% per year.
Risk objective	Needed volatility 8%. Volatility can be higher.
Time horizon	Phase I: 30 years to retirement. Phase II: 30–40+ years post-retirement. Phase III: Inheritance.
Liquidity	Save for deposit to buy home. Keep £2,000 in bank for emergencies. No other liquidity needs. No cash in pension.
Taxes	Maximise investing in pensions and ISAs.
Target asset allocation	80% global equity, 20% UK bonds, divided between gilts and corporate bonds.
Investment selection	80% of equity in global index tracker, 20% of equity across three global active funds. 50% of bonds gilts, 50% of bonds investment grade credit. All bonds in index trackers.
Trading rules	Stop loss −5%.
	Consider buying after a 10% drop in market.

Investment Policy Statement (IPS)	
Rebalancing	Every six months or when allocation exceeds target by 10%. Take profits at +10%.
Review performance	Every quarter. Consider deselecting active funds only based on at least 3-year track record or unexplained short-term drop.
Savings	Employer contributes 10% to pension, I contribute 10%. Current salary £40,000. Try saving in ISAs. When salary increases, use AVCs to boost contributions. Do not forget to carry forward annual allowance from previous three years.
Review IPS	Annually.

Summary

- Investment strategy is the plan of what you will do to increase the likelihood of achieving your target investment outcomes, in line with your risk tolerance whilst complying with your investment constraints.

- To formulate a strategy, understand the general financial goals for each phase of your life cycle, the characteristics of different investments and how to blend them into an asset allocation to match the return and risk objectives of each phase of your life cycle.

- Investment Policy Statement (IPS) outlines the investment objectives, constraints, strategy and rules for managing your portfolio.

- IPS can help with aggregating all your assets to form a holistic view of your wealth whilst keeping track of all your actions.

- Keep your plan flexible. While planning and following a plan are essential, reality is likely to make you change your plan.

CHAPTER 7
LIFECYCLE INVESTING

The investment objectives at different phases of life

'The journey of a thousand miles begins with a single step.'

Lao Tzu

The life journey of each person is unique. However, some phases in the path can be stylised, having similar investment objectives and constraints across individuals. Lifecycle investing can aid envisaging your financial goals during different phases of life and formulating an appropriate strategy.

We break the life cycle into three broad phases:

1   Accumulation.
2   Consolidation.
3   De-accumulation (decumulation).

Accumulation phase

The accumulation phase normally lasts from young adulthood (age of 25) to about 10 years before retirement (45 to 55, depending on your retirement age). In this phase, you are working, earning an income, investing and accumulating wealth. Some of this wealth should be saved for retirement.

The accumulation phase is divided into **early accumulation** and **late accumulation**.

Early accumulation

Early accumulation usually starts at young adulthood (25), lasting until early middle age (40). During this phase, the primary financial objectives focus on immediate needs, such as housing, car and starting a family. Emergency cash is important for large expenses, such as a car, education or a deposit on a house.

Net worth is small, but income is growing as you progress from a junior to a more senior job. A primary consideration is debt management, such as taking a mortgage for a house and repaying student loans. Children's private childcare and public school education could be a major expense, perhaps above mortgage payments.

You may have savings goals, like travelling, nice car, deposit on a house, education and retirement. However, retirement seems so far away, living expenses are high and income is low, so contributions into pension savings are relatively modest. You may be unable, or uninterested, to take advantage of your long-time horizon to start saving early.

Return objective

Your return objective is aggressive growth, beat inflation, target an annual average **excess return** (return above cash) of 5%, 6% or higher. Return objective should be linked to inflation, such as inflation or cash plus 5% or 6%.[1] An 'inflation plus' or 'cash plus' objective targets long-term *real* capital growth.

Alternatively, your return objective can be to maximise potential growth; not targeting a specific return. Adopting a strategy of investing only in equities, for example, does not target an explicit return. It depends on risk tolerance, utilising the long time horizon and low liquidity needs, which are satisfied by income from work. This is the phase to take investment risk.

Risk objective

Given the long time horizon and low liquidity needs from pension savings, risk appetite can be relatively high. An annual excess return of 5% to 6% should be aligned with an annualised volatility of about 10% to 12%, assuming Sharpe ratio of 0.50.[2]

A 1% risk-free rate is low, matching the current low-yield environment. A 'normal' level of risk-free rate is 3% to 4%. When risk-free rate is higher, the required risk level can be lower, as cash deposits generate better returns. However, it may coincide with higher inflation as the BOE tightens monetary policy. So, the total return objective might be higher as well (inflation + 4% equals 6% when inflation is 2%, but 8% when inflation is 4%).[3]

Investing only in equities requires a risk level of annualised volatility above 15%. This means accepting a possibility of losing over 20% in a single year.

Some investors should consider a conservative, low-risk strategy in their first few years of investing. Sometimes called the **foundation phase**, it aims to avoid bad investment experiences that might discourage you before you accumulate investment experience, building up your risk tolerance.

Tolerance for liquidity risk is high. You can invest in illiquid assets, reaping the liquidity premium.

Time horizon

Time horizon is typically between 15 and 20 years.

Liquidity

There are no liquidity needs from the pension. Income from work and cash reserves outside the pension should satisfy liquidity needs. The pension is inaccessible until the age of 55 anyway.

ISAs can be accessed. However, you need to return the withdrawal back into the ISAs in the same tax year to reset the tax-free allowance.

Investment strategy

The strategy is *aggressive* long-term real capital growth. This strategy can include only equities or a mix of mostly equities and other assets, including illiquid ones.

Late accumulation

Late accumulation usually starts at early middle age (40), lasting until about 10 years before retirement (45 to 55 as retirement age is typically between 55 and 65). During this phase, debt management gives way to wealth accumulation. The mortgage is shrinking, although you may still support your children and finance their education and, perhaps, their wedding.

Income from work should be higher than in the early accumulation phase. Net worth is growing. The primary goal is saving for approaching retirement. Time is flying fast. With increased income, you can, and should, significantly contribute into your pension. Consider a strategy of escalation of contributions: making small contributions initially and as salary rises increasing their proportion.

Return objective

Your return objective is growth, beat inflation, target an annual average excess return of 4% to 6% or higher. Return objective may be lower than that of the early accumulation phase, since contributions can grow the pension. But it is not necessarily so. Targeting high returns may still make sense since time horizon is sufficiently long and you may be more experienced and comfortable with investing. Having additional assets outside the pension can justify higher risk tolerance.

Risk objective

Time horizon is shorter than that of the early accumulation phase, but still long. Liquidity needs are low from pension savings. Anyway, the pension is inaccessible. Annualised volatility between 8% and 12% is aligned with the return objectives.[4]

Whilst you may keep a strategy of investing only in equities, consider shifting to a more diversified mix of assets, reducing downside risk. The time horizon may not suffice to recover from a severe market crash as this phase's end approaches.

Whilst tolerance for liquidity risk is still high, gradually start reducing the exposure to illiquid assets over time.

Time horizon

Time horizon is typically between 5 and 15 years.

Liquidity

There are no liquidity needs from the pension. Income and assets elsewhere should suffice.

ISAs can be accessed (see restrictions above in early accumulation).

Investment strategy

The strategy is long-term real capital growth. Focus on real return (beating inflation). Whilst still growth-oriented, strategy should be less aggressive, emphasising more on mitigating downside risk than in the early accumulation phase.

Consolidation phase

The consolidation phase usually begins 10 years before retirement (45 to 55) and ends at retirement. You have already accumulated assets in the pension. You have finished paying most of your debt, such as mortgage and tuition fees for children. Income from work is still high and expenses are lower, so maximise pension contributions.

This is the last stretch of the marathon. Make the most of annual allowances, aspiring to reach the lifetime allowance. Actually, most people can contribute the most into their pension during this phase.

With 10 years to go, start gradually de-risking the portfolio with a terminal asset allocation in mind. This process is called a **glide path**.

Terminal asset allocation is the asset mix you aim to hold at retirement. Whilst labelled 'terminal', it is not the journey's end since, after retirement, parts of the portfolio should remain invested. However, it is the end of the accumulation and consolidation phases.

For example, terminal asset mix can include 25% in cash to take as a tax-free lump sum. You may wish to purchase an annuity with, say, another 25% of the assets to provide a steady, secured income stream for the rest of your life. It is a way to mitigate longevity risk and satisfy minimum required needs. You should hold 25% in long-term gilts a number of years before retirement to do so.

Bonds and annuities share similar risks. When interest rates move down, annuity prices move up (and annuity rate down). Buying long-term bonds before retirement hedges changes in annuity price, in particular when bond yields are high.

Part of the portfolio can end up in income-generating assets for post-retirement. They target a yield benchmarked to annuity rate with the flexibility of selling them when requiring lump sums. An annuity lacks such flexibility. The trade-off is that investing for income requires taking investment risk, unlike an annuity.

Life expectancy is usually long after retirement. Hold some growth assets to preserve capital and keep pace with inflation. Retirement does not mean ceasing investing, but that needs, risk tolerance and strategy are likely to change.

The de-risking glide path should be gradual, avoiding selling assets after a drop, close to a trough, or buying assets after a rally, close to a peak. Doing it gradually over time averages buying and selling prices – so-called **dollar-cost averaging**.

A simple glide path linearly moves from current to terminal asset allocation. This mechanical approach does not need discretion. However, applying high-conviction discretion can help to opportunistically sell and buy assets after big price movements.

Another reason for de-risking the portfolio is sequential risk (timing of drawdowns). Overall average return can be good, but right returns in bad order can be detrimental. Nasty returns in the final ten years before retirement can hurt when portfolio size is big. A dynamic de-risking glide path can mitigate the impact of sequential risk.

Dollar-cost averaging

Dollar-cost averaging is buying or selling a fixed monetary amount of investments on a regular schedule, regardless of price. More investments are purchased when their price is low and fewer are purchased when their price is high. The price is averaged over time, minimising the risk of buying or selling at the wrong time.

Table 7.1 Illustrative linear glide path

Asset	T-10 %	T-9 %	T-8 %	T-7 %	T-6 %	T-5 %	T-4 %	T-3 %	T-2 %	T-1 %	T %
Equities	100	90	82	72	64	55	47	37	29	20	11
Long maturity bonds	0	3	8	11	16	19	23	27	31	34	39
Short maturity bonds	0	1	1	2	2	3	3	4	4	5	5
Corporate bonds	0	1	1	2	2	3	3	4	4	5	5
High yield bonds	0	1	2	3	4	5	5	6	7	8	9
REITs	0	1	1	2	2	3	4	4	5	5	6
Cash	0	3	5	8	10	12	15	18	20	23	25
Total	100	100	100	100	100	100	100	100	100	100	100

Note: T-n is n number of years before retirement (T)

Table 7.1 illustrates a linear 10-year glide path, moving from current 100% equity strategy to a strategy dividing the portfolio into four equal parts:

1   25% cash for a tax-free lump sum.

2   25% long-maturity bonds to purchase an annuity to satisfy minimum required income.

3   25% flexible income-generating asset mix (one quarter equity, one quarter long-maturity bonds, one quarter high yield bonds and one quarter Real Estate Investment Trusts – REITs).

4   25% growth-oriented asset mix (20% equity, 30% long-maturity bonds, 20% corporate bonds, 10% high yield bonds and 20% short-maturity bonds).

Return objective

The return objective is dynamic, shifting from current return target to annual excess return between 3% and 4%.

During the consolidation phase, the portfolio is transitioned from a growth outcome to income and growth outcomes. Accumulating cash for taking a cash lump sum and bonds for buying an annuity is a liability-hedging outcome.

Risk objective

Shifting from current risk level to an annualised volatility between 6% and 8%.[5]

The tolerance for liquidity risk is diminishing. Gradually sell illiquid assets (except for residential property) over the glide path.

Time horizon

Time horizon starts with 10 years, but shrinks as retirement is approaching. As retirement is getting closer, the time horizon shifts from medium term (about 10 years) to short term (about 1–2 years). Retirement is not the end of the time horizon (it is a new beginning; do not retire from something but retire into something). Parts of the portfolio should remain invested.

Liquidity

There are no liquidity needs from the pension, which is inaccessible until retirement. However, some of the pension gradually moves to liquid assets as per the terminal asset allocation.

Investment strategy

The strategy is dynamic following the glide path.

De-accumulation phase

The de-accumulation phase starts at retirement and continues until the end of life. After saving for many years, you deserve to enjoy the fruits of your labour. During this phase, you live off your savings, spending (de-accumulating) them.

This phase normally lasts from the age of 55 or 65 (your retirement age) to between 70 and 100 or even 120 (with good genes, healthy life and luck). This phase's length depends on your longevity.

Risk appetite is lower than in previous phases. However, because this phase can be long, the portfolio still needs to track inflation, preserving capital in real terms. Due to longevity risk, you are not sure how long you will need your portfolio to pay income. Some investment risk is needed to keep it going.

Income needs change during retirement. Expenses are typically higher in the first few years as you enjoy the start of retirement, drop as life becomes a bit more sedentary, and increase at the end to accommodate health issues and care. This shape of expenses is called **retirement smile**.

If you started withdrawing pension benefits, tax-efficient contributions into your pension are limited.[6] However, you can still tax-efficiently manage existing assets in your pension.

Your ISAs are fully available for accumulating and investing tax-efficiently. Increasingly, people continue working part-time or even full-time after retirement age. Some do so since they are still healthy, wishing to work. Others are forced to do so since they have not saved enough. You may have other income sources beyond your pension, such as rental property. As you may earn more than you spend, tax-efficient savings can still play a role.

Estate planning, such as gifting assets to your spouse or civil partner or family members and friends, can mitigate IHT. Consider using trusts, leaving assets to charities and taking a life insurance with its pay-out going into a trust.

The de-accumulation phase is divided into **early de-accumulation** and **late de-accumulation**.

Early de-accumulation phase

The early de-accumulation phase lasts as long as you are still relatively healthy and active. Some people continue working, either full-time or part-time, earning income after retirement age. This means that whilst your quality of life greatly depends on savings and assets that you have accumulated, you still have some leeway to do something if they are not sufficient.

Return objective

The return objective is income and capital preservation, mostly in line with inflation. Target return depends on the amount of accumulated savings and income level needed from the portfolio to maintain the desired standard of living.

For example, you need £40,000 annual income and your pension's size is £1 million. The return objective is 4% income. The portfolio needs to keep pace with inflation at 2% per year, meaning a 6% total return objective. This return objective might be aspirational, requiring an adventurous 10% volatility.[7]

With £1 million you will probably need to be satisfied with £30,000 income per year and perhaps a growth rate of only 1%, accepting erosion of the portfolio's purchasing power over time due to inflation. The new total return is 4% and a conservative risk level of 6%.[8]

Risk objective

To mitigate the risk of depleting the portfolio, it needs an annual volatility of 6% to 10%. Such volatility allows generating returns to cover income needs and keeping pace with inflation.

Sell any remaining illiquid assets, except for residential property, unless there are good reasons to retain them.

Time horizon

Time horizon could be over 30 years. By the time we retire advances in medicine can mean people will live longer than today. This is good news, but it is also bad news. You will need to be prepared to preserve some of your portfolio's capital for many more years. Keep investing after retirement, unless you take an annuity that will satisfy your financial needs.

Liquidity

You are drawing retirement benefits from the portfolio. It must hold cash, liquid investments you can sell to raise cash (drawing capital), income-generating investments (taking the natural yield) or an annuity.

Keep a cash reserve for emergencies, such as healthcare.

Investment strategy

The strategy is income and capital preservation.

Late de-accumulation phase

The late de-accumulation phase covers your last years, starting at the age of 80, 90 or 100. It depends on your health, lifestyle and activity level. At this phase, the main concerns are covering ongoing living expenses, care and healthcare.

Now, it is too late to find new sources of financial support (with rare exceptions of a financial windfall, such as inheritance – although you probably outlived most candidates for inheritance, lottery win or a property or business sale). You cannot work any more. You might be unable to make financial decisions due to health problems, such as dementia. The decisions you have taken during your life determine your financial security. You must be in a position of having sufficient assets remaining to provide for your financial needs at this life's late phase. And your finances should be simple, low maintenance.[9]

Longevity risk is acute. If you live longer than expected and run out of money, it is a dramatic problem.

The late de-accumulation phase finishes with the end of life. However, you may wish to leave assets for your heirs or a legacy by contributing to charities. Even at this final phase, you may still aim to preserve capital.

Return objective

The return objective is annual income of 2% to 3% and perhaps 2% capital growth.

Risk objective

The risk objective is to minimise downside risk, volatility of 6% to 8%.[10]

Time horizon

The time horizon could be over 10 years. You cannot know for sure.

Liquidity

You are drawing retirement benefits from the portfolio. Keep a cash reserve for emergencies, such as healthcare.

Consider gifting parts of your assets to mitigate IHT.

Investment strategy

The strategy is income and *conservative* capital preservation.

Dynamic investment strategy

Lifecycle investing demonstrates how investment objectives and constraints change during life. One key for successful investing is being dynamic, adapting to changing circumstances. Your strategy should be dynamic and adapt to your changing financial needs.

Your investment objectives

When planning for your future, take a conservative approach. After retiring, your savings need to generate an annual income. The required income level depends on whether you and your partner have other financial sources, such as State Pension, DB income, part-time job or rental properties, and your desired standard of living. Your portfolio size, its annual growth rate and time horizon limit the available income level.

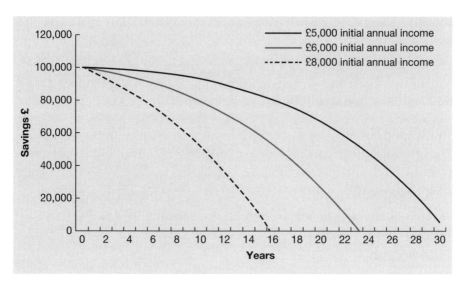

Figure 7.1 Pension exhaustion rates

Figure 7.1 shows how quickly your pension can be exhausted. It assumes a £100,000 initial portfolio, initial drawdowns growing at a 2% annual rate to keep up with inflation and 5% nominal annual portfolio growth rate. The initial drawing rate of 8% exhausts your portfolio in 15 years, but an initial drawing rate of 5% keeps it going for 30 years.

As a rule of thumb, most people need about half of their pre-retirement income to be satisfied at retirement.[11] When retired, some expenses fall. For example, mortgage and other debt should be paid off and you stop paying for children's education. Some other expenses may increase, such as heating, leisure costs and healthcare costs. Overall, however, it should be possible to maintain your pre-retirement standard of living with half the income you had before retiring.

Annuity rate can be used as a conservative estimate of expected annual yield from your portfolio. If annuity rate is 5%, you will generate an annual income of £25,000 on every £500,000 saved.[12]

Is £25,000 enough for you to live the way you desire post retirement? If yes, then your target saving amount at retirement is £500,000. If you need more, say, £40,000, you need to reach £1 million. Is that realistically achievable?

When you know the amount you want to save, work backwards, deriving your return and risk objectives. Given time and contributions, work out the target average annual return and risk level.

With increasing life expectancy, you will need to preserve your portfolio's capital for around 30 years after retirement. Your portfolio should at least keep pace with inflation. With 2% annual average inflation, post retirement your portfolio's minimum total return should be around 4% or 5%.

Now you are equipped with the tools to formulate your return and risk objectives, considering your investment constraints, for different phases of your life cycle. This is the first step in designing your investment strategy, fitting each phase. The next step is, with your strategy in mind, choosing and blending appropriate investments.

Summary

- Typical life phases are: (1) accumulation; (2) consolidation; and (3) de-accumulation. Each phase has different return and risk objectives, constraints and an appropriate strategy.

- During early accumulation, your time horizon is long and risk tolerance can be high. Seek aggressive growth and perhaps invest your entire portfolio in equities. Your target excess return should be 5%, 6% or higher, with a volatility level of 10%, 12% or higher. You can invest in illiquid assets.

- During late accumulation, your time horizon is shorter, but your income from work should be higher than early accumulation. Focus on growth, but with lower downside risk than previously. Your target excess return should be 4% to 6%, with a volatility level of 8% to 12%.

- During consolidation, start a 10-year glide path de-risking from current strategy to your target portfolio at retirement – the terminal asset allocation. Your target portfolio can include cash for a tax-free lump sum, long-term bonds to hedge the price of an annuity, income-generating assets and growth assets. Transition from a growth outcome to income and growth. Gradually reduce illiquid assets, except for residential property.

- During early de-accumulation, your portfolio should generate income. However, capital preservation and keeping pace with inflation are important. You are likely to need to continue investing after retirement. Your target return should be 4%, with a 6% volatility level.

- During late de-accumulating, your portfolio should generate income, as well as preserve capital. Longevity risk means you may live a long time and need your assets to safeguard your financial security.

Notes

1 Assuming an annual inflation rate of 2%, inflation + 5% translates into 7%.

2 Sharpe ratio = (return − risk free) ÷ standard deviation = excess return ÷ standard deviation; 10% = 5% ÷ 0.5; 12% = 6% ÷ 0.5.

3 The FCA sets assumptions for pension projections. The assumed annual inflation rate is 2.5%. The growth rates before inflation are 2% (lower), 5% (medium) and 8% (higher). The growth rates after inflation are −0.5%, 2.5% and 5.5%.

4 8% = 4% ÷ 0.50; 12% = 6% ÷ 0.50; assuming Sharpe ratio 0.50.

5 6% = 3% ÷ 0.50; 8% = 4% ÷ 0.50; assuming Sharpe ratio 0.50.

6 Once you take advantage of flexible drawdowns, your annual allowance drops from £40,000 to £10,000. This is unless you are already in an existing capped drawdown scheme.

7 10% = (6% − 1%) ÷ 0.50, assuming risk-free rate 1% and Sharpe ratio 0.50.

8 6% = (4% − 1%) ÷ 0.50, assuming risk-free rate 1% and Sharpe ratio 0.50.

9 Age UK is a charity dedicated to helping people over the age of 60. Its website at **www.ageuk.org.uk** has plenty of information not only about financial matters, but also about other topics, such as health, care, work, learning, benefits for pensioners (such as housing benefits, cold weather payments) and lifestyle. The website includes a free benefits calculator.

10 6% = (2% + 2% − 1%) ÷ 0.50; 8% = (3% + 2% − 1%) ÷ 0.50; assuming risk-free rate 1% and Sharpe ratio 0.50.

11 Age UK at **www.ageuk.org.uk** offers a free pension calculator helping to plan for retirement, including expected expenses and benefits.

12 £25,000 = 5% × £500,000.

CHAPTER 8
ASSET CLASSES

A concise guide to asset classes

'Know what you own, and know why you own it.'

Peter Lynch

The objective of this and the next two chapters is to cover the characteristics of different assets. When investing, you mix and match investments. Constructing an investment portfolio with relatively predictable behaviour requires an understanding of its building blocks.

Investing mainly involves buying **securities.** Securities are financial instruments representing ownership rights in publicly traded companies (stocks), creditor relationships with governments, corporations and other borrowing institutions (bonds), or rights to ownership as represented by derivatives (options). Securities are interchangeable, negotiable and tradable.

What is an asset class?

An **asset class** is a group of securities and investments sharing similar characteristics. They often behave similarly during different market conditions (regimes), and they share the same legal framework.

Traditional asset classes include equities (stocks), fixed income (fixed interest or bonds) and cash (money market). They make the majority of most portfolios. **Alternative investments** include non-traditional assets, such as property, commodities, private equity, hedge funds and infrastructure.

This chapter explains the characteristics of asset classes. The next two chapters focus on traditional investments and alternative investments.

The advantage of aggregating securities into asset classes is that instead of managing a universe of thousands of different securities, the focus turns to a manageable small number of asset classes.

There are a number of ways to invest in asset classes: select individual securities; outsource the selection to fund managers; and use passive index trackers aiming to track the performance of all the securities in each asset class.

For example, you want to invest 60% of your portfolio in equities, 30% in bonds and 10% in cash. You have £90,000 in your pension and £10,000 in a cash ISA.

In your pension, you buy for £30,000 an index tracker, tracking global equities, as represented by the MSCI World Index and for £30,000 an active equity fund aiming to outperform the FTSE 100 Index. That is 60% of your aggregated accounts invested in equities via two funds.

In your pension, you buy for £30,000 a bond fund, investing in both gilts and UK corporate bonds. That is 30% invested in bonds, using a single fund. In your cash ISA you hold £10,000 in cash.

And, that is it. You chose how to allocate your portfolio to different asset classes, implementing it using three funds and cash, all in a tax-efficient way. You do not need to select hundreds of stocks and bonds. But we are jumping ahead.

After defining your investment objectives and constraints, the next step is formulating an investment strategy. One of the main decisions of a strategy is **asset allocation** – which asset classes to include and exclude and how much to allocate to each one.

Next, decide how to access each asset class, such as through active funds or passive index trackers. To make informed decisions, first know the characteristics and roles of each asset class. And this is this chapter's focus.

Asset classification

Every asset in your portfolio should have a clear role. Everything else you buy has one. You buy a house for shelter, a car for transportation and a television for entertainment. Similarly, you buy investments to fulfil specific roles in your portfolio.

Some roles match the four investment outcomes: growth, beat inflation, income and hedge liabilities. Other roles focus on mitigating risks: diversification and protection. In short, roles are delivering outcomes and mitigating risks.

To understand the universe of assets and readily define their roles we classify them in categories, each with general roles in portfolios. The two sets of categories are **risk and conservative assets** and **real and nominal assets.** To add granularity, we also examine assets' different sources of returns and risks.

Risk and conservative assets

The asset universe is divided between risk and conservative assets. Risk assets, as their name suggests, include an element of high risk. Typically, their price is volatile, with a potential for attractive returns and agonising losses. Their role in portfolios is generating growth, so they are called **growth assets.**

Risk assets include equities, bonds with below investment grade credit rating (high yield), emerging market debt (EMD), commodities, private equity, aggressive hedge funds and managed products (funds) targeting equity-like returns, such as **Diversified Growth Funds** (DGFs).

Conservative assets exhibit lower risk relative to risk assets. Their returns are less volatile, often including a large income component. Their roles in portfolios are generating income, hedging liabilities, diversifying risk assets, as well as perhaps a potential for delivering growth, but lower than that of risk assets. The most conservative are called **safe-haven assets.**

Conservative assets include cash, government bonds of creditworthy countries (such as the UK, USA, Germany and Japan), investment grade corporate bonds, prime (high quality) property and defensive hedge funds.[1] Some currencies, such as US dollar and Japanese yen, and gold are considered safe-haven assets and may perform well during stressful market conditions.

Classification of some assets might change over time. For example, government bonds of countries such as Greece and Portugal turned from conservative to risk assets following the 2011 Eurozone sovereign debt crisis.

Real and nominal assets

One of investing's fundamental objectives is keeping pace with inflation. This is one of the strongest motivations to invest instead of holding cash.

Returns of some assets are positively linked to inflation or changes in expected inflation. When inflation rises, their prices rise. Their main role in portfolios is beating inflation or generating real returns. These assets are called **real assets.**[2]

The four classic real assets are inflation-linked bonds, property, commodities and infrastructure. Commodities and infrastructure are not common in most DC pensions. Normally, only institutional investors access them. Nevertheless, they are available for some individual savers.

Nominal assets generate returns or cash flows that are adversely affected by inflation. For example, long-term bonds are highly sensitive to inflation, which erodes the value of their cash flows. When inflation rises, their price tends to fall.

Whilst equity price can suffer from a sharp rise in inflation or hyperinflation, equity returns should be correlated with inflation over the long term.

The price of goods and services sold by corporations is positively linked to inflation and so are corporate revenues. However, production costs, such as labour and energy, are also correlated with inflation. Since the link between inflation and costs tends to lag the link between inflation and revenues, corporate profits (earnings) should be positively associated with long-term inflation, and so are equity prices.

Sources of returns

One way to understand assets' characteristics is exploring the drivers of returns. Asset classes are not investing's most fundamental building blocks. Each asset is a bundled exposure to **risk factors,** which are the sources of returns.

These returns are called **risk premiums,** market returns or **beta returns.** Such returns do not need active management. By exposing a portfolio to risk factors, it should attract systematic returns over time as a compensation for bearing risks.

This does not mean that dynamically rotating the exposures to risk factors cannot add value. Factor returns are cyclical and change over time. However, predicting which return will be higher or lower is difficult.

One of the biggest trends in asset management is moving from asset class investing to **factor investing.** Investors are looking for diversifying their portfolios across independent factors, rather than across potentially correlated and overlapping asset classes.

The three traditional risk premiums are **equity risk premium** (compensation for equity market risk), **term risk premium** (compensation for interest rate risk) and **credit risk premium** (compensation for credit risk).

Beyond the three traditional ones, other risk premiums are available. **Liquidity risk premium** compensates for illiquidity risk. Property, commodities and infrastructure all offer unique risk premiums. **Alternative betas,** often called **alternative** or

style risk premia, include exposures to other risk premiums, such as value, small size, momentum, quality, low beta and carry.[3]

Most assets mix a number of risk premiums. For example, equities in the energy sector blend equity and commodity risk premiums.

A portfolio harvesting different and balanced independent risk premiums should deliver a smooth return profile. When one factor does not perform well, others may perform better. On average, the chances of a multi-factor portfolio investing in some performing factors are higher than that of a single-factor portfolio.

Article 8.1

Factor in the changing investment cycles

By David Stevenson

Financial Times, 14 March 2014

Every fund manager will tell you their stockpicking methodology is superior to their rivals. But what they offer is different investing styles that tend to work better at different points in the economic cycle.

Passive funds are no different; a "smart beta" fund is just a tracker with an investment style overlaid. If you want a more defensive bunch of stocks, go for a low-volatility exchange-traded fund. Want more income? Go for an ETF where the weightings are based on dividend yield not market capitalisation.

The technical term for this is "factor-based investment styles". Over the past hundred years of stock market history, some factors have consistently done better than others.

One is momentum, which according to academic theory should not outperform for long, yet does – the annual Credit Suisse/London Business School global returns sourcebook shows momentum has been outperforming since 1900. Another is value; reliably defensive shares that pay consistent and rising dividends tend to outperform racier growth stocks – possibly because investors tend to pay too much for growth.

Then there are small-caps, which have consistently outperformed large-cap shares, despite the additional risk and volatility that they bring.

The problem with all of these factors is that they are only really consistent over long periods. Over 50 years, value investing with a focus on dividend-paying stocks has worked a treat. But over many individual five- or 10-year periods, value has underperformed, such as during the dotcom boom or after 2009. That's because over time different factors come into their own.

➡

Since central banks began printing money in earnest (late 2008 and early 2009), cyclical and high-beta shares have done the best. Growth has broadly outperformed value in recent years. Retailers, car dealers, housebuilders and others soared in the "dash for trash". High-beta sectors such as technology and biotech have boomed over the past couple of years.

Similarly, small-caps have turned in a barnstorming performance in recent years, but those with long memories will recall that small shares underperformed large ones for eight years out of 10 in the 1990s.

Factor investing is important when choosing funds, because any manager worth his salt will stick to an approach he believes in even if it isn't "factor of the month". Many well-known value-driven fund managers have had a bad few years, underperforming their benchmarks or peers because the main factor they use has underperformed. Examples include Tom Dobell at M&G Recovery or even Neil Woodford at Invesco.

Or take my own investment in Asian shares via Hugh Young at Aberdeen. Hugh is indisputably a great manager and the funds he runs have a cracking long-term record.

But his particular style is to target quality stocks with a value tilt and these have done relatively badly over the past few years.

Outperformance will certainly return one day, but what if you need your money out before that happens?

You could have a portfolio that comprises different factors, rather like the sprinters, climbers and time trialists in Terry Smith's Tour de France analogy.

So, for instance, in a core holding for developed world equities (tracked by something like the MSCI World index) you could have a low volatility or minimum variance ETF, which has a more defensive tilt than the benchmark.

For emerging markets, you might go for a value fund to take advantage of low valuations. These are much more widely available in the US – examples include the PowerShares MSCI Emerging Markets RAFI tracker (ticker PXH) – than they are here.

There are two problems with this approach. One is that it still requires you to second-guess which factors will work at which times in the cycle. You might buy a low-volatility strategy just as markets surge ahead. Such "tactical asset allocation" is in reality little different from market timing.

The other is that your fund might fail to deliver on its promised factoring. I recently analysed leading UK low-volatility ETFs, which suggested that many were actually no less volatile than mainstream products. Not all factor-based investment approaches are created equal.

Risk factors

The majority of risks and returns of most assets can be explained by a list of 10 fundamental risk factors.

1 **Real rate.** Changes in prevailing interest rates, excluding inflation.

2 **Inflation.** Changes in expected inflation. Expected inflation is already reflected in security prices. Therefore, changes in expected inflation, or unexpected inflation, affect asset prices.

3 **Investment grade spread.** Changes in the difference between yields of investment grade corporate bonds and government bonds.

4 **High yield spread.** Changes in the difference between yields of below investment grade corporate bonds and government bonds.

5 **Emerging market spread.** Changes in the difference between yields of emerging market debt and government bonds of developed countries.

6 **Developed growth.** Economic growth rate of developed economies.

7 **Emerging growth.** Economic growth rate of emerging economies.

8 **Size.** Risk associated with equities issued by companies with small market capitalisation.

9 **Commodities.** Changes in commodity price.

10 **Currency.** Changes in exchange rates between base currency and foreign currencies.

By understanding the exposures of assets to these risk factors, you can envisage assets' expected behaviour during different market conditions, how they should behave with respect of each other and to which risks a portfolio mixing them is exposed.

Because each of these risk factors is independent and systematic, it attracts a risk premium. Exposing your portfolio to each risk factor should generate a different market return, independent of a fund manager's skill.

For example, your portfolio is invested 50% in UK equities and 50% in gilts. It should benefit from equity risk premium and term premium. Over the long term equities are expected to appreciate as the economy and corporate earnings grow. Gilts are expected to pay interest as you lend money to the government.

Even if you do not use fund managers to select securities, your portfolio is still expected to generate beta returns, which are not dependent on any manager.

Alpha

Another source of return comes from active management. Fund managers aim to generate returns above the benchmark (beta returns) through active investment decisions. This excess return is called **alpha.**

Active investment decisions include three groups:

1   **Asset allocation.** Deviating from the benchmark's asset allocation.
2   **Security selection.** Holding different securities from those of the benchmark.
3   **Market timing.** Going in and out of the market.

For example, assume your benchmark is 50% equities and 50% bonds. One way to try to outperform is by holding 60% equities and 40% bonds. You will benefit if equities outperform bonds and lose if equities lag bonds.

Another way to try to beat the benchmark is by investing in only 20 out of the 100 stocks in the universe of the FTSE 100 Index. If your 20 stocks perform better in aggregate than the other 80, you win. If you picked underperforming stocks, you lose.

Finally, you can try to time the market by staying in cash when you think the market will fall and investing when you think it will rise. Get it right and you are a hero; get it wrong and you are a zero.

Whilst beta returns do not need skill (although rotating among beta returns does need it), generating alpha depends on talent. Luck has a huge impact, but it is hardly sustainable. Therefore, alpha is more expensive than beta.

The challenge with alpha is that managers effectively claim the market is wrong. They believe they have an edge over the market by better estimating the fair value of investments.

For example, a stock price is £10. This is the price the market collectively assigns to it. Thousands of buyers and sellers buy and sell stocks at different prices, until they reach this price. The fund manager claims: 'No, the market is wrong, the correct price should be £15,' and buys the stock. The manager may be right and make money or wrong and lose or not make money.

In a Las Vegas casino the house always has an advantage. Even when playing black and red on the roulette, zero is green. This ensures the house has a statistical edge since both black and red lose every time the ball falls on zero.[4]

This is analogous to active management. The first reason is that trading securities involves transaction costs – managers' returns need to pass this hurdle. The second reason is that each trade has two sides – a buyer and a seller. It is a zero sum game. For every winner on one side there is a loser on the other side. The odds, therefore, are against the manager. The market, like a Las Vegas casino, has an edge.

Alpha and beta

After the asset allocation decision, the next decision is how to access each asset. Here, the choice is between alpha, beta or blending both.

The beta decision is how to allocate – expose the portfolio to which betas. The alpha decision is selecting securities, choosing fund managers or just sticking with beta returns.

Beta returns are natural returns coming with different assets. Often, they can be accessed passively through index trackers. Alpha returns are based on active investment decisions. They come with skill or luck.

For example, you decide to expose 50% of your portfolio to equities and 50% to bonds. This is the beta decision. You then decide to split equities, half in active funds and half in an index tracker, whilst for bonds you use an index tracker. This is the alpha decision.

Most investments, such as active funds, mix alpha and beta. For example, an active fund aiming to outperform the FTSE 100 Index includes a large exposure to UK equities as represented by the index. The fund manager usually has a tracking error constraint with respect of the index so the fund's performance does not deviate too much from that of the index. This is beta return.[5]

The manager aims to outperform the index by holding a portfolio with different securities and weightings from those in the benchmark. This is alpha return. Alpha can be negative, as managers might underperform (**manager risk**).

Ensure you pay extra fees of active management for alpha, rather than for beta. You can access beta cheaply without paying rich fees. Some managers generate returns by exposing funds to alternative betas, such as value and small caps. This is another return source that might appear as alpha, but does not justify alpha's full fees. This insight motivated some investors to move to factor investing.

Summary

- Each asset in your portfolio should fulfil a role. Some roles match the four investment outcomes: growth, beat inflation, income and hedge liabilities. Other roles focus on mitigating risks, such as diversification and protection.

- Risk assets deliver growth. Conservative assets deliver income and diversification. Real assets hedge inflation.

- Beta returns are natural returns coming with exposure to financial markets. They can be accessed passively and cheaply. Alpha needs skill. It costs more than beta.

Notes

1 The classification of property is not straightforward. Property can suffer capital losses. However, over the long term, high-quality property tends to appreciate in value and generate rental income.

2 Not to confuse with real assets referring to physical or tangible assets, such as commodities and property. Most financial assets are intangible.

3 The Fama–French three-factor model, developed by Eugene Fama and Kenneth French in 1993, added value and size factors to market factor used in CAPM, to explain equity returns. $r = r_f + \beta(r_m - r_f) + \beta_s \text{SMB} + \beta_v \text{HML}$, where return (r) equals CAPM return plus returns from loadings of investment on small-minus-large (SMB) and high-minus-low (HML) book-to-value factors.

4 Most roulette tables also include a green double zero, giving the house an additional edge. There are 38 numbers on the table (including 0 and 00) but a straight bet pays off 35 to 1. If you put £1 on every number you bet £38. A winning number is paid only £35 plus the original £1. The house has a profit of £2.

5 Most active equity funds would have a beta between 0.80 and 1.20 with respect of the benchmark and a tracking error between 2% and 6%. This means that a large portion of the fund's return is determined by the benchmark return. Enhanced indexing typically has a tracking error of about 2%. Perfect index tracker has a tracking error of 0%. In practice, however, tracking error is never nil.

CHAPTER 9
TRADITIONAL INVESTMENTS

A concise guide to traditional asset classes

'Price is what you pay. Value is what you get.'

Warren Buffett

Most investments in your portfolio are likely to be traditional investments. The main traditional asset classes include:

1 Equities.

2 Fixed income.

3 Cash.

They are likely to make up the lion's share of your portfolio. In this chapter we focus on their characteristics and roles in portfolios.

Equities

Equities (shares, stocks) represent partial ownership in the company issuing them. When you own a stock you are the proud owner of part of a business. Through stocks you participate in the business' growth prospects.

Companies primarily raise capital through issuing either shares (ownership, capital, equity) or bonds (borrowing, liabilities). To raise capital from the public, the company lists (quotes) its shares on the stock exchange through an **Initial Public Offering** (IPO). Creation of securities is done on the **primary market**. After the IPO, shares trade on the **secondary market** between buyers and sellers.[1]

Equity returns

'Stock price movements actually begin to reflect new developments before it is generally recognized that they have taken place.'

Arthur Zeikel

Equity total returns consist of two components:

1   Dividends.
2   Changes in price (capital gains or losses).

Companies can compensate shareholders by paying them cash dividends, coming out of the company's profits. The two rights of shareholders of **common stocks** are receiving dividends and voting at shareholders' meetings. Dividends are not mandatory.[2] Companies are supposed to pay them only when profitable and their Board of Directors decides to do so.

UK companies normally pay dividends twice a year. The ratio between the dividend and stock price is **dividend yield**. For example, a company pays a dividend of £0.50 on each of its shares. If the share price is £12.5, the dividend yield is 4%.[3] When receiving dividend as a shareholder, you can either use it as income or reinvest it back into your equity holdings.

The second component of equity returns is changes in price (price appreciation). You buy a stock for a certain price. When selling it you either make a profit if its price increased or lose money if its price decreased.

For example, you bought a stock for £10. You received dividends of £0.20 whilst holding it and sold it for £12. Your total return is 22%, made up of 2% dividend yield and 20% price appreciation.[4,5]

Equity price reflects the value the market collectively assigns to the company. If the market thinks a company will do well in the future, exceeding expectations, more buyers than sellers of its stock may push its price upwards. If the market thinks the company will not do well and its financial results are disappointing, more sellers than buyers may push its share price downwards.

Whilst the forces of supply and demand set equity price, the forces of fear and greed drive sellers and buyers. Equity prices often reflect stories, perceptions, predictions and speculations about the future. When it looks rosy, optimistic and euphoric buyers push the stock market upwards. When it looks gloomy, pessimistic and panicky sellers push the stock market downwards. Fear can be paralysing. You can leave logic behind when fear drives the market.

Sentiment is an important driver of share price over the short term, whilst fundamentals should drive price over the long term. Buyers and sellers overreact to daily good and bad news, causing share prices to fluctuate. When momentum is positive, more buyers jump on the bandwagon, pushing prices further up. The opposite occurs when momentum is negative, causing prices to overshoot.

Over the long term, however, daily news and noise wash out. Price is linked more closely to the company's financial conditions and the general economy.

Share price stabilises when it satisfies all buyers and sellers. The so-called **equilibrium price** clears the market, as everyone gets the price they want – not too low to attract new buyers and not too high to attract new sellers. It is an abstract price as stock prices constantly change.

This is how the stock market works. Numerous buyers and sellers buy and sell securities, moving their prices due to forces of supply and demand. That is economics in a nutshell.[6]

Price and value

Market forces set price. Fair value, in theory, is how much a stock should be worth. However, in practice, value is subjective. Your valuation is what you think a stock is worth, based on your assumptions. Reality is the perception of the seer.

The **dividend discount model** (DDM) evaluates stocks as the present value of future cash flows (dividends) and eventual selling price (terminal value).[7]

The timing and size of cash flows are uncertain. Investors estimate (guesstimate) cash flows by appraising the company's future financial fortunes. If a company does well, its dividends may increase; if it does poorly, its dividends may decrease. Each investor may reach a different value due to different assumptions.

Then, investors buy and sell the stock, moving its price. There is only one price, there is only one true value, but each investor may derive a different valuation.

Often, instead of dividends, **free cash flows** (FCF) to shareholders are used in a **discounted cash flow** (DCF) model.[8] FCFs estimate the cash the company generates after spending on maintaining and expanding its operations.[9]

Whilst DDM and DCF models calculate stocks' **intrinsic value**, relative valuation compares stock price to peers. The premise is that similar companies should have similar value, unless there are good reasons they should not.

One common relative valuation ratio is **price-to-earnings** (P/E).[10] For example, if a British company in the oil exploration sector has P/E of 10, whilst the sector's average is 15, the stock may be undervalued. Its price may converge with the average. The question is: why is the company under-priced? Perhaps its business prospects or management are weak.

If you think value is higher than price, buy the stock. It is, apparently, undervalued. If you think value is lower than price, sell the stock. It is, apparently, overvalued. Luckily, price is more volatile than value, creating investment opportunities.

Whether you gain or lose depends on whether your valuation is correct. Even if your valuation is correct, price might not converge to it since the market disagrees with your valuation or it might be due to changes in the conditions of the company or the economy.

The future commercial fortunes of each company depend on both its performance and that of the overall economy. If the economy grows, the demand for goods and services the company sells increases and it may boost profitability. So its stock price can go up. If the economy slows, the opposite occurs. When buying a stock you make two investments: one in the company and a second in the economy.

The risk associated with a single company is called **idiosyncratic risk**. By holding a sufficient number of stocks of companies with different businesses, you can remove (diversify away) the risk associated with any individual stock. Typically, you need at least 30 lowly correlated stocks to do so. You are left with market risk (beta risk), which is un-diversifiable (**systematic risk**). This risk is associated with the overall market. You cannot diversify it by only buying stocks.

UK equities

The UK equity market is represented by two common indices: FTSE 100 and FTSE All Share. FTSE 100 Index is a **market-capitalisation index** representing the performance of the 100 largest companies traded on the **London Stock Exchange** (LSE).

Market capitalisation means each stock's weight in the index is calculated by multiplying the number of outstanding stocks each company issues by the stock price. The FTSE All Share Index represents a larger number of stocks, consisting of some small capitalisation stocks excluded from the FTSE 100 Index.

Global equities

The UK economy is an open economy, including a number of multi-national conglomerates. A large share of British companies' revenues comes from overseas, both from developed and emerging economies.[11] Nevertheless, when investing in equities, it is recommended that you adopt a global approach, including equities from around the world.

The US equity market is by far the leading and most developed worldwide. Over half of the global equity market capitalisation is made of US equities.[12] They comprise thousands of listed companies, some of which are the largest, most well-known companies internationally.

Often, the direction of the US equity market dictates the direction of global equity markets. *When the US sneezes the world catches a cold.* The question is whether other markets can decouple.

The US equity market has the longest, most reliable history of prices, data and research. The three common indices representing the US equity market are the Dow Jones Industrial Average (DJIA), NASDAQ Composite Index and S&P 500 Index.[13]

Investing in overseas equities is fairly easy. You can buy equity funds and index trackers of stocks in North America, Europe, Japan, Pacific and emerging markets. Including foreign equities expands your investment opportunity set and adds diversification. You can participate in global economic themes, such as China's swift development over the last two decades (although it has already started a secular slowdown), the rise of India and the recovery of Europe. Mind you, when investing overseas, currency risk can have a big impact on results.

The equity universe is divided between developed and emerging markets. **Developed markets** include the USA, Western Europe, Japan, the UK, Canada and Australia. Emerging markets include Brazil, Russia, India, China (abbreviated to BRIC), as well as numerous other countries.

Emerging markets offer potentially higher returns with higher risks compared with developed counterparts. Whilst often considered a single block, **global emerging markets** (GEM) are a heterogeneous group of economies with diverse characteristics. They should at least be divided into three main regions: Asia, Latin America (LATAM) and Europe. Economies that are not emerging yet are termed **frontier markets**.

A popular index for global developed equities is MSCI World Index. MSCI Emerging Markets Index covers emerging markets. MSCI World All Country Index (MSCI AC World Index or ACWI) includes both developed and emerging markets. MSCI offers regional equity indices (such as MSCI North America, including the USA and Canada, and MSCI Latin America).[14]

Sector, style and size

Equities are often categorised not only by regions and geographies, but also by sectors, styles and sizes. Sectors are the industry in which the issuing company operates, including: energy, materials, consumer discretionary, consumer staples, healthcare, financials, information technology, telecommunication services and utilities.[15]

Styles include value (stocks whose price is deemed below fair value) and growth (stocks with a potential for growing earnings at above-average rate compared to the market).[16] Sizes include large caps, mid caps and small caps.

Academic research and empirical evidence suggest that over time, value stocks and small cap stocks outperform the general equity market, as well as stocks with positive price **momentum** (winners are expected to continue winning) and **quality** stocks.[17] This outperformance, however, is patchy, as these types of stocks can undergo long periods of underperformance.

Had they outperformed all the time, investors would have bought them, pushing their price upwards and eliminating their superior performance. When there is an obvious or risk-free investment opportunity (called **arbitrage**), investors quickly take advantage of it and it disappears. Nothing good lasts forever.

The characteristics and roles of equities

The roles of equities in portfolios are growth, as well as dividend income. Equities make the bulk of growth assets in most portfolios. Whatever your objectives are, equities are likely to play an important role in your portfolio.

Equities are fairly liquid; in particular, those of large companies operating in developed markets. Small capitalisation stocks and emerging market equity are less liquid, but still more so than many other assets.

Liquidity depends on trading **volume**. Securities and financial markets that are traded frequently and in large quantities are more liquid as more buyers and sellers interact. Liquidity leads to **price discovery**. As the number of transactions is larger, more securities exchange hands and prices are determined and published more often.

Most equity markets are **efficient**. This means numerous buyers and sellers trade them, their prices are published throughout the day and markets and companies are heavily researched.

Equity prices react quickly to news. According to some theories (**Efficient Market Hypothesis** – EMH, which was developed by Nobel laureate Eugene Fama) equity prices reflect all historic information (weak EMH), instantly reflect all new publicly available information (semi-strong EMH) and perhaps even all private information, including illegal insider trading (strong EMH).

According to EMH, it is challenging, or maybe impossible, to beat equity markets through active security selection, in particular net of fees and transaction costs. If you believe in EMH, avoid active funds.

The **random walk theory** claims equity prices change following a random walk. Past movements cannot be used to predict the future and active management is fruitless.

In practice, however, equity markets are not completely efficient. One proof is bubbles and crashes, demonstrating inefficiency or at least lapses of inefficiency. Another proof is anomalies, such as **January effect** (seasonal anomaly where markets tend to rise) and weakness in May (*sell in May and go away*).

Equity markets do not follow a complete random walk as evidenced by superior performance of momentum and trend following strategies. Whilst, undoubtedly, it is difficult to generate alpha in equity markets, it is possible.[18]

The main source of equity returns is the **equity risk premium** (ERP). ERP is the return equity investors require as compensation for investing in risky equities compared to safe-haven assets, such as government bonds or cash. Historically, ERP has been about 4% or 5% on average above the risk-free cash rate. Therefore, cash +4% or 5% is commonly defined as equity-like returns.

ERP changes over time. When investors demand a higher compensation for taking equity risk, ERP rises. It pushes equity's price downwards (higher discount rate in present value calculations). Lower price today means higher returns in the future. The opposite occurs when investors are less risk averse, demanding a lower ERP. Higher price today means lower returns in the future.

The three main risk factors of developed equities are developed economic growth, inflation and commodity prices. Commodities are an important input for corporations, as well as output for some.

For emerging market equity, the main risk factors are developed economic growth, emerging market economic growth, inflation, commodity prices and currency exposure.

Emerging economies are heavily dependent on developed ones; hence, their exposure to the developed economic growth factor. Many emerging economies are commodity exporters (Russia, Brazil) or importers (India, China). Their equity markets are greatly affected by commodity prices.[19]

Investment principles

Benjamin Graham was an investor and author of the classic books *Security Analysis* and *The Intelligent Investor*. Considered the father of security analysis and value investing, he advocated three principles for equity investing.

1 **Always invest with a margin of safety.** Buy equities with a significant discount to intrinsic value (fair value).

2 **Expect volatility and profit from it.** When investing in stocks, volatility is part of the deal. Instead of exiting the market when it falls, see it as a buying opportunity. Seek investments that were unfairly punished in a correction and are undervalued relative to potential. Two strategies to mitigate the negative effect of market volatility are dollar-cost averaging and mixing stocks and bonds.

3 **Know what kind of investor you are.** Are you an active, enterprising investor or a passive, defensive investor? Active investors seriously commit time and energy and actively manage their portfolios. Passive investors use passive index trackers. Are you a speculator or an investor? Investors look at stocks as part of a business and shareholders as owners. Speculators buy expensive pieces of paper.

Value investing is not just looking for bargains. Rather, it is a philosophy of performing in-depth fundamental analysis, pursuing long-term results, limiting risk and resisting crowd psychology.

Many stock pickers follow a philosophy of investing in stocks of good businesses managed by competent management, with potential for sustainable earnings growth (stock price reflects the future, not the past and present) at a reasonable price. Price is the cornerstone of every sound investment decision.

It is relatively easy to invest in equities. You can invest in individual stocks, active funds and index trackers.[20] Unless you are an active investor, committed to researching and selecting stocks, go with funds, either active or trackers.

This was an awfully concise summary of the mechanics of equities. Equity investing is a popular, fascinating subject, with countless books and research aiming to explain the behaviour of equity markets, suggesting various trading strategies. If you are interested, there is plenty more to read on this topic.

Fixed income

The fixed income market covers diverse types of debt securities, mostly bonds. Bonds represent loans (IOUs). The bond's issuer borrows money. Investors in bonds lend money to the issuer. In return, the issuer contractually promises to pay its creditors interest, in the form of coupons, and to repay the loan's principal when the bond matures.

Bonds are negotiable securities. Lenders trade bonds for a price. Some bonds are publicly traded on exchanges, whilst most are traded only **over-the-counter** (OTC).[21] Once again, forces of supply and demand set bonds' price, based on the issuer's estimated ability to service the payments due and general economic conditions.

Borrowers include governments, corporations, government agencies, local authorities and supranational organisations (such as the International Monetary Fund – IMF). Therefore, the fixed income market is much bigger than the equity market. The number and variety of bond issuers is large and each one issues several bonds, each with different features, terms and maturities. Conversely, only corporations issue equities and normally every company issues a single type of common stock.

Yield to maturity

Yield to maturity (YTM), or **redemption yield**, is the discount rate equating the present value of the cash flows of a bond (coupons and principal) with its current price. YTM is the bond's **internal rate of return** (IRR).

When holding a bond to maturity without selling it, assuming it does not default, YTM is your realised total return. Higher bond price means lower YTM, whilst lower bond price means higher YTM.

For example, a bond's price is £1,050. It pays 5% annual coupons on its £1,000 **face value** (principal) and its maturity is three years. The YTM is 3.22% since when using it as a discount rate in a present value calculation, we get £1,050.[22] The bond is traded at **premium** because its YTM is lower than its interest (coupon) rate and its price is higher than its face value. When buying a bond at a premium, your expected return is lower than its coupon rate.

The same bond's price is now £950. Its YTM is 6.9%.[23] The bond is traded at **discount** and its YTM is higher than its interest rate. Your expected total return when holding it to maturity is higher than its coupon rate.

When evaluating the bond's interest rate, use YTM, not the coupon rate, since YTM considers the bond's price.[24]

Yield curve

The **yield curve** (term structure of interest rates) consists of YTMs of bonds with the same credit quality but different maturities.

For example, in the USA, the yield curve includes the yields of 3-month, 2-year, 5-year, 10-year and 30-year Treasury bonds.[25]

The yield curve shows the interest rates investors demand for holding bonds with different maturities. It represents the term premium. The steepness of the yield curve is often measured by subtracting a short-maturity yield, such as 2-year yield, from a long-maturity yield, such as 10-year yield.

For example, if 10-year gilt yield is 2.2% and that of 2-year gilt is 0.7%, the steepness of the gilt yield curve is 1.5%.

The government bond curve is used as a reference to price debt instruments, such as mortgage rates, as well as liabilities of DB pension schemes. It is also used to predict changes in economic activity.

Government bonds

National governments issue bonds. The two main sources of money for governments are tax proceeds and borrowing in capital markets via bonds. Governments can also print money, but this causes inflation and devaluation of the currency. Government bonds are called **sovereign debt** or, colloquially, **govies**. The government bond market is often called the rates market.

The British Government issues **gilts**, the US Government issues **Treasuries**, the German Government issues **bunds** and the Japanese Government issues Japanese Government Bonds (JGBs).[26]

Gilt price heavily depends on prevailing interest rates and inflation. The price and YTM of govies are set by supply and demand of bonds. When the economy slows down, the market expects low inflation and central banks to reduce interest rates to reflate the economy. Under these conditions, govies are attractive. Investors buy them, pushing their price up and YTM down. The opposite occurs when the economy expands.

A slowing economy is bad news for equities since corporate earnings are expected to fall as demand for goods and services wanes. The same economic forces have the opposite impact on the price of equities and govies. Equities should strive in economic expansion, whilst govies should strive in economic recession.

This is one reason blending equities and govies can generate a smoother return profile. Equities deliver growth in good times, whilst govies offset some of equities' negative returns in bad times.

Government bond investors are part of a pessimistic bear camp. They hope for bad economic news since this should benefit their asset class. Equity investors are part of an optimistic bull camp. They hope for good economic news as this should benefit their asset class.

You should be neither a bear nor a bull. Aim to be realistic. Include both assets in your portfolio to benefit from the different roles they play.

The characteristics and roles of government bonds

Government bonds are the main conservative assets in portfolios. Their roles are generating income, hedging liabilities, mitigating downside risk (providing some protection), as well as diversifying equity risk.

Govies should perform well in times of **flight to quality**. During financial stress investors tend to panic, selling all risk assets, such as equities, to seek safety in high quality, safe-haven assets, such as govies. Investors dump all risk assets indiscriminately, pushing pairwise correlations towards one, causing all risk assets to fall in tandem.

Govies can provide some degree of protection to offset a drop in equity markets during stressful market conditions. To generate enough returns, the govies should have long duration; otherwise, price movements are small. The govies need firepower. Do not bring a knife to a gunfight; bring a bazooka.

For example, if a bond's duration is 8 years, when yields fall 0.50% during a flight-to-quality episode, the bond returns about 4%. With only 1-year duration, the return is 0.5%. Cash with nil duration cannot generate capital gains.

Govies are liquid. You can use them as a source of liquidity in your portfolio.

Government bond markets are highly efficient. Usually they do not include a large number of securities (narrow breadth) since there is only one issuer in each country (the government). Generating alpha in this market is challenging.

The main tools for fund managers to add value are duration and yield-curve positioning. When expecting rates to rise, hold short-duration bonds, since their price is less sensitive to rising rates. When expecting rates to drop, hold long-duration bonds to benefit from capital gains. Short-duration bonds offer a lower yield (**carry**) than long-duration bonds.

Yield-curve positioning aims to benefit from changes in the yield curve's shape. Yields across the curve rarely move in a similar way (**parallel shift**). The curve's short end is normally more volatile than the long end. When the difference between long- and short-term rates increases, the yield curve **steepens** and when the opposite occurs, it **flattens**.[27]

Fund managers position portfolios to benefit from expected changes in the curve's shape. For example, you expect a monetary tightening with short-term rates rising faster than long-term rates. You adopt a **barbell** strategy of selling short-term bonds and buying long-term bonds. This position should benefit from the change in the **spread** between yields of short-term and long-term bonds.[28]

The main source of government bond returns is **term premium**. Bonds with longer maturities normally offer higher yields as compensation for higher interest rate risk. The yield curve is typically upward sloping. A flat or downwards sloping (inverted) yield curve often implies the market expects low economic growth (perhaps a recession) with low inflation (perhaps deflation).

The two main risk factors of govies are real rate and inflation. They drive the majority of performance.

The common index for UK gilts is FTSE Actuaries UK Conventional Gilts All Stocks Index. Its factsheet is available online and includes the index's performance, volatility and characteristics, such as redemption yield (YTM), modified duration and top holdings. FTSE Russell offers a series of gilt indices with different maturities.[29]

Global government bonds

Consider including in your portfolio govies issued by foreign governments, not only the British Government. This enhances diversification, benefiting from different monetary cycles of other countries.[30]

One lesson from the 2011 European debt crisis and 2015 Greek tragedy is to globally diversify govies. Prices of sovereign debt of supposedly creditworthy developed countries can drop surprisingly and quickly.

However, when investing in foreign bonds, currency exposure can dominate returns. It can even reclassify bonds from conservative to risk assets as their volatility can more than double due to currency movements. Therefore, currency risk of foreign bonds should be hedged back to your base currency (British pound).

Inflation-linked bonds

Inflation-linked bonds, commonly called indexed-linked gilts or informally **linkers,** have a principal linked to inflation. When inflation rises, the principal's value rises and, consequently, the coupons, which are a fixed percentage of the principal. Instead of focusing on nominal yield, investors in linkers focus on real yields.

The primary issuers of linkers are governments. All G7 governments, as well as others, use linkers as part of their borrowing programmes. Non-government issuers are fairly rare. In the UK a number of utility companies issue linkers as their pricing structure is statutorily linked to inflation.

For long-term savers, linkers whose maturities match the saver's time horizon are as close as it gets to a risk-free asset. Cash is not risk-free in this context because of duration mismatch. When the value of long-term liabilities changes due to changes in interest rates or inflation, the value of cash does not change as such. However, the value of duration-matching linkers does.

Breakeven inflation rate is the difference between yields of standard govies and linkers with the same maturity. The breakeven rate observes the market inflation expectations over the bonds' maturity.

For example, 10-year gilt yield is 4% and that of a 10-year linker is 2%. The market expects an annual inflation rate of about 2% over the next 10 years.[31] Use the breakeven rate to gauge the market's expectations of future inflation.[32]

If you think inflation is likely to be higher than the breakeven, buy linkers instead of nominal (standard) govies. If you think inflation is likely to be lower than the breakeven, buy govies instead of linkers.

Linkers are conservative assets. Their main roles in portfolios are delivering real income, keeping pace with inflation, hedging liabilities and diversifying equity risk.

Linkers are liquid. Similar to government bonds, the number of securities in the universe is small, as governments issue most linkers. Therefore, alpha opportunities through active management are limited.

The main return sources for linkers are real rates and changes in expected inflation. Since linkers remove inflation risk, they are less risky than govies. Linker's yields are normally below those of comparable govies (unless deflation is expected). As always, lower risk equals lower expected return.

Linkers' main risk factor is real rate. Changes in inflation are not a risk.

The common index for UK linkers is Barclays Capital UK Government Inflation-Linked Bond Index. The index's factsheet is available online. Barclays Capital offers a series of bond indices.[33]

Corporate bonds

Companies mainly borrow in capital markets by issuing corporate bonds, so-called **credit**. Since corporations might go bust, they need to compensate investors by offering a spread over the yield of govies with similar maturity. Corporate bonds are called **spread products**.

Corporate bond's YTM is that of an equivalent government bond plus a spread. The spread reflects the ability of the issuing corporation to generate enough cash flows to service its debt.

The higher the creditworthiness of a corporation, the lower the spread it needs to offer to persuade investors to lend it money. Performance of credit is derived from that of the underlying, reference govies and changes in the spread.

When the economy is doing well, spreads tend to *narrow* due to better chances of corporations paying their debt. Investors demand a lower credit risk premium. The yields of underlying govies, however, can rise in such circumstances. When the economy struggles, the opposite occurs. Spreads tend to *widen*, whilst the underlying government bond rates can drop.

Corporate bonds' returns are determined by which of these two opposing forces has the upper hand: narrowing or widening spreads or rising or dropping rates.

Credit shares some qualities with equities. Both depend on the issuing company's commercial fortunes. If a company is profitable, it can generate cash to pay dividends to shareholders and interest to bondholders. If the company is not profitable, both shareholders and bondholders might suffer.

One difference between shareholders and bondholders is that shareholders participate in the company's upside as, in theory, the share price can appreciate endlessly. Bond price, however, is capped since the spread of corporate bonds narrows when the company is doing well, but it rarely turns negative.[34]

Shareholders are more risk seekers than risk-averse bondholders. For example, if a company is in financial distress, shareholders might encourage company's management to take risky projects to potentially boost depressed equity price. Bondholders, however, would encourage management to use prudence, avoiding risky projects to reduce bankruptcy risk and potential default on bonds.[35]

Credit rating agencies, such as Moody's and Standard & Poor's (S&P), publish **credit ratings** reflecting their assessment of the ability of issuers to meet their debt obligations.

Investment grade (IG) rating means the issuer is unlikely to default on its debt. Below investment grade means the issuer is speculative – default risk is higher than that of IG issuers.[36]

A change in credit rating affects bond price and YTM. Deteriorating rating means the bond is riskier, its YTM usually increases and its price drops. Improving rating means the opposite.

Spreads of IG corporate bonds typically range between 1% and over 2.5%, depending on credit rating and economic backdrop.

In stressful economic conditions, default risk increases as more companies might face financial difficulties. During the 2008 crisis, spreads surpassed 5.5% and then narrowed sharply as the economy stabilised. With hindsight, which is a wonderful thing, the depth of the crisis was a once-in-a-lifetime buying opportunity for credit.

The characteristics and roles of corporate bonds

The classification of corporate bonds as conservative or risk asset depends on their credit rating. Investment grade credit is considered conservative, whilst low-rated credit can be considered risk asset.

However, high rating is not a guarantee of no default. For example, in 2008 Lehman Brothers, the US investment bank, infamously went bankrupt, defaulting on its bonds, even with an investment grade rating.

The roles of credit in portfolios are generating income, hedging liabilities and potentially delivering growth when price appreciates. Corporate bonds can produce higher income than comparable govies because of the spread.

Credit's liquidity depends on market conditions. In the past, banks used to hold an inventory of corporate bonds, providing liquidity. However, after the 2008 crisis, banks have scaled down on their proprietary trading. They do not hold an inventory of corporate bonds as they used to due to stricter regulations and capital requirements. Accordingly, the credit market is not as liquid as it used to be. This means transaction costs of trading corporate bonds are higher than in the past.

The credit market is relatively inefficient compared to the government bond market. It includes many different issuers, issuing different bonds with different features (such as callable bonds and convertible bonds).[37] This offers active management ample opportunities to add value.

The tools available for fund managers to add value include selecting duration, issuers, credit rating and bonds with different features and yield curve positioning. This all lends itself to opportunities for alpha generation by active managers. However, since transaction costs are higher than in the past, active management faces headwinds as costs eat into performance.[38]

The main return source for corporate bonds is **credit risk premium**. Corporate bonds normally have shorter maturities than those of govies, so the term premium is lower for credit.

Credit's main risk factors are real term, inflation, credit spread and developed economic growth. The latter is a common risk factor for both equities and credit. This explains why these two asset classes can be highly correlated, in particular at times of stress as during the 2008 crisis.

The common index for UK credit is Markit iBoxx £ Non-Gilts Index or Markit iBoxx £ Corporates Index.[39]

High yield

Investment grade bonds offer a relatively tight spread over govies. They do not need to offer high compensation to induce investors to buy them. It is a different story, however, for bonds with below IG credit rating, often called speculative, high yield or **junk**. Such bonds must offer a wide spread to attract investors due to material default risk.

High chances of default can cause volatility of spreads. When financial markets go through stressful periods, such as recessions, vulnerable corporations can default. High yield bond prices can fall significantly during such times, as spreads might widen. When financial markets calm down, spreads can narrow, generating capital gains.

The typical high yield spread over govies is between 2.5% and 4%, depending on credit rating and economic conditions. However, spreads can abruptly reach 10% levels and even over 17% at crises.

In the early 1990s' recession, the 2000 high-tech bubble burst, the 2008 crisis and the 2011 European sovereign debt crisis, high yield bond yields widened, reflecting fears of defaults. However, following each of these crises, yields narrowed back to 'normal' levels. Investors who did not sell their well-diversified high yield holdings usually prevailed.

During periods of low yields, cash offers low returns, as do govies and IG bonds. Investors seeking higher yields flock into riskier assets, such as high yield.

However, high yield is a risk asset, not a conservative one. High yield is more correlated with equities than it is with govies and IG bonds. The volatility of high yield is closer to that of equities than to that of govies and IG bonds. There is a downside to investing in high yield.

The roles of high yield in portfolios are income, growth and diversification with govies and IG credit. High yield is a growth asset of fixed income. It can offer high total returns made of carry and price appreciation. Like every risk asset, its total returns might be negative. High yield can substitute some of the equity allocation as a growth asset, but with a lower downside risk.

The risk factors of high yield are real term, inflation, IG credit spread, high yield spread and developed growth. High yield shares commonalities with the fortunes of the equity market.

The US high yield market is by far the largest and deepest in the world. When investing in this asset class, it is recommended to take a global approach. Investing across the USA, Europe and the UK allows for diversification and choice, offering alpha opportunities for managers.[40] When investing globally, hedge the currency exposure back to your base currency.

The high yield market is far less efficient than other equity and bond markets, allowing managers to add value through active management.

A common index for the global high yield market is Markit iBoxx Global Developed Markets Liquid High Yield Index.[41] Barclays Capital offers a series of high yield bond indices.[42]

Emerging market debt

Emerging market debt (EMD) includes bonds issued by the governments of emerging countries and corporations operating in such countries. Since EMD is generally riskier than peers issued in developed economies, it offers higher yields to attract investors.

Many emerging economies are on different monetary cycles compared to developed ones. In 2015, for example, whilst the US Federal Reserve (Fed) was on a moderate tightening cycle of monetary policy, some central banks in emerging economies were on an easing cycle (cutting short-term rates). This provides opportunities for capital gains when developed bonds face potential capital losses, as well as diversification benefits.

EMD is a risk asset, whose price can be volatile. It is not as volatile as it was a number of decades ago, as many emerging economies got inflation under control and defaults of emerging sovereigns are not as common as they used to be. But still, defaults occur and emerging economies can run into financial difficulties, such as Russia in 1998, causing a global financial crisis.

EMD is susceptible to downside risk. During flights to quality investors might dump their EMD, causing a drawdown.

EMD is divided into hard and soft currency. **Hard currency** is denominated in foreign currencies of developed economics, such as the US dollar. The currency is more stable, but the issuing government cannot print money to pay off its debt.

Soft currency is denominated in local currencies of emerging economies. The currency is more volatile, but governments can print money to pay off debt. Doing so can cause an inflationary spiral, currency devaluation and a drop in EMD's price.[43]

EMD's roles in portfolios are income and growth. EMD can diversify holdings in govies and IG corporate bonds.

The risk factors of EMD are real term, inflation, emerging spread, developed growth and emerging growth.

EMD is a relatively inefficient market, offering fund managers opportunities to add value through active management. Active management is important to manage EMD's risks.

JP Morgan offers popular EMD indices, such as the JP Morgan Emerging Market Bond Index Plus (EMBI+).[44]

Investing in bonds

Choose from individual bonds, active funds and index trackers.[45] Since trading individual bonds is not as easy as trading equities, and since many pension and ISA platforms do not offer individual bonds, funds and trackers are the easiest route. Use individual bonds to hedge specific liabilities.

One major difference between bonds and funds is that you can hold individual bonds to maturity, realising the YTM notwithstanding defaults. Funds, however, are priced on a daily basis. Their holdings are **marked to market** and fund managers tend to trade securities, rather than holding them to maturity.[46]

Consider index trackers for gilts and linkers. For IG credit, use active funds or trackers. High yield and EMD can be accessed through trackers, but active management can enhance returns and manage risks.

You are likely to invest mostly in UK gilts and IG credit. Linkers can be used to hedge inflation, in particular when you expect it to rise above the breakeven rate. High yield and EMD can be included in your portfolio, but they are less common.

Instead of selecting from different types of fixed income, you can use **aggregate bond funds**, mixing gilts and IG credit. **Strategic bond funds** allow their managers freedom to select securities from across the fixed income spectrum. **Multi-asset credit funds** typically invest dynamically across the entire credit universe.[47]

Cash

Cash is king. It is the most liquid asset. At times of financial stress or stagflation, cash does not lose money, as do many other assets.[48] Whilst considered a risk-free asset, cash can generate negative returns in real terms and it can be a risk asset when considering long-term liabilities.

Cash funds are often called **money market** funds. The two important cash rates in the UK are the BOE's base rate and **LIBOR**. These rates are used as a reference for different financial instruments, variable cash ISAs, bank deposit rates and variable mortgage rates.

In a low-yield environment, cash delivers meagre returns. Savers face challenges since bank deposits deliver low yields, potentially below inflation. Low cash rates are good for borrowers but bad for savers.

Saving for retirement needs investing. Investors seeking yields turn to riskier assets with longer maturities or lower credit quality, as well as to equities. When yields of cash and govies are low, investing becomes more important for securing your financial future.

The role of cash in your portfolio includes stable returns, income and liquidity. When you fear financial markets are heading to a tumble, consider shifting assets into cash. Cash may not generate high returns, but it does not lose money.

However, before selling investments and moving money to cash, remember that timing the market is extremely difficult. With the benefits of a long time horizon it is usually better to stay invested, riding through market falls, rather than trying to get in and out. Getting it wrong can hurt performance, as well as generate avoidable transaction costs by churning the portfolio. Time in the market is usually superior to timing the market.

Summary

- Equities are portfolios' main risk assets. They deliver dividend income and potential price appreciation.
- You can access equities via individual securities, active funds and index trackers. Unless you are willing to commit efforts to research individual stocks, use funds and trackers.
- IG corporate bonds, high yield bonds and emerging market debt are fixed income investments offering higher yields than those of govies, as well as higher potential total returns and losses.

- Invest in bonds through funds. Use index trackers for gilts and linkers. Consider index trackers or active funds for IG credit. Active funds are recommended for high yield and EMD.
- Cash is the ultimate liquidity source. In a low-yield environment, savers need to invest to generate sufficient long-term, inflation-beating returns.

Notes

1 The company does not raise additional capital on the secondary market. When you buy a share on the secondary market, the money goes to the seller, not to the company.

2 **Preferred stocks** have higher claim on the company's assets and dividends than do common stocks. Preferred shares usually have a fixed dividend that must be paid before payment of dividends to holders of common stocks. Preferred stocks do not have voting rights.

3 $4\% = £0.50 \div £12.50$.

4 $22\% = £0.20 \div £10 + £12 \div £10 - 1 = 2\% + 20\%$.

5 **Ex-dividend** means the shareholder owning the stock on the ex-dividend date (ex-date) will receive the dividend payment, regardless of who currently owns the stock. When the ex-date is declared, the stock price usually drops by the amount of expected dividend.

6 Another source of equity returns is **share repurchase** or buyback, where companies buy their own stocks from the market. This reduces the number of outstanding stocks, creates demand, signals that the company's management thinks the stock price is undervalued and can push the stock price upwards. Companies can use cash to buy back stocks instead of paying dividends. When borrowing costs are low, corporations might use debt to buy their own shares.

7 $PV = \Sigma[D_t \div (1 + r)^t] + TV \div (1 + r)^t$. According to the Gordon Growth Model $PV = D_1 \div (r - g)$ where D_1 is dividend next year, r is required rate of return and g is constant annual dividend growth rate $(r > g)$.

8 $PV = CF_1 \div (1 + r) + CF_2 \div (1 + r)^2 + \cdots + CF_n(1 + r)^n$.

9 $FCF = EBIT (1 - \text{tax rate}) + \text{depreciation & amortisation} - \text{change in net working capital} - \text{capital expenditure}$. EBIT is earnings before interest and tax.

10 P/E divides equity price by earnings per share (EPS). For example, if the price is £10 and EPS is £1, then P/E is 10. Earnings are usually after-tax income. Earnings and the circumstances relating to them indicate whether the business is profitable and successful.

11 Research by Capital Group shows that 77% of the turnover of FTSE 100 is derived from sales overseas. Of the 77%, 30% comes from emerging markets, 19% from the USA, 17% from Europe, 5% from Japan, 4% from the rest of Asia and 2% from Canada.

12 The largest country weights in the MSCI World Index are the USA 57%, Japan 9%, the UK 8%, France 4%, Switzerland 4%, Canada 4%, Germany 3% and Australia 3%. The weights change over time.

13 DJIA is a price-weighted index with stocks of the 30 largest industrial companies in the USA.

14 Factsheets of MSCI indices are available online. Check **www.msci.com**.

15 The largest sector weights in the MSCI World Index are financials 21%, information technology 14%, healthcare 13%, consumer discretionary 13% and industrials 11%. The weights change over time.

16 Value stocks commonly have high dividend yield, low price-to-book ratio and low price-to-earnings ratio. GARP stands for growth at a reasonable price.

17 Quality can be defined in many ways. High ratio of gross profits to assets, sustainable earnings momentum, high return on equity (ROE), and low debt-to-equity ratio are some quantitative indicators of quality. Qualitative indicators include market positioning, business model, corporate governance, financial strength and management.

18 The **Adaptive Market Hypothesis** (AMH), developed by Andrew Lo, attempts to reconcile EMH and behavioural finance. During periods of regime change, market participants adapt to new rules causing temporary irrational market behaviour.

19 Often, the global emerging equity market universe is divided across commodity importers or exporters and countries with capital account surplus or deficit.

20 It is also easy to invest in equities through the derivatives market. Listed futures and options are available on individual stocks and indices.

21 OTC means the security is not traded on a formal exchange, but rather via a dealer network. Broker-dealers negotiate with one another over computer networks or phone to trade OTC securities. Many debt securities are OTC, traded by investment banks. Bond investors need to speak with the bank that makes the market in the bond to get a quote.

22 $£1,050 = £50 \div (1 + 3.22\%)^1 + £50 \div (1 + 3.22\%)^2 + £1,050 \div (1 + 3.22\%)^3$.

23 $£950 = £50 \div (1 + 6.9\%)^1 + £50 \div (1 + 6.9\%)^2 + £1,050 \div (1 + 6.9\%)^3$.

24 Current yield is the annual coupon rate divided by bond price. It is not YTM and does not reflect the bond's total return.

25 The current yield curve is available on Bloomberg at **www.bloomberg.com**. The *Financial Times* offers a free website with market data, including bond rates at **markets.ft.com**. The Research Division of the Federal Reserve Bank of St Louis offers plenty of current and historic data on US and international markets at **research.stlouisfed.org**.

26 The website of the UK Debt Management Office (DMO) at **www.dmo.gov.uk** includes information and data on gilts, including current rates.

27 In a **bear steepener** long-term rates rise faster than short-term rates, in a **bear flattener** short-term rates rise faster than long-term rates, in a **bull steepener** long-term rates fall faster than short-term rates and in a **bull flattener** short-term rates fall faster than long-term rates.

28 The positions of this pair trade should be adjusted for durations. Say the duration of short-term bonds is 2 years and that of long-term bonds is 10 years, for every 1% on the long term, you need 5% on the short term to have a similar magnitude of returns.

29 Check **www.ftserussell.com**.

30 Global bond funds specialising in government bonds are available. Citi WGBI (World Government Bond Index) is a popular index series for global govies. The countries with the largest weights in the index are the USA 33%, Eurozone 32%, Japan 22% and the UK 7%.

31 The breakeven rate is affected by additional factors, such as tax treatment of different bonds, supply and demand forces and liquidity premium. Hence, breakeven does not purely reflect inflation expectations.

32 Yields of index-linked gilts and other information on UK linkers are available from the UK Debt Management Office at **www.dmo.gov.uk**. YTM is called **redemption yield** at DMO's website.

33 Check the website of Barclays Capital dedicated for indices at **index.barcap.com**.

34 The maximum total return for a bondholder is the interest and capital repayment plus capital gain, which is limited. Rates of govies can turn negatives, as it did for Switzerland and Germany in 2015. When yield is negative, investors are paying the government to keep their money and give it back at maturity. Instead of return on capital it is return of capital.

35 The pecking order dictates that bondholders have priority over shareholders on the company's assets in case of bankruptcy. Assets might be sold and shareholders will get proceeds only after all debt has been paid off.

36 IG: Aaa to Baa for Moody's and AAA to BBB for S&P. Below IG: Ba and below for Moody's and BB and below for S&P.

37 **Callable bonds** come with a call option for the issuer, which can redeem or call the bond before its maturity. **Convertible bonds** come with an option for the investor to convert the bond into the issuer's equity. Convertible bonds are a hybrid security, lying between equity and fixed income.

38 Due to higher transaction costs, active corporate bond strategies have a higher hurdle to pass. This leads to a proliferation of **buy and maintain** strategies where trading is minimised.

39 The index's daily performance is available on **markets.ft.com**. Information on the index, its characteristics and past performance are available at the websites of ETFs tracking it. Check **www.ishares.com/uk**.

40 The country weights in the global high yield market consist of USA 64%, Italy 8%, Germany 5%, UK 5%, France 4%, Luxembourg 4% and Spain 2%.

41 Information on the index, its characteristics and past performance are available at the websites of ETFs tracking it.

42 Check the website of Barclays Capital dedicated for indices at **index.barcap.com**.

43 The value of a currency depends on demand and supply. When governments print money, money supply can cause currency devaluation since more of it is available.

44 Information on the index, its characteristics and past performance are available at the websites of ETFs tracking it. Check the website of JP Morgan for information on the index at **www.jpmorgan.com**.

45 Listed futures are readily available on government bonds issued by countries like the USA, UK, Germany and Italy.

46 The price of a fund is valued based on valuations or most recent prices of its holdings.

47 We have not covered large segments of the fixed income market, such as securitised debt (for example, Asset-Backed Securities – ABS, Mortgage-Backed Securities – MBS, and Collateralised Loan Obligations – CLOs), Floating Rate Notes (FRNs) and many other types of bonds. Leveraged loans are another fixed income asset class, although it is often considered an alternative investment.

48 Stagflation is an economic condition where inflation is high, economic growth is stagnating (slowing down) and unemployment can be high. Central banks are conflicted since lowering rates to reflate the economy can further increase inflation.

CHAPTER 10
ALTERNATIVE INVESTMENTS

A concise guide to non-traditional assets

'Old age isn't so bad when you consider the alternative.'

Maurice Chevalier

Whilst traditional asset classes make up the bulk of most portfolios, other assets can complement them, adding additional sources of return and enhancing diversification. Alternative investments (AI or alternatives) include non-traditional assets, such as:

1 Property.
2 Commodities.
3 Private equity.
4 Hedge funds.
5 Infrastructure.

Many other types of AI exist, for example leveraged loans, insurance-linked securities (ILS), timber and art. However, they are rarely accessible on DC pensions and ISAs.

Historically, alternatives were held exclusively by institutional investors and high net worth individuals (considered sophisticated investors) due to their relative expensiveness, complexity, limited regulatory oversight and illiquidity.

Most alternatives covered in this chapter, however, can be readily accessed in some form through regulated funds. You can do so with relatively small amounts, in a liquid, transparent and cost-effective way.

Property

'Buy land, they're not making it any more.'

Mark Twain

Unlike financial securities, property is bricks and mortar. It is tangible; you can touch it. It is different from other investments in many senses.

Everyone needs property – the public sector, corporations and individuals. Property is used across three broad categories: residential, commercial and industrial.

Property investing can play both a role in your investment portfolio and as a separate retirement solution. Owning your house and a portfolio of residential properties to let are two long-term savings solutions.

Property plays such an important role in financial planning that the next chapter focuses entirely on residential property. Also, you cannot own residential property in your pension – it is not a regular investment, but much more than that.

One challenge of property investing is that each property is expensive. You need a lot of money to buy a building. However, investing in property as part of your portfolio is feasible. The two common means are property funds, investing in direct commercial real estate (CRE), and Real Estate Investment Trusts (REITs). These can be considered as two separate asset classes.

Direct property

Direct property funds pool together the money of many investors to purchase ownerships in properties. Pooling assets allows each investor access with a relatively small sum of money, diversification and professional management.

Direct property funds typically invest in a diversified portfolio of CRE, selected from across the retail, office, industrial and other sectors. Some funds specialise in specific regions, such as the UK, Europe, USA and Japan.[1]

The roles of CRE in portfolios are income, growth, keeping pace with inflation and diversification. Properties generate rental income by leasing them to tenants, paying the proceeds to investors.

Income divided by property price is called **rental yield**. For example, a £2 million property with a £5,000 monthly rent has a 3% rental yield.[2]

Property prices and rental income tend to appreciate when the economy grows, with increasing demand for office space, commercial areas and industrial zones.

Prices and rents can fall when the economy slows down. They should keep pace with inflation over the long term.

One main risk of property is illiquidity. Selling property can be a lengthy process. Property investing involves high transaction costs. The stamp duty in the UK when buying non-residential property above a certain price has a highest rate of 5%. Property is appropriate only for a truly long-time horizon.

Property is not a financial asset. Companies issue equities and bonds to raise capital to finance their business. Property, instead, is needed for the operations of companies and the economy. Therefore, the factors affecting property performance differ from those affecting the performance of financial assets. This adds diversification to portfolios that include property.

The common index for UK CRE is the IPD UK Monthly Property Index.[3]

REITs

REITs are pooled vehicles investing in property. After raising capital from investors through an IPO to invest in property, they trade on the stock exchange. Over the short term, they exhibit equity-like volatility, with high correlation with the equity market. Over the long term, however, they should have higher correlation with the property market.

REITs pay high dividends, so they can fulfil a role of an income source in portfolios, as well as growth and diversification with other assets. Legislation normally forces REITs to pay out most of their profits as income.

REITs are a way to access the property market in a liquid way. The price of liquidity is high volatility. Transaction costs of REITs are much lower than those of direct property. Stamp duty in the UK when buying REITs is 0.5%.[4]

Similar to local versus global equities, globally investing in REITs brings benefits of enhanced diversification and a wider investment opportunity set.[5]

Currency risk is part of global investing. As REITs are a risk asset, hedging currency exposure depends on your view on currencies. If you think the British pound is likely to appreciate, hedge the foreign currency. If you think the pound is likely to depreciate, leave the foreign currency unhedged.

The common index for UK REITs is FTSE EPRA/NAREIT UK Index. FTSE Russell offers a series of REIT indices, covering different regions.[6] You can easily follow some of the indices using ETFs or invest via active funds.[7]

Commodities

Commodities are essential resources and agriculture products. They include basic, in-demand, commercially used goods, supplied unbranded, without qualitative differentiation across the market. This means a barrel of oil is the same as the next barrel of oil from the same type.

The commodity universe includes three broad categories: energy (such as oil and gas), metals (**base metals** such as copper, **precious metals** such as gold) and agriculture (**grains** such as wheat, **softs** such as sugar, **livestock** such as cattle).

Hard commodities refer to natural resources that are mined or extracted (such as silver, coal) and **soft commodities** include grown, perishable agriculture and livestock (such as corn, hogs).

Oil is one of the most important commodities. Its price greatly affects the global economy. In the corporate sector, energy is the input of industrial and transportation corporations, for example. It is the output of corporations in the energy sector. Consumers use energy to warm houses in the winter and to drive cars. The world is addicted to fossil fuel.

The US consumer is the most powerful global economic force. Consumer spending makes about 70% of the GDP of the USA, the world's biggest economy. When the oil price drops, the US consumer is left with more disposable income. When the consumer buys more goods and services, it lifts corporate earnings and the stock market.

Oil price is linked to inflation. A higher oil price translates into higher inflation whilst a lower oil price translates into lower inflation. Changes in oil price can affect the real economy and different asset classes, across equities and bonds.

Gold is another important commodity. Gold is the ultimate safe asset and storage of value. When financial markets crash, investors tend to buy gold.

Gold/copper ratio

The **gold/copper ratio** divides the gold price by the copper price. This ratio has a strong inverse link with the equity market's performance. Copper is an industrial metal. When its price falls, it indicates a slowing economy. Gold is often used to hedge against uncertainty. When its price falls, it is a bullish signal. The ratio is an indicator of sentiment in the global economy. A falling ratio is positive.

Commodities are risk assets. Their roles within portfolios are growth, hedge inflation and diversification.

Some events affect commodities differently from the way they affect equity markets. When a disaster strikes, such as a war in the Middle East, the supply of oil is disrupted, moving its price upwards. The same event can have a negative impact on equity markets.

Commodity prices tend to follow long **super cycles**. The dynamics of supply and demand in commodity markets are slow, taking years to impact prices. For example, China has been a large tailwind for commodity prices for decades, as its economy grew at a fast pace, demanding large quantities of commodities for its industrialisation and urbanisation. China has started slowing down and so has its demand for commodities, adversely impacting their prices.

An example on the supply side is the US journey to energy independence, thanks to the shale oil boom and fracking technology.

Most commodity funds trade futures contracts on commodity indices. The funds do not directly trade the underlying commodities. The prices and behaviour of futures can differ from those of direct commodities (cash, physical or **spot** market).

The three sources of commodity futures' returns are changes in commodity prices (spot price), returns from rolling futures contracts (**roll yield**) and yield on cash held as collateral for the futures (**collateral yield**).[8]

Investing in commodities takes a global approach. Since commodities are risk assets, hedging currency exposure is not mandatory. Commodities are priced in US dollar and have an inverse relation with its value.

The two common commodity indices are Bloomberg Commodity Index (BCOM) and S&P Goldman Sachs Commodity Index (GSCI). GSCI Light Energy Index is often used to limit the index's exposure to oil and gas.[9]

Equity commodities

Investing in commodities is not as common as other asset classes in DC pensions and ISAs. Investing in companies within the commodity sector is more usual. Often, funds investing in such companies are called **natural resources**.

However, investing in stocks of companies in the commodity sector is equity investing, not direct commodity investing. Nevertheless, over the long term, these stocks should have a correlation with commodity prices. An indirect exposure to commodities is often better than not having one at all.

A common commodity equity index is S&P Commodity Producers Oil & Gas Exploration & Production Index.[10] You can easily follow the index using ETFs.

Private equity

Private equity refers to companies whose securities are not listed (unquoted) on the stock exchange (quoted equities are public equity). Whilst it is called *equity*, private equity includes both stocks and debt.[11]

Investing in private equity firms is not typically available for retail investors since it requires large minimum investments, a long investment horizon and hefty fees. However, you may be able to tax-efficiently invest in unquoted companies through the Enterprise Investment Scheme (EIS) and Seed Enterprise Investment Scheme (SEIS).

Retail investors can readily invest in listed equity of companies operating in the private equity sector. The advantages are accessibility, liquidity and indirect exposure to private equity. The disadvantages are large exposure to public equity, impure access to private equity and limited universe of only listed private equity firms.

Private equity is a risk asset. Its risk level and potential returns are higher than those of public equities. Private equity investing heavily depends on the skill of managers of private equity firms to choose successful investments. In fact, tapping manager skill is a prerequisite condition to justify investing in this asset class.

The common index for listed private equity is the S&P Listed Private Equity Index.[12] You can easily follow the index using ETFs.

Hedge funds

Hedge funds tend to hit the news due to billionaire hedge fund managers and spectacular failures of some funds. They are also famous for generating high returns for the rich.

Hedge funds are not an asset class. They are a group of actively managed funds with a number of characteristics distinguishing them from funds that are distributed to the general public.

Most hedge funds are unregulated, as they are often incorporated offshore in places like the Cayman Islands. This allows managers flexibility with investment techniques and strategies – free your manager.

Regulated funds sold to retail investors in the UK, USA and Europe have restrictions on the way they manage assets. The regulations' objective is protecting investors' interests by forcing fund managers to diversify, control risks and be transparent.

Traditionally, hedge funds have not been sold to the wide retail market; only to qualified or accredited investors, considered sophisticated. Therefore, they could avoid such restrictive regulations.

Three areas where hedge funds have more freedom than regulated funds are:

1 Short selling.

2 Derivatives.

3 Leverage.

Whilst you, as an individual investor, are unlikely to use these techniques, it is important to comprehend them. These concepts are helpful not only to understand hedge funds, but also to explain subjects that we will discuss later on.

Hedge funds can **short** securities. Shorting is borrowing a security you do not own, selling it and profiting if its price declines when returning it to the lender. Simply put, shorting is a way to benefit from falling prices.

For example, you borrow and sell a stock for £1,000. Its price falls to £800. You buy it in the market for £800 and return it to the lender, profiting £200. Nice. But had the stock price climbed instead to £1,200, you would have lost £200. Had it rallied to £3,000, you would have lost £2,000.

When buying a stock, the maximum loss is the money invested. When short selling, your loss could be, theoretically, infinite since stock price can rise unlimitedly.

Buying a security is called **going long**. It benefits from increasing price. Regulated funds normally cannot go short – hence, their name **long-only funds**. Hedge funds can freely short securities, potentially benefiting from both upwards and downwards price movements.

Hedge funds have flexibility using **derivatives**. Derivatives are financial instruments deriving their price from other assets. Forward, futures, options and swaps are common derivatives. Listed derivatives are standardised and traded on exchanges. Others are customised, traded directly between parties or through a bank's intermediation, and are called over-the-counter (OTC).

Long-only funds are regularly limited using derivatives for **efficient portfolio management** (EPM) purposes only. Hedge funds can use them more liberally, including speculating.

Hedge funds can use **leverage** (gearing). Long-only funds are restricted in using leverage since it increases risk. Leverage is borrowing money to invest or synthetically using derivatives for leverage.

For example, you want to invest £1 million in the stock market. One way is investing the full amount. If the stock market appreciates 10%, your return is 10%. If it drops 10%, you lose 10%. Your position is **funded** because you committed the entire capital. Simple.

Another way is using leverage. You do not have £1 million, only £100,000. You borrow £900,000 for 5% interest. If the stock market moves up 10%, you make a return of 55% on your investment, net of borrowing costs.[13] But, if the stock market drops by 10%, you lose 145%.[14] Oh dear!

Leverage is a double-edged sword. It amplifies returns to the upside and downside. This is the dark side of leverage – you can lose more than you own. Remember: never invest more than you can afford losing in risky investments.

Leveraged positions are **unfunded** since you commit only a fraction of the capital. You can use derivatives for unfunded positions since you get an exposure without committing all the capital to back it up.

Unregulated hedge funds are generally unavailable in DC pensions and ISAs for retail investors. However, regulated versions are available, in particular in SIPPs. These versions do not enjoy the full freedom of unregulated funds.

Hedge funds' performance greatly depends on fund manager skill. Therefore, diligently select them. Their investment strategies range widely; they can be opaque and illiquid, and they can be pricier than long-only funds.

Hedge funds can be a risk or conservative asset, depending on their strategy and level of aggressiveness or defensiveness. They can fulfil different roles in portfolios, depending on each fund's characteristics. Since they are not an asset class, each fund should be treated on a case-by-case basis.

Often, hedge funds are classified as return enhancers or risk diversifiers. **Return enhancers** are normally more aggressive, aiming to generate high returns. **Risk diversifiers** are normally more defensive, aiming to add diversification benefits.

Most hedge funds fall under one of four broad categories of strategies: global macro, equity long/short, event driven and market neutral. Another related category is managed futures or CTAs (Commodity Trading Advisors). Hedge funds can be further categorised by single or multi manager, single or multi strategy and single fund or fund of funds (FoF).

FoFs conduct fund selection and can offer a diversified exposure to hedge funds. However, they might be expensive due to a double layer of fees, one at the FoF level and one at the underlying funds' level.

Hedge funds seem cool. Billionaire hedge fund managers often appear in the news, talking about how they made millions for investors. You hear less about hedge funds failing or just delivering disappointing returns.

Hedge funds used to be sold as delivering equity-like returns with bond-like volatility. However, their volatility can be misleading. It is sometimes based on smoothed returns of illiquid investments that are infrequently priced or they conceal risks, such as counterparty, liquidity and fat-tail risks.

One philosophy is investing only in what you understand. Investing in hedge funds requires expertise. If you do not have the time and resources to study hedge funds before buying them, steer clear.

A common family of hedge fund indices is HFRI.[15]

Hedge fund benchmarks

Hedge fund benchmarks suffer from a number of biases. **Survivorship bias** is when only successful hedge funds are included in the index; failed ones are deleted. **Backfill bias** is when a hedge fund joins the index its track record is added; but only successful funds are added. **Selection bias** is due to hedge fund returns being self-reported and funds with poor performance do not report. **Valuation bias** is when funds use their own valuation models to report performance.

Infrastructure

Infrastructure is essential buildings and structures required for the functioning of society and the economy. It includes systems of transportation (roads, railways), water, electricity (the electricity grid), telecommunications, energy (gas, oil pipes) and sewage.

Infrastructure projects and structures tend to be capital-intensive, high-cost investments. The government funds projects publicly, but private or public-private partnership (PPP) funding is common, allowing investors to participate.

Investors in infrastructure receive a long-term stream of cash flows. For example, the owner and operator of a toll road collecting cash flows. Infrastructure investing has gained popularity as institutional investors were looking for long-duration investments to hedge long-term liabilities. Declining bond yields made infrastructure an attractive alternative to bonds.

For retail investors, infrastructure investing is typically available via listed infrastructure. Infrastructure funds invest in stocks of companies operating in the infrastructure sector. This is equity investment, but over the long term it should be correlated with the underlying infrastructure projects.

Listed infrastructure is a risk asset. It exhibits equity-like volatility since it is publicly traded equities.

Common indices for listed infrastructure are the Macquarie Global Infrastructure Index series, which is offered by FTSE Russell, and the S&P Global Infrastructure Index.[16] You can easily follow the Macquarie index using ETFs.

Liquid alternatives

Often, alternatives are unlisted, illiquid and expensive. Property, private equity, hedge funds and infrastructure in their unlisted form are accessible mainly to large institutional investors and high-net-worth individuals.

We are after practical solutions that you, as a retail investor, can easily implement in your portfolio. Liquid or listed alternatives are therefore suggested wherever possible.

Listed alternatives are traded on a stock exchange. They exhibit equity-like volatility. Arguably, they are not truly alternatives. Rather, they are equities in their respective sectors. Investing in listed alternatives abandons the liquidity premium and some of the diversification benefits and characteristics of the underlying alternatives.

This is correct. However, given the choice between tapping listed alternatives and excluding alternatives, I opt for the former.

Adding listed alternatives to your portfolio expands its investment opportunity set, enhances diversification and accesses the underlying alternatives' special risk factors. Whilst impure and indirect, it should work over the long term. You do need, however, the appropriate risk tolerance to live with the volatility.

When adding investments to your portfolio, there is a trade-off between benefits and complexity. Adding small allocations to esoteric investments you do not fully understand, requiring significant due diligence, might not be worth it.

If the allocation is small, potential benefits are small anyway, whilst added complexity can be burdensome. If you add alternatives, allocate enough to make them count so potential benefits merit the added complexity.

Article 10.1

Wealthy investors' alternative direction

By Laura Suter

Financial Times, 25 March 2014

Very wealthy investors increasingly are moving into the liquid alternatives market, looking to gain a piece of the traditional hedge fund and private equity action, but at a fraction of the cost and illiquidity.

Liquid alternatives (also known as "retail alternatives") package alternative strategies such as long/short or hard-asset investing inside heavily regulated mutual funds. Advisers are leading the shift as clients search for diversification and uncorrelated returns in their portfolio.

Still scarred by the plummet of almost all assets in the 2008 financial crisis, investors are looking for less volatile, uncorrelated returns from their existing holdings. While hedge funds and private equity strategies are open to those that meet the "accredited investor" definition of having a net worth of at least $1m or who earn at least $200,000 a year, those who fall short of these requirements have previously been locked out of the alternatives market.

A survey by MainStay, a New York Life company, found high-net-worth individuals on average have one fifth of their portfolio in alternatives, with most (65 per cent) investing through mutual funds, followed by 40 per cent using exchange traded funds (ETFs) and 38 per cent managed funds.

The market has grown in recent years to hit $270bn at the end of 2013, according to Strategic Insight. The MainStay research found that financial advisers were the main way very wealthy investors discovered more about liquid alternatives.

Alternatives are being used to gain diversification and investment growth in high-net-worth investors' portfolios, but 60 per cent are also using alternatives to protect principal capital, according to MainStay.

"Advisers and clients are looking for tools for risk management; they are looking for additional sources of returns outside of the stocks-bond-cash traditional asset matrix, and they are looking for additional diversification to build better portfolios," says Rick Lake, portfolio manager of the Aston/Lake Partners Lasso Alternatives Fund.

As the market has seen a flood of assets, managers have responded with a flood of products. Brian Strachan, a managing director of private wealth at Morgan Stanley, says the number of liquid alternative products grew from 400 at the start of 2013 to 800 at the end of the year. That figure is expected to double again this year. "You have to really do your research to make sure you are in the right investment and asset class," he says.

This proliferation of products means the selection process for advisers is not easy. Pedigree matters a lot, say the experts. "Liquid alternatives run by experienced hedge fund managers outperform the rest," says Mr Lake. Academic studies support this, with a paper from London Business School finding that experienced hedge fund managers running mutual funds outperform their competitors by up to 4.1 per cent per year, net of fees.

Certain alternative strategies lend themselves better to a liquid structure than others, says Jason Katz, a managing director of private wealth at UBS Wealth Management. "Long/short equity, managed futures and global macro strategies fit better in a liquid alternative than private equity, distressed assets and fixed income arbitrage."

While track records are scrutinised in the world of traditional investments during the selection process, they cannot always be used for liquid alternatives, says Mr Katz. "The challenge is that many of these vehicles have a fairly short lifespan of five, six or seven years at best," he says.

Instead, one way to assess managers is to look at the record of any previous funds they ran, the experience of the portfolio managers and how long the portfolio manager has been with the asset manager.

One benefit of liquid alternatives, compared with their more illiquid counterparts, is that the fees are lower. While not as low as traditional mutual funds and ETFs, they are offered at a fraction of the cost of "true" alternatives, which typically charge a 2 per cent upfront management fee and 20 per cent of any performance generated.

However, these fees can be justified if the performance backs them up, says Mr Strachan. "The fee issue goes away based on performance – people are willing to pay for good performance," he says. "I don't really get a big fee objection [from clients], because it is part of a total portfolio, but as more products come into the market, lower fees are going to come," he says.

Mr Lake predicts more mutual fund products will come from the private fund world. Hand in hand with this will be a steep learning curve for advisers to better understand the market, he says. "We will see the adviser world linking with outside resources and expertise to help navigate the world of liquid alts."

Summary

- Property funds and REITs are pooled vehicles, allowing you to add a diversified exposure to property to your portfolio. Property plays roles of income, growth, hedging inflation and diversification.

- Direct property needs a long investment horizon since it is illiquid and expensive. REITs are not as expensive as direct property is and can be included, even when the horizon is shorter.

- Commodities can add a source of growth to portfolios, their price keeps up with inflation and they diversify equities as they react differently to some events.

- Private equity is mainly accessible through listed private equity in DC pensions and ISAs. It is a risk asset whose role is growth.

- Hedge funds are not an asset class. They are unregulated, actively managed funds that can use flexible investment techniques, such as shorting, derivatives and leverage. Retail investors mostly access regulated hedge funds.

- Hedge funds can enhance returns and diversify risk, depending on their investment style. They heavily depend on manager skill, so selection requires extra diligence.

- Infrastructure is accessible to retail investors as listed infrastructure. It has the volatility of public equities. Over the long term it should deliver exposure to underlying infrastructure.

- Listed alternatives are a practical way to access alternatives for retail investors. They are liquid, transparent and normally affordable. Whilst listed alternatives exhibit equity-like volatility, including them can be better than not accessing alternatives at all.

- When considering adding new types of investments to your portfolio, consider the trade-off between benefits and complexity. Adding a small allocation to a complex investment has limited benefits whilst adding complexity. Add investments only if they can impact results.

Notes

1 KPMG offers free reports on the property market on its website at **www.kpmg. com/uk.**

2 3% = 12 × £5,000 ÷ £2,000,000.

3 The index's factsheet is available on the website of MSCI at **www.msci.com.**

4 Check **www.gov.uk** for rates of **Stamp Duty Reserve Tax** (SDRT), which applies to buying REITs, UK equities and options to buy shares, amongst others.

5 The countries with the largest weights in the FTSE EPRA/NAREIT Developed Index are the USA 52%, Japan 12%, Hong Kong 8%, UK 7% and Australia 6%.

6 The factsheets of the indices are available on the FTSE Russell website at **www. ftserussell.com.**

7 The European Public Real Estate Association (EPRA) at **www.epra.com** offers free research and indices on REITs.

8 Excess return indices include only changes in spot price and roll yield. Total return indices also include the collateral yield.

9 The factsheets of the indices are available online. Check **www.bloombergindexes. com** and **us.spindices.com**.

10 The index's factsheet is available on the S&P website at **us.spindices.com**.

11 Investment strategies in private equity include leverage buyouts, venture capital, growth capital, distressed investments and mezzanine capital.

12 The factsheet of the index is available on the website of S&P at **us.spindices.com**. A quarterly benchmark of private equity (unquoted) is produced by Cambridge Associates and is available free at **www.cambridgeassociates.com**.

13 $55\% = (10\% \times £1{,}000{,}000 - 5\% \times £900{,}000) \div £100{,}000$.

14 $-145\% = (-10\% \times £1{,}000{,}000 - 5\% \times £900{,}000) \div £100{,}000$.

15 Information and performance of HFRI indices is available on the website of Hedge Fund Research at **www.hedgefundresearch.com**.

16 The factsheets of the indices are available on the FTSE Russell website at **www. ftserussell.com** and the S&P website at **us.spindices.com**.

CHAPTER 11
RESIDENTIAL PROPERTY

Bricks and mortar

'Don't wait to buy land, buy land and wait.'

Will Rogers

If you own your house, you are materially exposed to residential property. The vast majority of most people's wealth is tied up in their house. Owning a house is not solely an investment. It has numerous non-monetary rewards, such as shelter and safety for you and your loved ones. It is much more than numbers and financial planning.

Investing in residential property is different from other investments for three main reasons:

1 We are all investors in residential property, either as owners or tenants. We simply need to live somewhere.

2 Residential-property investing falls outside financial market investments held in pensions, ISAs or bank accounts. It is an alien world with different rules.

3 Mortgage financing for residential property facilitates leverage.

This chapter is dedicated to residential property. The focus is on two broad topics:

- owning your main home
- buy-to-let.

This book does not aspire to be a guide to property investing – there are numerous dedicated guides and publications on this subject. Rather it will look at the main considerations when investing in property, with a particular emphasis on its role in long-term saving for retirement.

Owning your house

Should you buy or rent?

Buying your house is a huge commitment. It is expensive. You need to commit time and energy to maintaining it. Maintenance costs can be high. Mortgage financing can be risky. You give up flexibility since you cannot relocate as easily as when renting. Property's value can fall. Buying may be more expensive than renting. It is not for everyone.[1]

However, owning a house has advantages. You will have a place to live – a roof over your head, before and after retirement. When retiring, you might struggle finding income to pay rent. Owning your house allows you to live rent-free.

Over the long term, UK residential property tends to outpace inflation, appreciating in value. The British population increases, as is the demand for properties, whilst supply in prime locations is restricted. Price appreciation, of course, depends on location, location, location.

Try jumping onto the property ladder as soon as possible. It might be more difficult to do so in the future.

Figure 11.1 shows the UK average house price since January 1991. Over nearly 25 years the average house price appreciated by about 270%.

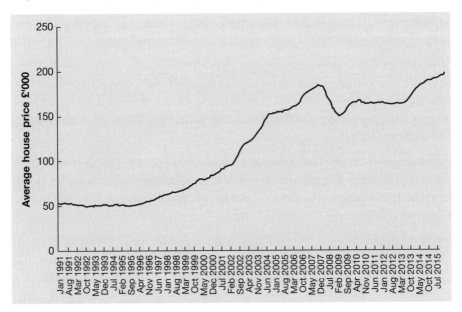

Figure 11.1 UK average house price

Source: Nationwide House Price Index. January 1991 to December 2015. Based on monthly returns, seasonally adjusted

Note, however, that from 1991 to 1996 and from the end of 2007 to 2013 house prices fell or moved sideways. Like other investments, residential property can go through years of falling or flat prices.

Your house is a way to accumulate wealth and cash . The simplest way is after retirement, when the children have left home, to downsize by selling it and buying a smaller house.

Another way to access the equity in your home when you are over 55 is **equity release**. One type of equity release is a **lifetime mortgage**. This is a mortgage on your home but, instead of making repayments whilst you are alive, your estate repays the capital and interest when you die or you do so when moving a house.

A **home reversion** is another equity release product, where you sell your home or part of it to a provider for a lump sum or regular payments. You can live in your home for the rest of your life, as long as you maintain and insure it.

You can raise cash at relatively attractive borrowing costs on your owned house by re-mortgaging it (homeowner loan). If your house is worth £200,000, for example, you can take a £10,000 mortgage to buy a new car. You can then repay the loan over a number of years.

Interest rates on mortgages are typically lower than those on personal and credit card loans since mortgages are safer for lenders. Your house is the collateral (security). The principle of high risk, high return works the opposite way. When borrowing money, the lower the risk for the lender, the lower the rates demanded to compensate for risk. This is a basic principle of banking and credit.

Buying your house with a mortgage is akin to disciplined saving. Investments in your house can potentially increase its value and improve your quality of life. Rent payments are not saving since you buy a perishable service (housing) without accumulating ownership. On the other hand, your monthly mortgage repayments accrue ownership.

Each mortgage payment in a **capital and interest mortgage (repayment mortgage)** consists of capital repayment and interest. The capital repayment is saving as you increase ownership in your house (equity) over time, reducing the outstanding mortgage (debt).

Mortgage payments are not as tax efficient as is a pension since they do not benefit from a tax relief. You also cannot deduct them as expenses for tax purposes. But they are tax efficient because you are usually exempt from CGT on your house.[2]

Your house's potential price appreciation and other financial and non-financial benefits of home ownership can make it worthwhile.

Mortgages

Whilst properties are relatively expensive, leverage makes it feasible for some long-term savers to buy residential properties.

Leverage is buying property with borrowed money. For example, you want to buy a property for £200,000. You saved £50,000 for a down payment (deposit) and borrow £150,000 with a mortgage at a 3% annual interest. Assume the property's price appreciates by 8%. Your net profit is £16,000 − £4,500 = £11,500, a 23% return on your investment.[3,4]

One advantage of residential property is that leverage is relatively easy to accommodate because of mortgages. Mortgage is a legal agreement between you, the borrower, and a lender, usually a bank or a building society. You receive a loan from the lender to buy the property. You promise to repay the loan with interest. Your property is the collateral for the loan.

The lender takes title to your property with the condition that the title's conveyance becomes void when you repay your debt. That is, if you do not repay your mortgage, the bank can repossess your property.

Organising a mortgage is relatively simple. Most steps are completed online and via the phone. Facilitating leverage in your pensions and ISAs, on the contrary, might be impossible. Residential property allows leveraging yourself. But do so prudently.

Importantly, do not take a mortgage but plan a mortgage. It must fit your needs and circumstances.

Mortgage features

When choosing a mortgage, consider its rate, costs and features. Different mortgages come with different terms and conditions.[5] Choosing the right mortgage is an important decision. If unsure, take professional advice.

According to rules from 2014, lenders and brokers must offer advice by recommending the most suitable mortgage for you. If you are uncertain about the advice, seek a second opinion. Use the ample sources of free mortgage advice.

How much can you borrow?

Buying a property is an immense monetary commitment; probably the largest you have made. You need to save for a deposit and borrow the reminder of the agreed price.[6] The deposit and amount you can borrow minus the costs determine the budget for purchasing the property.[7] Then, ensure you can afford it – you need sufficient income to pay the ongoing mortgage payments, including a sensitivity analysis in case the mortgage rate changes.

The amount you can borrow depends on several factors. Namely, the mortgage's purpose (main home, additional property or buy-to-let); what you plan to do with the loan (first-time buyer, move house, re-mortgage, borrow more); mortgage's term (normally up to 25 years); property's location; your income (normally, lenders lend up to 4 or even 4.75 times your annual salary); your outgoings (expenses); your credit score; and **loan-to-value** (LTV) ratio.[8]

LTV is the ratio between the loan and property's price. For example, if you borrow £150,000 to buy a £200,000 property, LTV is 75%.[9] The higher the LTV, the riskier is the mortgage for the lender.

Use a free online mortgage calculator. After entering your basic information it calculates how much you can borrow, which mortgage deals are available for you and your monthly payments.

Rates

One of the most important factors when choosing a mortgage is its interest rate. It depends on current market conditions and the risk to the lender based on assessing your capacity to repay the loan. The assessment considers the LTV, the property, your finances and the mortgage's characteristics.

Types of mortgages

Mortgages come with different rates and features, each with pros and cons.

Variable rate mortgages' rates are – you guessed it, variable, changing based on a formula. A **tracker mortgage** tracks the BOE's base rate plus a spread. If the base rate increases you pay more, if it decreases you pay less.

For example, 2% spread above the base rate when it is 1% means a 3% rate. After an **initial period**, ordinarily two to five years, the spread can significantly rise. If you want out before the initial period finishes, you might pay a penalty.

Lifetime or **term trackers** have no initial period. You have flexibility to early repay and terminate the mortgage when you wish.

The advantage of trackers is that rates tend to be initially lower than those of fixed-rate mortgages. Rates are transparent since they are linked to the base rate. Lifetime and term trackers offer valuable flexibility of early repayment and switching (re-mortgaging) without penalties.

The disadvantage is interest rate risk. Ensure that you can absorb higher rates. Otherwise, unable to make the mortgage payments, you might lose your property. Most mortgage calculators can calculate monthly payments for different interest rates.[10]

Another type of variable mortgage is a **discount mortgage**. Discount mortgages do not track the base rate but the lender's **standard variable rate** (SVR). The discount applies to the initial period and then, normally, the rate moves to the much higher SVR. The lender can change the SVR independently of the base rate – SVR can even increase when the base rate decreases.

The advantage is potentially lower rates than fixed-rate mortgages. The disadvantage is rates are not as transparent as those of trackers.

Fixed-rate mortgages offer a fixed rate for the deal's initial period, usually one to five years. Typically, mortgages come with an **initial rate** during the initial period, afterwards it jumps significantly higher. During the initial period, early repayment charges are imposed if you want to switch mortgages.

The advantage of fixed rate is that payments remain constant when interest rates rise. The disadvantages are that fixed rates may be higher than current variable rates and you are locked in the mortgage for the initial period. Exiting before involves a penalty.

A fixed-rate mortgage is like selling a bond. When interest rates rise, you benefit since your loan is worth less, as it is more competitive. When interest rates fall, you are worse off since your loan is worth more. When inflation increases, you benefit since it erodes the loan's value. The opposite occurs when inflation drops.

Your fixed-rate mortgage is a liability (like a short bond) you can hedge by buying gilts with similar maturity to that of the mortgage. The values of the mortgage and gilts should move in the opposite directions when interest rates change.

Table 11.1 shows the monthly payments for different interest rates and repayment periods (terms) on £100,000.

This is an example of a simple sensitivity analysis to gauge whether you can withstand an increase in interest rates on a variable mortgage. Use such calculations to compare fixed and variable mortgages.

The choice of mortgages depends on your outlook on rates. If you expect rates to rise, a fixed-rate mortgage can be beneficial. It matters when rates will rise since, in the meantime, you might pay more on a fixed mortgage. If you expect rates to remain low, a variable-rate mortgage can be advantageous.

Table 11.1 Monthly payments for mortgage rates and repayment periods

Payments (£)	2%	3%	4%	5%	6%
10 years	928	977	1,027	1,079	1,132
15 years	649	698	750	803	858
20 years	510	560	613	669	727
25 years	427	479	533	591	652

Source: Mortgage calculator of BBC Homes

Check the spread between fixed and variable-rate mortgages. Wide spread (fixed above variable) means the lender expects rates to rise. Narrow spread implies the lender expects rates to remain stable or decline.

Offset mortgages offset your savings held with the lender against the mortgage so you pay less interest. For example, with a £150,000 mortgage and £70,000 savings with the lender, you pay interest only on £80,000. However, monthly payments include repayments on the full amount, so you repay your mortgage earlier, reducing interest payments.

The advantages are earlier repayment, flexibility of accessing your savings and, potentially, a significant tax advantage. Normally, you pay income tax on interest on savings. Offsetting the interest on the mortgage is tax efficient since you earn no interest and pay no tax.

With an offset mortgage you retain full control of your savings. You do not need a cashback facility.

The disadvantage of offset is that rates might be higher than those of other mortgages. Whether it is worthy depends on the savings amount you deposit with the lender. It needs to be sufficiently large to justify higher rates. If you are a high-rate taxpayer and cannot put more money in ISAs and pensions, an offset mortgage can be useful to reduce tax.

An offset mortgage can be used to save money for a deposit for buying another property, whilst reducing interest payments on your existing mortgage.

Fees and costs

Mortgages typically come with fees and costs, beyond interest payments. The provider charges an **arrangement fee** (**product fee** or **completion fee**) for the product. It normally ranges between nil and £2,000.

A **booking fee** may be charged when applying for a mortgage and might be non-refundable, even if the mortgage falls through. It can be up to £250.

A **valuation fee** is paid for surveyors to evaluate the property. A basic **valuation report** costs between £150 and £1,500, depending on the property's value. Lenders usually require a valuation report. It is designed to assess the property's reasonable price, considering any needs for repairs and replacements.

However, you may get your own surveyor or pay extra to the lender's surveyor to check not only the value of the property, but also its state. You can choose between a **Homebuyer Survey** and a more comprehensive **Full Building Survey**.

These surveys provide details on construction, condition, needed repairs and matters requiring further investigation. The full report is usually recommended if the property is in bad shape or you are concerned about subsidence, for example. A Homebuilder Survey is suggested to ensure you are buying a property without any obvious skeletons in the closet. When buying an expensive property, it is wise to spend some more on an appropriate survey to mitigate risks.

Buying a property with hidden defect is a low probability high impact risk. The survey's cost to mitigate the risk is worthwhile. Say the probability of serious defect is 2% and the cost of fixing it is £100,000. The expected loss is 2% × £100,000 = £2,000 which is more than the survey's cost.

Most lenders require you to insure the property during the mortgage's term. Obligatory insurance usually covers only the building, but some lenders insist on content insurance as well.

These are the main charges, but others may exist. Add all the charges to the mortgage's total costs. Sometimes, you can borrow and defer charges (including stamp duty) by adding them to the mortgage. Whether it is profitable depends on whether you have cash, the time value of money and your opportunity cost – how much money you can make on the money whilst having it.

Early repayments

Flexibility to make early repayments is an option. Options in finance, and generally in life, are valuable. You never know when flexibility will come in handy.

Early repayment allows you to repay your mortgage and re-mortgage to another one, if you find a better deal, or reduce or terminate it, if you accumulate cash. For example, if you receive a bonus or an inheritance.

However, it is not always sensible to early repay, even when cash is available. It depends on the opportunity cost and potential returns on the cash.

For example, your outstanding mortgage is £150,000; its rate is 3% without penalties for early repayment. You win £150,000 in the lottery. One possibility is paying off your mortgage, saving 3% interest payments or £4,500 annually.

Instead, you can use the £150,000 to pay as a deposit to buy another property with an expected 6% net total return. You can use the money to invest in the stock market with an 8% expected total return. You can do whatever you like with the money.

You cannot borrow from the bank such an amount at this rate to invest in the stock market. When taking out a mortgage, you specify reasons for the loan. But now that you have a mortgage, you do not need to prematurely terminate it. You are free to do what you want with the money.

Early repayment charges normally range between 1% and 5% of the early repayment's value. Sometimes it is financially sound to pay the penalty to re-mortgage to a better deal. For example, saving more than 1% after considering all switching costs whilst the penalty is 1% can be beneficial.

When making an early repayment you can normally choose between shortening the mortgage's term and keeping it. Shortening the term leaves monthly payments the same, but you pay less interest overall. Keeping the term the same reduces monthly payments. If you struggle with payments, opt for the latter.

Interest only or repayment

In a capital and interest mortgage (repayment mortgage), every monthly payment includes interest on the outstanding loan and capital repayment of some of the principal. Capital repayments reduce the outstanding mortgage every month. Over the term of the mortgage, typically up to 25 years, you repay it, ending up owning the property outright.

The advantage is reducing the interest portion as capital is paid over time. The disadvantage is monthly payments are larger than those of an interest only mortgage.

Interest only mortgage includes only interest in the monthly payments. The capital is repaid at the term's end.

The advantages are deferring the repayment (time value of money), monthly payments are lower and inflation erodes the loan's value. The disadvantage is you do not reduce capital and pay more interest over the mortgage's life.

You must show the lender how you can repay an interest only mortgage at its term's end. Examples of repayment plans include cash saved in savings accounts or ISAs; stocks and shares ISAs; pensions; **investment bonds** (a single premium life insurance policy where you invest a lump sum in with-profits or unit linked funds until surrender or death); **endowment policies** (life insurance contract designed to pay a lump sum after a specific term or on death where you pay regularly and your money is invested in with-profits or unit linked funds); and other assets.

Investment bonds

Check the websites of insurance companies for more information on investment bonds and endowment policies. Explore **International Investment Bonds**. These are offshore solutions allowing you to invest a lump sum in pooled funds and tax-efficiently withdraw a certain amount (such as 5%) each year of the original investment over a specific term (such as up to 20 years). You can use the withdrawals to contribute to your pension, benefiting from a tax-relief.

Shopping around

Mortgage deals and rates are available online. You can get a **mortgage promise** (**decision in principle** or **agreement in principle**) even before finding a property.

After completing an online questionnaire, the lender conducts a credit search on you. You are informed whether and how much you can borrow. The final mortgage depends on finding a property, completing a valuation, finalising the mortgage with the lender and exchanging contracts.

When taking out a mortgage, the most important factors are the rate and features. The lender's identity is less important. You are not buying a car where brand is significant. The lender should just show you the money. So, shop around.

Buy-to-let

If you buy a property with a mortgage, let it and its rental income less expenses cover the mortgage payments, by the end of the term of the mortgage, you can fully repay it. You end up owning the property. Owning a number of properties at retirement can be an income source. It can be a pension solution or complement savings.

You can make all the right actions when saving for retirement – saving in ISAs, maximising pension contributions and investing in financial markets. Yet, it may still be insufficient to deliver the income needed for your desired post-retirement standard of living. Buy-to-let properties can supplement your pension.

This materially differs from investing in capital markets. It requires a different skillset, time and energy. This is not for everyone. However, it can be a rewarding retirement solution.

The UK buy-to-let market has flourished because of a combination of attractive returns on residential properties, low borrowing costs and plummeting saving and annuity rates.

The advantages of buy-to-let are potentially lucrative returns, access to leverage via mortgages and a source of capital and income. It is not dependent on financial markets, fund managers or insurance companies. It is your business.

But buy-to-let does not come without risks. The main disadvantages include properties standing vacant (voids); capital intensity (down payments and renovations); demand for hard work, being a landlord and engaging agents, lawyers and tenants (dealing with people is difficult); leverage risk (properties can be repossessed); illiquidity; and poor property selection.

Building a portfolio of buy-to-let properties can take years and considerable efforts: saving for deposits, locating properties, arranging mortgages, renovating and letting. After retirement, you may be uninterested or unable to manage properties. Nudging tenants might call you frequently with problems. You can use a property management company, but it adds costs and it still requires oversight.

Before embarking on this adventure, carefully think whether it fits your lifestyle and personality.

Finding a property

The first step is locating a property to buy. Location is critical. Think what kind of tenants you want. Families normally prefer unfurnished houses, with a garden, parking space, at least three bedrooms and nearby schools. Being in a good school's catchment area is valuable. Young professionals normally seek local amenities, such as restaurants and transportation. Students search for clean and comfortable flats close to campus.

Students may appreciate a tenancy agreement allowing them to sublet the property. This enables them to locate and share with flatmates.

Knowing the area helps with choosing the best location. That is why people tend to buy properties close to where they live. It also helps to reach them easily. The downside of doing so is lack of diversification, due to large exposure to one area via the main residence.

Think whether it would be easy to sell the property eventually. A ground floor flat could be a disadvantage due to security issues and lack of privacy. A top floor flat could be problematic due to stairs and high temperatures in summer. A flat high up in a building with a lift might mean an expensive service charge, which usually the landlord pays.

Flats in purpose built blocks usually come with hefty service charges. Conversions normally have no or low service charges, but the flats' floor planning might be awkward.

Whether the ownership is freehold, leasehold or a share of freehold impacts the value. Ask your solicitor to explain to you the rights and obligations of each.

It is not only how the flat looks, but also how its building looks. You have control on refurbishing a flat, but you depend on neighbours to refurbish a building.

Is the property on a busy road with buses? Is it close to a noisy railway? Is it walking distance from train and bus stations? Does it have parking or is it easy to park near it? Is it over a noisy pub with smokers standing below its window? Is it next to a school with noisy children? Are the buildings near it residential, commercial or public? Ask yourself all these questions before buying.

Form good relationships with local estate agents. They are the main source for properties. Take your time to study the market's dynamics. View many properties before deciding. Do not rush – this is a big decision.

Choose between a relatively cheap and shabby property, in an up-and-coming area, in need of possibly expensive and time-consuming renovations, and a more expensive property in good condition, that can be let out quickly. Having a good and trustworthy builder can tilt the balance. Property developers' rough calculation is that a refurbished property's final value should be at least purchase price, plus work's cost plus 20%.

Haggle for price. If you are not reliant on selling a property to buy another, you are **chain free**. This can be an advantage when negotiating a price. Ideally, being a cash buyer who does not need a mortgage could be a bigger advantage.

Buy a property in which you would live yourself. You can buy a property with the potential of moving into it after retirement if you downsize your house.

Consider buying properties to gift to your children at a later stage to help them getting onto the property ladder, increase the chances they will live near you after you retire and mitigate IHT.

Calculate price per square foot or metre. This allows you to compare property prices across different locations and types. Ensure that the property's floor plan makes sense – measurements might be inaccurate.

Down payment

Either save cash for a deposit over time or use the tax-free lump sum from your pension when retiring. It may be sufficient to buy a property outright without a mortgage.

Contemplate re-mortgaging your house to borrow a deposit, whether it is mortgage-free or by increasing an existing mortgage. The mortgage rate on your house will be lower than that on a personal loan. The quality of collateral (your house) makes it less risky for lenders.

Balance between the time it takes to save a bigger deposit (lowering LTV) and leverage risk of high LTV. Buying a property as early as possible can be an advantage if its value appreciates. This is the same principle of starting to save early. However, buying early may mean lacking time to save enough to reduce LTV, leading to higher borrowing costs. Trade-offs are everywhere.

Mortgage

Buy-to-let and residential (owner occupier) mortgages are different. Lenders look at prospective rental income to more than cover the mortgage payments. Most lenders demand monthly rental income of 125% of monthly mortgage payments. The deposit should be between 25% and 40% of the property's value.

Buy-to-let mortgage rates tend to be higher than those of residential mortgages, reflecting the borrower's higher default risk. First, you are likely to save your home before buy-to-let property in case of inability to pay the mortgage. For example, due to rising interest rates, loss of a job or excessive indebting. Second, there are risks of bad tenants and difficulties in letting properties.

Over recent years, buy-to-let rates have fallen in line with residential rates. But depending on LTV, buy-to-let rates can be 1% to 2% higher than equivalent residential mortgages. Shop around for a suitable deal, fitting your needs.

Having an existing mortgage on your home may affect your borrowing capacity. If you do not have a mortgage on your home, or if it is small, consider using your home to take a residential mortgage for a buy-to-let instead of a buy-to-let mortgage. This is called a **homeowner loan** and it is a way to release some equity from your house. The rate may be better. However, you are risking your home if you cannot repay your mortgage.

Use a broker to find a mortgage or approach lenders directly. Brokers search the whole market, whilst lenders offer only their products. A broker's advice costs money (£400 to £500). Some lenders offer buy-to-let mortgages only via brokers.

The internet offers plenty of information on mortgages. It is easy to compare rates and lending terms.

Mortgage comparison websites (or commercial websites comparing any other financial products) can add costs to mortgages to cover their commission. They might exclude some mortgage providers. Conduct your own comparison by visiting websites of major mortgage providers, comparing deals. It takes time, but it can save money.

Interest-only mortgage

Commonly, borrowers take a repayment mortgage when buying a home and interest only when buying-to-let. Interest only mortgages have tax benefits, as interest is tax deductible on buy-to-let (landlords' mortgage interest relief).

This might change, however, with changes phasing in between 2017 and 2020. Landlords might no longer be able to deduct the cost of their mortgage interest from rental income. The government may allow a tax credit equivalent to basic rate tax (20%) on interest, reducing profits from buy-to-let for some landlords.

Another advantage of interest only is lower monthly payments. For example, on a £150,000 mortgage at a 3% rate and 25-year term you pay £718 per month with repayment and £375 per month with interest only.[11]

You can use the extra cash to cover maintenance costs. After 25 years when it is time to repay the principal, the potential appreciation in the property's value (although you do not sell it) and inflation should help with repayment.

After 25 years, assuming 2% average annual inflation rate, a £150,000 mortgage is worth £91,430 in today's values.[12] That is about 40% less.

Number crunching

Rents are seasonal. In August, for instance, you may get a higher rent due to demand from overseas relocations and students looking for residence ahead of the start of the academic year. In winter rents might be lower. When entering a tenancy agreement, you set the rent for the agreement's term.

Similar to bond yields, property's valuation metric is **rental yield** – estimated annual income expressed as a percentage of property price. For example, you are a cash buyer buying a property for £200,000. The rent is £1,200 per month or £14,400 per year.[13] *Gross* rental yield is 7.2%.[14]

Compare the rental yield with other investments, such as cash deposits and gilts, for an objective cross-investment valuation. In particular, 10-year gilt yield should be the benchmark for properties.

For example, if rental yield is 7.2% and 10-year gilt yield is 2%, property appears better valued.

However, account for costs, including mortgage payments, maintenance costs, insurance, ground rent, service charges, estate agent fees (plus VAT), as well as estimated vacancy periods when the property does not pay rent.

Say you need a mortgage for the £200,000 property. You put a 25% deposit (£50,000), taking a £150,000 mortgage. At a 3% fixed rate on interest only you pay £375 per month (£4,500 per year). Maintenance costs and insurance are about 10% of rent (£1,440 per year). Your net rental income is £8,460, giving a 4.2% rental yield.

Add estate agent fees at another 10% of rent (£1,440 per year), and rental yield drops to 3.5%.[15,16] Instead, hiring a management company, which tenants call with problems, comes with a fee of about 15% of rent (£2,160 per year). Being hands-on and dealing with the property can save fees. However, be prepared to give up some spare time. Hiring a management company drops the rental yield to 3.2%.[17]

Bargain with estate agents on their fee. There are many agencies, creating competition. If you purchase your property through an agency, you may get a discount on the fee for letting it. Always haggle – everything is negotiable in business.

This still looks favourable compared to 2% yield of 10-year gilts. However, consider the risks of the property standing vacant (assume two-month vacancy per year), tenants missing payments, major works needed at the property and property's illiquidity.[18] Gilts are a relatively safe investment, whilst buy-to-let has risks and it requires extensive efforts. And this is yet before taxes.

Taxes

Stamp Duty Land Tax (SDLT) is due when buying a property, whether it is residential or buy-to-let. Calculate SDLT using the online calculator at **www.tax.service. gov.uk/calculate-stamp-duty-land-tax**. From April 2016 a 3% extra stamp duty on second homes and buy-to-let applies.[19]

Income tax is due on rental profits. Rates are the same as those on income and interest on savings. Deduct certain costs, called **allowable expenses**, from gross rent to calculate net rental profits.

Costs include property's repair, letting agent fees, landlord insurance, mortgage interest payments, council tax and travel expenses to and from the property. Capital expenditures, such as purchase price and renovations beyond repairs of wear and tear, are not allowable expenses. Losses on rental income can be carried forward to set against future profits.

Until April 2016 landlords benefited from a 10% wear and tear allowance, even if they did not incur actual expenditures. This was scrapped and replaced in April 2016 with a relief enabling landlords to deduct costs they actually pay.[20]

Deductible interest does not need to be on a buy-to-let mortgage. A mortgage on your home can qualify. You must show which interest payments were for the buy-to-let.

CGT applies when selling a buy-to-let (an additional 8% surcharge applies to residential property, so the rates are 18% and 28%). For CGT purposes, deduct some expenses associated with buying and managing the property. These include SDLT, fees to solicitors, estate agent and surveyors.[21]

Letting the property

Properties in the UK typically are let through estate agents. However, new avenues, such as Airbnb, offer new flexible ways for short-term letting.[22] Short-term letting may be profitable and you cut out the middleman.

Holding company

Consider incorporating a company to own buy-to-let properties. It can reduce tax and make it easier to pass ownership to children.

When you own buy-to-let properties, rental profits are taxed at your marginal tax rate. Capital gains are taxed at 18% or 28%. When a company owns a property, rental profits and capital gains are taxed at the Corporation Tax rate of 20% (corporation tax will decrease from 20% to 17% in 2020).

When taking money out of a company, you pay income tax (if drawing a salary) or dividend tax in addition to the 20% Corporation Tax already paid.[23] Keeping profits in a company enables you to invest them in new properties at relatively benign tax rates. Growing a property portfolio may be more tax-efficient in a company.

Transferring existing properties into a company might be a disposal for CGT purposes, incurring a potential SDLT.[24] This is likely to be tax inefficient.

Gifting personally held buy-to-let properties to children incurs CGT on the basis of market value. The gift may be a **potentially exempt transfer** for IHT purposes. That is, there is no IHT on the gift if you survive for seven years.

If you incorporate a company to buy rental properties, you could make your children shareholders. They need to pay tax on dividends, capital distributions or sale of shares.[25]

Consult your accountant or solicitor before establishing a company.

Summary

- Residential property is part of everyone's financial planning.

- Leverage property by investing through mortgage financing.

- Accumulating a portfolio of buy-to-let properties could be a retirement solution or complement your pension.

- Gifting properties to your children can help them financially, mitigate IHT and increase chances of them living near you after retirement. You can use a buy-to-let property as your home after retirement if you plan to downsize your existing house.

- Consider incorporating a company to hold buy-to-let properties to mitigate taxes.

Notes

1 *The Telegraph* offers a free online buy or rent calculator at **www.telegraph.co.uk**. It calculates after how many years you can breakeven by buying.

2 No CGT is levied when selling your main home if you have one home and you have lived in it for all the time you have owned it; you have not let part of it; you have not used part of it for business only; the grounds are less than 5,000 square metres; and you did not buy it just to make a gain. Check **www.gov.uk** for details on CGT on your home and **private residence relief**.

3 Price appreciation: £16,000 = £200,000 × 8%; annual interest payment: £4,500 = £150,000 × 3%.

4 23% = £11,500 ÷ £50,000.

5 Check **www.nationwide.co.uk** for a guide on mortgages. Many lenders offer free guidance on mortgages online.

6 First-time buyers can get up to £3,000 from the government to help buy a property through a **Help to Buy ISA**. You will need to save £200 each month and the government adds 25% on top. If you have a Help to Buy ISA you can transfer it into the new Lifetime ISA that will be introduced in 2017 or continue saving in both. However, you will only be able to use the government bonus from one to buy a house. **London Help to Buy** scheme helps Londoners to buy a property with just a 5% deposit and a mortgage as low as 55%. Check **www.gov.uk** and **www.helptobuy.gov.uk** for Help to Buy ISA and London Help to Buy.

7 Costs include stamp duty, mortgage arrangement fee, valuation fee, legal fees (including property searches), surveys, removal costs, home repairs, furniture and extras (light bulbs, door mats and so on).

8 Similar to a credit rating of a company, a credit score is a numeric expression of an individual's creditworthiness. It is used by lenders to assess the likelihood

that the individual will repay debts. You can get a free credit report and score from Experian at **www.experian.co.uk**.

9 75% = £150,000 ÷ £200,000.

10 The website of BBC Homes at **www.bbc.co.uk/homes** offers a mortgage calculator with flexibility to input the mortgage repayment period and interest rate to calculate the monthly payments.

11 Ibid.

12 £91,430 = £150,000 ÷ $(1 + 2\%)^{25}$.

13 Rent per month = rent per week × 52 ÷ 12.

14 7.2% = 12 × £1,200 ÷ £200,000.

15 To calculate estate agent fees multiply the weekly rent by 52 and take 10% (or the estate agent fee) of the sum.

16 3.5% = (12 × £1,200 − 12 × £375 − 10% × £14,400 − 10% × £14,400) ÷ £200,000.

17 3.2% = (12 × £1,200 − 12 × £375 − 10% × £14,400 − 15% × £14,400) ÷ £200,000.

18 You can take an insurance against your tenant failing to pay rent (rent guarantee insurance).

19 Check **www.gov.uk** for SDLT rates and a free online calculator. SDLT no longer applies in Scotland and instead you pay Land and Buildings Transaction Tax when buying property.

20 Check **www.gov.uk** for details on taxation of buy-to-let and property in general.

21 If buy-to-let was used at any point as your single or main residence during the last 18 months of ownership, it can qualify for a tax break known as **private residence relief**. This makes it free of CGT over this time period. From April 2019 the window for paying CGT on property will be cut from 10–22 months to 30 days after the transaction.

22 Check legislation banning short-term letting. For example, the Greater London Council Act 1973 bans letting out properties for less than three months, unless homeowners have a planning permission.

23 When closing a company you could carry out **members' voluntary liquidation** and pay CGT on any capital left. But 20% Corporation Tax on gains must be paid first.

24 When a company buys a property worth over £500,000, the stamp duty is 15%, unless the property will be let out commercially to third parties and then the standard SDLT applies.

25 If any children under the age of 18 received income from the company, the parents would be liable for the tax due.

CHAPTER 12
INVESTMENT HISTORIC PERFORMANCE

To predict the future understand the past

'Those who cannot remember the past are condemned to repeat it.'

George Santayana

This chapter will review assets' historic performance. Formulating an investment strategy requires investing in assets based on expectations on how they are likely to perform in the future. To predict future performance, first understand the past.

The best guide to the future is history. It provides probabilities. If an investment behaved in a certain way 80% of the time, it is fair to assume it is *likely* to continue doing so. The challenge is using the right past since investments behave differently during different pasts.

The objectives of this chapter are exploring and demonstrating assets' characteristics. So far we have discussed how they should behave. Now we will see how they behave in practice.

We are using a relatively short 17-year recent history to simply illustrate assets' behaviour. This is hardly sufficient to draw any conclusions, which require a much longer track record.

Traditional assets

Figure 12.1 shows the cumulative performance of three traditional asset classes: UK equities (FTSE 100 Index), gilts (iBoxx £ Gilts Index) and cash (UK Cash LIBOR TR 1 Month Index).[1] Inflation rate (UK RPI Index) is also included.[2]

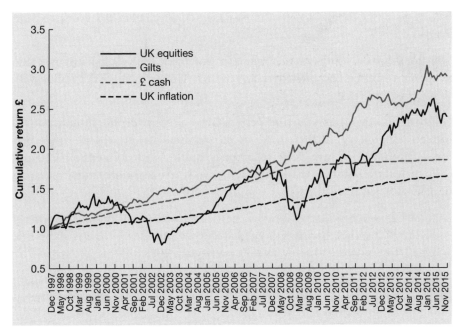

Figure 12.1 Historic performance of UK equities, gilts, cash and inflation

Source: Bloomberg. FTSE 100 Index, iBoxx £ Gilts Index, UK Cash LIBOR TR 1 Month Index, UK RPI Index.
January 1998 to December 2015. Based on monthly total returns, measured in £

Performance is based on monthly total returns of indices representing the assets. Each asset is assigned the value of £1 at the end of December 1997. The figure shows how £1 would have appreciated or depreciated over time.

UK equities have experienced periods of impressive gains, such as up to 2000, from 2002 to 2008 and from 2009 to 2015. They have also experienced impressive declines, such as from 2000 to 2002 and in 2008.

Relative to lines representing performance of gilts and cash, the line representing UK equities is bumpier. This demonstrates the higher volatility of equities compared to conservative assets.

The large declines illustrate equities' downside risk. During the 2000 high-tech bubble burst, the FTSE 100 Index fell over 42% between January 2000 and March 2003. In the 2008 crisis the index lost about 40% between July 2007 and February 2009. These drawdowns measure the fall from peak to trough.[3]

Such 40% drawdowns just before retirement can be disastrous without time to remain invested. If you have time, after every crash the market eventually recovers.

It can take a long time, but so far in history the equity market has recovered from every drop.

The index's worst month was the infamous September 2008 when it lost over 12% as Lehman Brothers collapsed. Investors thought it was the end of the world. Well, the world did not end.

Equity returns depend on the time period. Over the entire period, equities outperformed cash, but lagged gilts. However, during some periods, equities underperformed both gilts and cash. Yet in other times equities outperformed both gilts and cash, such as the last three years. This is risk – you can make more money investing in risk assets, but you can also lose. Timing is critical.

Gilts have experienced a secular rally over the entire period. This is not surprising. As Figure 12.2 shows, 10-year gilt yield at the beginning of 1998 was above 6%, going all the way down to as low as 1.3% on January 2015.

Gilts' strong performance was due to a combination of carry (yield) and capital gains. When yield was at a level of about 5%, this was a big part of gilts' total returns.

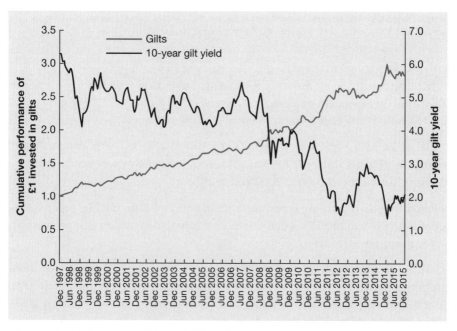

Figure 12.2 10-year gilt yield and gilt performance

Source: Bloomberg. iBoxx £ Gilts Index, UK Generic Govt 10Y Yield. January 1998 to December 2015. Based on monthly total returns, measured in £

Then, capital gains kicked in because of a series of reductions of the base rate by the Bank of England (BOE). In the 1980s inflation fell; after the 2000 crisis the BOE cut rates to reflate the economy; and after the 2008 crisis the BOE further cut rates, as well as engaged in quantitative easing (QE).

According to the BOE, QE is an unconventional form of monetary policy where a central bank creates new money electronically to buy financial assets, like government bonds. This process aims to directly increase private sector spending in the economy and return inflation to target.

In the future, if the UK economy expands, rates are expected to rise. If the UK economy remains sluggish – in a Japan-like scenario – rates might stay low. In any case, gilts are not projected to perform as they did in the last two decades.

Notice the line representing gilts' performance is smoother than that of equities, but bouncier than that of cash. Gilts are more volatile than cash, but not as risky and volatile as are equities.

Finally, the line representing cash is smooth. Cash is hardly volatile. It has been losing ground relative to inflation since 2008. When the BOE aggressively cut its base rate following the 2008 crisis, cash started lagging inflation.

Figure 12.3 shows the historic base rate and cash performance. The base rate fell off a cliff from a level of 5% to 0.5% in 2008. Notice how the cash performance line's gradient flattens after 2008.

Cash performance over the entire period is not bad. However, with the base rate's current low level, cash is anticipated to deliver low returns until the BOE lifts the base rate. In a low-yield environment, cash is not king.

These magnificent collapses in the base rate and gilt yield explain why deposit, mortgage and annuity rates fell so sharply during recent years. The big questions are when they will rise and which new levels they will reach – what is a 'normal' level? The impact of 'normalisation' of short- and long-term rates on pensions, savings and investing will be remarkable.

Table 12.1 shows the annualised return, annualised volatility, Sharpe ratio and maximum drawdown of each asset between January 1998 and December 2015. The table confirms what Figure 12.1 is showing. Gilts delivered better risk-adjusted performance, with higher return and lower risk compared to UK equities over this specific time period.

Table 12.2 shows the same statistics but for the *last three years*. During different times, assets exhibit different results. Returns and volatilities are **non-stationary**, they change. UK equities dominated gilts during this particular time.

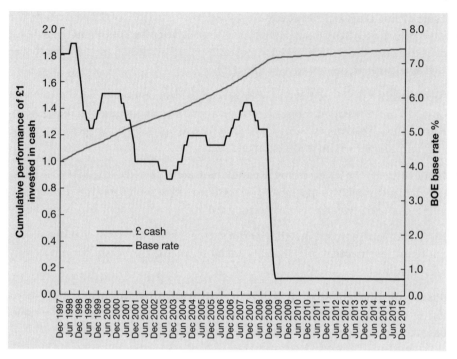

Figure 12.3 The base rate and cash performance

Source: Bloomberg. UK Cash LIBOR TR 1 Month Index, UK Bank of England Official Bank Rate. January 1998 to December 2015. Based on monthly total returns, measured in £

Table 12.1 Annualised return, volatility, Sharpe ratio and max drawdown

	UK equities	Gilts	£ cash	UK inflation
Return pa %	4.9	6.0	3.5	2.8
Volatility pa %	14.2	5.4	0.7	1.3
Sharpe ratio	0.10	0.47	–	–
Drawdown %	−43.6	−5.9	0.0	−3.7

Source: Bloomberg. FTSE 100 Index, iBoxx £ Gilts Index, UK Cash LIBOR TR 1 Month Index, UK RPI Index. January 1998 to December 2015. Based on monthly total returns, measured in £

Table 12.2 Annualised return, volatility, Sharpe ratio and max drawdown

	UK equities	Gilts	£ cash	UK inflation
Return pa %	6.0	3.3	0.5	1.9
Volatility pa %	11.5	6.6	0.0	1.1
Sharpe ratio	0.48	0.43	–	–
Drawdown %	−12.0	−6.1	0.0	−0.8

Source: Bloomberg. FTSE 100 Index, iBoxx £ Gilts Index, UK Cash LIBOR TR 1 Month Index, UK RPI Index. January 2013 to December 2015. Based on monthly total returns, measured in £

Table 12.3 Correlation matrix

	UK equities	Gilts	£ cash	UK inflation
UK equities	1.00	−0.15	−0.07	0.05
Gilts	−0.15	1.00	0.08	−0.14
£ cash	−0.07	0.08	1.00	−0.04
UK inflation	0.05	−0.14	−0.04	1.00

Source: Bloomberg. FTSE 100 Index, iBoxx £ Gilts Index, UK Cash LIBOR TR 1 Month Index, UK RPI Index. January 1998 to June 2015. Based on monthly total returns, measured in £

Correlation

Correlation between each pair of assets is a statistical measure of how they linearly move in relation to each other.[4] It ranges between −1 and +1. Perfect negative correlation of −1 means every time one asset moves in one direction the second asset moves in the opposite direction. Perfect positive correlation of +1 means every time one asset moves in one direction, the second asset moves in the same direction. A correlation of zero means no correlation between assets.[5]

Correlation does not mean causality; it does not say whether one asset's movement affects that of the other. It only measures the tendency to move in the same or opposite direction on average.

Table 12.3 is a **correlation matrix**. The results match the theory. Equities and gilts have a negative correlation as expected since same factors have an opposite impact on their performance.

Gilts and inflation have a negative correlation as inflation negatively affects gilts. Equities and inflation have a slightly positive correlation, as performance of equities should keep up with inflation over the long term.

Additional assets

Figure 12.4 shows the performance of four asset classes: global equities (MSCI World Index), UK IG credit (iBoxx £ Non-Gilts Overall Index), global high yield (BofA Merrill Lynch Global High Yield Index) and UK property (UK IPD TR All Property Index).

High yield and global equities can be highly correlated. High yield exhibits material drawdowns, such as that in 2008. Investors who did not panic and sell at the bottom, benefited from a strong recovery.

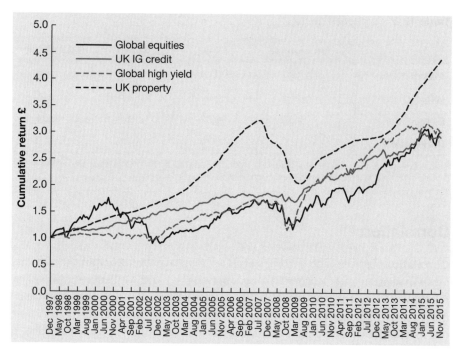

Figure 12.4 Performance of equities, high yield, UK IG credit and property

Source: Bloomberg. MSCI World Index, iBoxx £ Non-Gilts Overall Index, BofA Merrill Lynch Global High Yield Index, UK IPD TR All Property Index. January 1998 to December 2015. Based on monthly total returns, measured in £, except for high yield measured in $

IG credit is much less risky than is high yield. However, it has some correlation with equities as similar factors affecting the two asset classes.

Commercial property's performance seems smooth. However, because property is illiquid and properties are not traded on an exchange, the index returns are often based on appraisals (valuations). Appraisals are sticky since frequently they are based on last available price, not on current prices, which are not always available due to infrequent transactions.

The index returns are **serially correlated** (autocorrelated); meaning this month's return influences next month's return. The index's true volatility is understated because of that.

As always, be critical about what is presented, understanding the logic behind it.

Finally, Table 12.4 shows the return and risk statistics of the four asset classes, whilst Table 12.5 shows their correlation matrix.

Table 12.4 Annualised return, volatility, Sharpe ratio and max drawdowns

	Global equities	UK IG credit	Global high yield	UK property
Return pa %	6.4	6.2	6.3	8.6
Volatility pa %	15.2	5.0	9.5	4.0
Sharpe ratio	0.19	0.55	0.30	1.30
Drawdown %	−49.0	−8.7	−33.6	−36.7

Source: Bloomberg. MSCI World Index, iBoxx £ Non-Gilts Overall Index, BofA Merrill Lynch Global High Yield Index, UK IPD TR All Property Index. January 1998 to December 2015. Based on monthly total returns, measured in £, except for high yield measured in $

Table 12.5 Correlation matrix

	Global equities	UK IG credit	Global high yield	UK property
Global equities	1.00	0.14	0.54	0.14
UK IG credit	0.14	1.00	0.31	0.06
Global high yield	0.54	0.31	1.00	0.15
UK real estate	0.14	0.06	0.15	1.00

Source: Bloomberg. MSCI World Index, iBoxx £ Non-Gilts Overall Index, BofA Merrill Lynch Global High Yield Index, UK IPD TR All Property Index. January 1998 to December 2015. Based on monthly total returns, measured in £, except for high yield measured in $

The return and risk statistics corroborate the observations from the chart. Based on volatilities, global equities and high yield are risk assets, whilst UK IG credit and property appear to be conservative. However, UK property can exhibit material drawdowns, like that between 2007 and 2009, and its reported volatility does not necessarily reflect its true risk (for example, volatility does not reveal liquidity risk).

When comparing the volatility of global equities with that of UK equities (in the previous section), note that UK equities are somewhat less volatile. Even though global equities are more diversified, the UK equity market is relatively defensive.

The correlation matrix shows the high correlation between global equities and high yield. Whilst there are no negative correlations, all the assets have imperfect correlation, which is important for diversification.

Summary

- Equities are volatile, exhibiting large drawdowns. You do not want to lose 40% just before retiring.
- Gilts have enjoyed a remarkable bull run. However, they are not expected to repeat it in the coming years, as yields are currently low and might rise.
- Cash has low volatility. But it can have low returns, lagging inflation during some periods.
- The 10-year gilt yield has come down from a level of over 6% in 1998 to below 2% in 2015. The base rate has come down from a level of over 7% in 1998 to a level of 0.5% in 2015. This is a low-yield environment. No wonder deposit, mortgage and annuity rates have fallen.
- Relative performance of different assets depends on the specific time.
- Correlation measures the tendency of assets to move in the same or opposite directions.
- High yield is a risk asset. As you should not judge a book by its cover, do not judge an asset by its name. Even when they are called bonds, studying their behaviour reveals the characteristics of assets.
- Returns of property indices can hide their true volatility. Returns are based on appraisals, not on daily prices. Always think critically about what you are presented with. Apparent facts can hide the truth.

Notes

1 This index shows the total return (TR) of 1-month British pound LIBOR.

2 UK RPI (Retail Price Index) is available on the website of the Office for National Statistics at **ons.gov.uk**.

3 Maximum drawdown measures an investment's peak-to-trough fall during a specific time period. Drawdown demonstrates downside risk. However, it is based on historic experience during the measuring period.

4 $\text{Covariance}_{(x,y)} = \Sigma(x_i - \mu_x)(y_i - \mu_y) \div n$ where x_i and y_i are the returns of x and y at time i, μ_x and μ_y are the mean returns of x and y, and n is the number of returns. $\rho_{(x,y)} = \text{Covariance}_{(x,y)} \div \sigma_x\sigma_y$, where $\rho_{(x,y)}$ is the correlation between x and y, σ_x and σ_y are the standard deviations of x and y.

5 Correlation of zero does not necessarily mean that there is no relationship between assets. It means no linear relationship. The assets can have a non-linear relationship.

CHAPTER 13
DIVERSIFICATION

The proven way to reduce portfolio risk

'The only investors who shouldn't diversify are those who are right 100% of the time.'

John Templeton

We are back to, 'Do not put all your eggs in one basket.' It captures the essence of diversification. If you put all your eggs in one basket and drop it, they all break. You are left with nothing (or with a mess). Conversely, if you spread your eggs across different baskets, by dropping one you do not lose everything.

This is the same with investing. Since nobody knows for certain how different assets will perform in the future, spreading investments across various assets reduces risk. When one falls, others may rise.

Diversification works only if different assets behave differently. If they all move in tandem, falling or rising together at the same time, there is no point diversifying. If you drop all your baskets, all your eggs break.

Luckily, different assets possess different characteristics. They behave differently under different market conditions.

In this chapter we will demonstrate what happens when blending a number of assets. We will see that when blended correctly, the risk of the mix is lower and its return pattern is smoother than those of its parts. We will then move to some simple calculations of a portfolio's expected return and risk.

Typically, there are no free lunches in finance. To get something, you need to either pay or take a risk. But it is said, 'Diversification is the only free lunch.' This is because it reduces risk without sacrificing all returns and it does not cost any fees. When offered something for free, take it.

Blending

When imperfectly correlated assets are mixed, the portfolio return is the weighted average of the individual assets' returns, but portfolio volatility is lower than the weighted average of the individual assets' volatilities.

Figure 13.1 shows the performance of UK equities, gilts and a blend of 60% UK equities and 40% gilts. This figure empirically reveals the effects of diversification.

The performance of the mix is between those of equities and gilts. Its volatility is lower than that of equities. Blending equities and gilts over this particular time period was exceptionally beneficial. It generated a return in line with the better performing asset (gilts) but with a lower risk than that of equities.

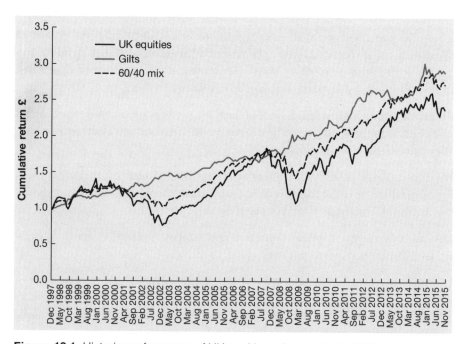

Figure 13.1 Historic performance of UK equities, gilts and their 60/40 mix

Source: Bloomberg. FTSE 100 Index, iBoxx £ Gilts Index. January 1998 to December 2015. Based on monthly total returns, measured in £

Table 13.1 Annualised return, volatility, Sharpe ratio and max drawdown

	UK equities	Gilts	60/40 mix	40/60 mix
Return pa %	4.9	6.0	5.7	5.9
Volatility pa %	14.2	5.4	8.5	6.1
Sharpe ratio	0.10	0.47	0.26	0.40
Drawdown %	−43.6	−5.9	−21.9	−11.8

Source: Bloomberg. FTSE 100 Index, iBoxx £ Gilts Index, UK Cash LIBOR TR 1 Month Index. January 1998 to December 2015. Based on monthly total returns, measured in £

Table 13.1 shows the return and risk analytics of equities, gilts and 60/40 mix, as well as a 40/60 mix. The 60/40 mix has a return in line with that of gilts, a lower volatility than that of equities, with a superior Sharpe ratio than that of equities.

The volatility of the 60/40 mix is 8.5%. It is lower than the weighted average volatilities of UK equities and gilts of 10.7%.[1]

A different mix, such as 40% equities and 60% gilts, gives a different return and risk profile. By changing the blend you can control your portfolio's return and risk. This is an important observation. We will get back to it later.

Calculating expected return and risk of blended portfolios

The expected return of a portfolio grouping a number of assets is simply the weighted sum of the assets' expected returns. Put differently, the portfolio's expected return is the sum of the weight of each asset times its expected return.

For example, assume a portfolio with 60% equities and 40% bonds. Say equities' expected return is 8% and that of bonds is 5%. The portfolio's expected return is 6.8%.[2]

$$r_p = \Sigma(w_i r_i)$$

Portfolio return (r_p) equals the sum of (Σ) the weight of each asset i (w_i) times the return of asset i (r_i). Simples.

It is more involved for volatility. In the 1950s, Nobel laureate Harry Markowitz developed **Modern Portfolio Theory** (MPT). Markowitz showed that the volatility of a portfolio is not simply the weighted average of its assets' volatilities.

The key for diversification is imperfect correlation (correlation below + 1.0). When two assets are imperfectly correlated, blending them produces a portfolio with volatility lower than the weighted sum of the two assets' volatilities. The total is less than the sum of the parts.

Calculating portfolio volatility is more complex than calculating expected return.

One definition before we dive into the formula: **variance** is standard deviation squared (or standard deviation is square root of variance). Whilst standard deviations are not additive, variances are. Now we are ready.

Portfolio variance is calculated by multiplying the squared weights of assets by their corresponding variances. Then adding twice the weighted average variance of each asset pair multiplied by the correlation between each pair.

This is a mouthful of what appears to be gobbledygook. An example can clarify.

In the 60% equity and 40% bond portfolio the standard deviation of equities is 15%, that of bonds is 5% and the correlation between the two assets is 0.20.

Portfolio standard deviation = square root of portfolio variance = square root of $60\%^2 \times 15\%^2 + 40\%^2 \times 5\%^2 + 2 \times 60\% \times 40\% \times 15\% \times 5\% \times 0.20 = 9.6\%$.

Another way to look at it is that the formula has two parts. The first part sums the squared weight of each asset times its variance. The second part sums for each different pair of assets, twice their weights, times their standard deviations times the correlation between them.

$$\sigma_p^2 = \Sigma w_i^2 \sigma_i^2 + \Sigma\Sigma w_i w_j \sigma_i \sigma_j \rho_{ij}$$

Portfolio variance (σ_p^2) equals the sum of (Σ) the squared weights of each asset i (w_i^2) times its variance (σ_i^2) plus for each asset i different from asset j $(i \neq j)$ the sum of $(\Sigma\Sigma)$ the weights of assets i and j $(w_i$ and $w_j)$, times the standard deviations of assets i and j $(\sigma_i$ and $\sigma_j)$, times the correlation between them (ρ_{ij}).

The formula validates that the smaller the correlation between assets, the lower is portfolio volatility, as the formula's second part is smaller. If correlation is perfectly positive (+1.0), portfolio volatility is the weighted sum of individual assets' volatilities. With perfect correlation diversification benefits disappear.

The good news is that this is the most complicated mathematical calculation in this book. You now know how to calculate the expected return and volatility of portfolios. What you need is the expected returns, volatilities and correlations of your portfolio's assets. We will get to it in the next chapter.

Three-asset standard deviation

To illustrate the formula one final time, we will calculate portfolio volatility with three assets. Assume a portfolio of 60% equities, 30% bonds and 10% cash. Equity's volatility is 15%, that of bonds is 5% and that of cash is 1%. The correlation between equities and bonds is 0.20, that between equities and cash is 0.00 and that between bonds and cash is 0.10. The portfolio volatility is 9.4%.

$$\text{Portfolio's volatility} = \text{square root of } 60\%^2\,15\%^2 + 30\%^2\,5\%^2 + 10\%^2\,1\%^2$$
$$+ 2 \times 60\% \times 30\% \times 15\% \times 5\% \times 0.20 + 2 \times 60\% \times 10\% \times 15\%$$
$$\times 1\% \times 0.00 + 2 \times 30\% \times 10\% \times 15\% \times 1\% \times 0.10 = 9.4\%$$

Adding 10% cash reduced portfolio volatility from 9.6% to 9.4% because cash has lower volatility than equities and bonds and due to better diversification across three assets instead of two. Cash can reduce risk.

What does this mean to you as an investor? Considering investments in portfolio context

When considering each asset's risk, do not consider it in isolation but in portfolio context. Assess the impact of investing in each asset on your overall portfolio.

For example, say you are risk averse and do not want to invest in equities since they are terrifyingly risky. You hold a portfolio of 100% bonds with 5% volatility.

How does adding a small allocation to equities impact the portfolio?

The volatility of equities is 15% and the correlation between equities and bonds is 0.20. By allocating 5% to equities and 95% to bonds, portfolio volatility is 4.95%.[3] Counter-intuitively, adding a risky asset actually reduced portfolio risk thanks to diversification benefits.

The expected return of bonds is 5% and that of equities is 8%. The expected return of the 100% bond portfolio is 5% and that of the 95% bonds and 5% equities is 5.1%.[4]

Adding some equities increased expected return and reduced risk. You improved your portfolio's Sharpe ratio: higher expected reward for each unit of risk.

Equities in portfolio context in this example are a risk diversifier and return enhancer.

Local versus global diversification

Global diversification is usually beneficial. Equity and bond markets across the globe undergo different economic regimes, leading to imperfectly correlated performance.

Over the last number of decades, the benefits of global diversification have diminished with tighter integration of financial markets, closer cross-border trade relations and greater coordination amongst central banks. Globalisation and technology are two forces bringing markets closer and enhancing information flow. But still, global markets do not move in unionisation.

The Eurozone's formation, for example, has advanced integration of equity and bond market across Europe. Nevertheless, even within the Eurozone, different markets behave differently.

Take, for instance, the bond and equity markets of Germany versus those of Southern European countries, such as Spain, Italy and, particularly, Greece. Germany and these countries have experienced diverging economic fortunes since the 2008 and 2011 crises, delivering distinctive return and risk profiles. There is still merit for global diversification, even within the union.

As a UK-based investor, consider global diversification. Admittedly, the UK is an open economy, with the majority of companies' revenues coming from overseas. The local equity market is developed and diversified. Therefore, going global does not make a huge impact. However, at times there is a large divergence between the UK, global developed and emerging equity markets.

Figure 13.2 compares the performance of UK equities, global developed equities, excluding the UK, and emerging market equity (EME). Whilst, during some periods, the performance of UK and global equities is nearly identical, it differs substantially during other times (partially due to currency movements). UK equities and EME can be correlated, but their performance diverges markedly.

When investing globally, do not neglect currency risk. It's a manageable risk since, in most cases, you can hedge it.

Multi-asset investing

Increasingly, funds follow a multi-asset strategy. These funds blend different asset classes to benefit from diversification; flexibility to dynamically invest across different assets; and harvest a wide range of lowly correlated return sources.

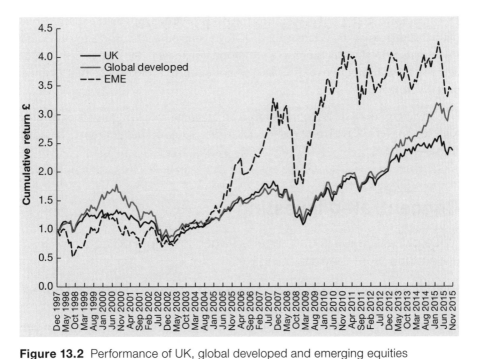

Figure 13.2 Performance of UK, global developed and emerging equities

Source: Bloomberg. MSCI UK Index, MSCI World ex UK Index, MSCI Emerging Markets Index. January 1998 to December 2015. Based on monthly total returns, measured in £

Armed with assumptions about return, risk and correlation of assets, you can combine them into a mix with a targeted return and risk profile or a specific outcome. Hence, some funds are labelled **outcome-oriented**.

'Balanced funds' have, historically, offered old-fashioned multi-asset investing in the UK. These funds often follow an allocation of 60% equities and 40% bonds. However, the overwhelming majority of their risk and return is driven by equities. Equities are more volatile and their expected return is higher than that of bonds. Therefore, over 90% of the 'balanced' funds' risk and return could come from equities – hardly balanced.

A new generation of multi-asset funds is **Diversified Growth Funds** (DGFs). DGFs are the sexy version of balanced funds. They enjoy more flexibility with their asset mix, some use dynamic asset allocation to enhance returns and mitigate risks and some use sophisticated derivative-based strategies. DGFs are not hedge funds since they are regulated, usually they are more transparent and liquid than hedge funds and, typically, they are not as expensive as hedge funds.

DGFs are active strategies. Their return and risk profile depends on the specific style of their fund managers. When using a DGF, you outsource the asset allocation and investment selection decisions to a professional manager. You can diversify manager risk by blending two to three DGFs – not more, to avoid over complexity and over diversification.

One advantage of DGFs is that they target an outcome matching the needs of most long-term savers. A return of cash + 4% to 5% is appropriate for most phases in the saver's life.

Concentrated investing

'Wide diversification is only required when investors do not understand what they are doing.'

Warren Buffett

Remember our basket and eggs. Well, another approach is put all your eggs in one basket and then watch that basket. Just do not drop it.

Diversification reduces some risk, but the return of your portfolio is the average return of its underlying investments. Diversification's objective is not to make you rich. Rather, it is delivering a smoother return profile and increasing the probability of reaching your objectives, if they are reasonable.

To make a lot of money from investing concentrate, do not diversify. Placing a small number of high-risk bets with high potential reward is the way to generate high returns. This is also a way to suffer large losses when getting it wrong.

Ordinarily, if something appears too good to be true, it is not true. If you identify an investment that seems to be a certain bet – it cannot go wrong – think again. Had it been such a good investment, others would have invested in it, pushing its price upwards, evaporating the opportunity.

I am not saying there are no unique investment opportunities. There are. But be careful and sceptic. Concentration can come not only with high rewards, but also with a high price. You can pay dearly for mistakes.

On the other side of the diversification spectrum sits over-diversification. If you overly diversify your portfolio, by holding a very large number of funds and assets, you might end up holding the entire investment universe – an expensive closet tracker. Diversification should be not too little and not too much.

Three buckets

If you are an expert in a field, having an edge over the market in some area of expertise and you can identify unique investments, by all means invest. Investing in private enterprises, property or exclusive projects can generate higher returns than usually are available in public capital markets. Informational advantage can be turned into profits in the right hands.

But do not forget the principle of diversification. Ensure that whatever happens you secure a minimum standard of living. Never risk what you cannot afford to lose.

Split your assets amongst three buckets. The first is a **safe bucket**. It holds conservative assets to maintain a *minimum* standard of living. Use an annuity to secure some income for the rest of your life, keep cash reserve and own your insured home. Minimise volatility and downside risk. Whatever happens, you will have enough on which to live.

A second bucket is a **market bucket**. It holds long-term savings in a diversified portfolio, invested in capital markets to maintain your *current* standard of living when retiring. Its objective is your target return. This bucket follows the investment principles we cover in this book.

The third bucket is a **speculative bucket**. It invests in your area of expertise in a concentrated way. It can hold a private business or buy-to-let properties. This bucket's objective is to potentially *upgrade* your standard of living. But, even if losing the third bucket, the other two buckets secure your financial future. Its objective is your desired return. Here, dream big. *If you do not aspire to great things, you will not attain small things.*

Summary

- Since nobody knows for sure how assets will perform in the future, diversify across different assets.
- The prerequisite for diversification is imperfectly correlated assets.
- By blending assets, you reduce risk and set your portfolio's expected return and risk profile.
- A portfolio's expected return is the weighted sum of its individual investments' returns. Calculate a portfolio's expected risk using a formula that accounts for individual investments' volatilities and correlations.
- Consider assets' risk in portfolio context, not on a standalone basis. What matters is how adding an asset impacts the portfolio's risk and return.

- Normally, global diversification has rewards. Mind the currency risk.
- Multi-asset investing benefits from diversification across asset classes, as well as from a wide investment opportunity set, the flexibility to dynamically change the asset allocation and the ability to target a desired outcome.
- To generate very high returns, concentrated investing is needed, not diversification. However, concentration comes with risks. Concentrate only when having a high conviction.
- Divide your wealth across safe, market and speculative buckets, which have different roles and potential impact on your wealth.

Notes

1 $10.7\% = 60\% \times 14.2\% + 40\% \times 5.4\%$.

2 $6.8\% = 60\% \times 8\% + 40\% \times 5\%$.

3 $4.95\% =$ square root of $(95\%^2 \, 5\%^2 + 5\%^2 \, 15\%^2 + 2 \times 95\% \times 5\% \times 5\% \times 15\% \times 0.20)$.

4 $5.1\% = 95\% \times 5\% + 5\% \times 8\%$.

CHAPTER 14
EXPECTED RETURN AND RISK

Forward-looking expected return, risk and correlation

'Prediction is very difficult, especially if it's about the future.'

Niels Bohr

Asset allocation is the process of appropriating capital to each asset class. It broadly sets the portfolio's risk and return profile and, as such, it is the heart of investment strategy. It should match your return objective, risk tolerance and investment constraints, in particular time horizon and liquidity needs.

Asset allocation should mix assets based on how they are likely to perform in the future, not based on how they have performed in the past. To do so, we need a crystal-ball framework to predict the future.

Government's assumptions

Each year, pension administrators need to give DC savers an illustration of the pension they may get when they retire. The illustration is known as **Statutory Money Purchase Illustration**. The law requires pension managers to provide it, based on assumptions laid down by the government. The assumptions should be detailed in your annual **Pension Benefit Statement**.

Whilst you can rely on these assumptions, we aim to generate independent forecasts that are better connected to current market conditions.

Capital market assumptions

Designing a long-term asset allocation aligned with your investment objectives starts with forming projections about the long-term prospective return, risk and correlations of assets that you consider including in your portfolio. These expectations are called **capital market assumptions** (CMAs) since they estimate how different capital markets (equities, bonds, cash) are likely to behave in the future.

It is important to know how assets tend to behave to understand their characteristics. However, past returns cannot just be simply projected into the future to estimate future returns as they differ from period to period.

Future likely returns depend on where we are now in the economic cycle. When assets are expensive, the expected return is low, and vice versa. This is what the CMAs are trying to capture.

CMAs are formulated for asset classes, not individual securities. When formulating an investment strategy, you choose in which assets to invest, not individual securities yet.

First make the beta decision on how to allocate to different asset classes. Then make the alpha decision on which securities to buy in each asset or outsource it to fund managers. Security selection follows asset selection.

In the next sections we explore how to estimate the future likely returns, risks and correlations of asset classes so you can blend them into an asset allocation fitting your needs. Prophesising about the future is challenging but, nevertheless, we will go through a relatively straightforward way to do so. It might be technical, but it is worthwhile. Use the expected returns to manage your expectations about what your portfolio is likely to achieve over the long term and plan accordingly.

Expected returns

Formulating CMAs is challenging. Unfortunately, looking at historic returns and extrapolating them into the future can be misleading.

Figure 14.1 shows the cumulative performance of the S&P 500 Index since January 1928. US markets have a reliable long historic track record, easy for studying the behaviour of assets over the long term with a statistically significant number of observations.

Statistical significance

Statistically significant means the likelihood that a conclusion of a statistical calculation or hypothesis testing is caused not only by mere random chance. To reach statistical significant conclusions from an experiment, you need the sample size to be sufficiently large. For example, calculating standard deviation or correlation requires at least 36 or 60 returns for it to be statistically significant.

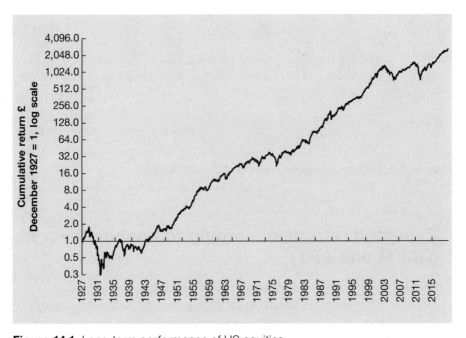

Figure 14.1 Long-term performance of US equities

Source: Bloomberg. S&P 500 Index. January 1928 to December 2015. Based on monthly total returns, measured in $

As Figure 14.1 shows, equities can move up, sideways or down at different times, for different lengths of time and at different paces. Can you tell how they are likely to behave over the next 10 years, based on how they have behaved in the past? It is a guess.

Figure 14.2 shows the annualised return of the S&P 500 Index during each decade. Whilst the average annual performance over the entire period since January 1928 is 9.4%, performance swings from decade to decade. The average performance in the last four decades deviated substantially from the long-term average. Past performance is hardly a reliable indicator of future results.

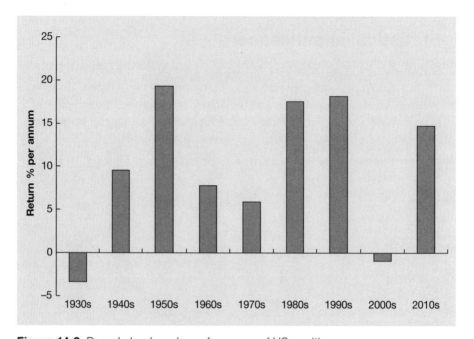

Figure 14.2 Decade by decade performance of US equities

Source: Bloomberg. S&P 500 Index. January 1928 to December 2015. Based on monthly total returns, measured in $

Expected returns according to finance theory (CAPM and APT)

Finance theory offers a number of methodologies to calculate assets' expected returns. Two common ones are the **Capital Asset Pricing Model** (CAPM) and **Arbitrage Pricing Theory** (APT). Unfortunately, both have faults and their results are unreliable.

CAPM relates expected return with risk as measured by beta. According to CAPM, the return of an asset (r) equals the risk-free rate (r_f) plus the product of the asset's beta (β) and the market risk premium (market's return, r_m, minus risk-free rate).

$$r = r_f + \beta (r_m - r_f)$$

According to CAPM, which is a single factor model, markets compensate investors only for un-diversifiable risk.

APT, which is a multi-factor model, relates expected return of an asset with its exposure to different risk factors (RF). The exposures (loadings) use the asset's betas with respect of each risk factor.

$$r = \beta_1 RF_1 + \beta_2 RF_2 + \cdots + \beta_n RF_n$$

Since we cannot use past returns to formulate CMAs, we need a simple forward-looking methodology, based on readily available data.

Arguably, the simplest, most intuitive approach to formulate asset classes' expected sustainable returns is breaking them down into their building blocks – their separate drivers. We estimate the expected return of each building block and aggregate them to formulate each asset's expected return.

Our aim is using observable market data, telling us what the market collectively thinks about assets' future performance over the long term (5–10 years). Not relying on our subjective views, we let the data speak for itself, implying expected returns for us.

Equities

Equities' sustainable, long-term expected return is made of three building blocks:

1   Dividend yield (carry).
2   Earnings growth (momentum).
3   Re-pricing (valuation).

The first building block is straightforward. **Dividend yield** is cash payments to shareholders. When looking at a stock market, the dividend yield of the index representing the market is the relevant figure.

For example, the dividend yield of the FTSE 100 Index is currently about 4.0%.[1] When aggregating all the dividends of the index's constituents and dividing the sum by the index's price, the ratio is approximately 4.0%.

The second building block is **earnings growth**. Share price reflects the present value of future dividends. Dividends are paid out of company's earnings. The pace of earnings growth is, therefore, part of equity's return.

Whilst it is difficult to predict the rate of earnings growth for a single company or over the short term, it is easier doing so for the entire market over the long term. We assume that, over the long term, trend earnings growth is linked to general trend economic growth (nominal GDP growth rate).

However, earnings grow more slowly than GDP because growth of existing corporations explains only part of GDP growth. Historically, earnings growth in the USA lagged GDP growth by about 2% annually. This figure differs across different markets and across different regimes.[2] To simplify, we apply a 2% dilution factor between trend nominal GDP growth and earnings growth.

In the UK, for example, the average annual *real* GDP growth rate has been 2.6% since 1948.[3] With BOE's 2% target inflation rate, trend *nominal* GDP growth rate is about 4.6%. This means an estimated 2.6% earnings growth after deducting the dilution factor.[4]

Instead of trend nominal GDP growth rate, you can use economic forecasts. Future trend economic growth might be slower than historically due to slowing developing economies and aging population in the developed world. Free sources of economic forecasts are available online.[5] However, forecasting GDP growth is challenging; many of the forecasts prove incorrect.

The third and final building block of equity return is **re-pricing**. It captures the price the market currently assigns to the stock market.

One metric indicating the valuation of the equity market is **price-to-earnings ratio**. P/E expresses the relationship between share price and earnings per share (EPS). For example, if the share price is £10 and EPS is £0.50, P/E is 20. Price reflects 20 years of earnings.

P/E tends to revert back to its long-term mean, unless there is a structural change, justifying the stock market to be more expensive or cheaper than it has been in the past. For example, new technologies, like the advent of the internet, can explain a higher market P/E since companies can permanently increase productivity.

If long-term average P/E is, say, 15 and current P/E is 20, the market is rich. If current P/E is 10, the market is cheap. P/E is likely to revert back to its 15 level. We do not know when it is going to happen. We do not know if it is going happen. But we assume it is likely to happen eventually.

Since we are estimating returns over the long term, including P/E mean reversion as part of expected returns is sensible. Empirical evidence shows that when P/E is very high, equity market performance over the next 10 years is much lower than when P/E is very low. It actually works over the long term.[6]

Figure 14.3 shows the rolling 10-year annualised performance of US equities and their cumulative performance superimposed. The level of rolling return at each point is average annualised performance during the previous 10 years. For example, the average return in the previous 10 years up to December 2015 was 8.3%.

The chart reveals how equity returns swing like a pendulum. Optimism pulls stocks to unsustainable highs and pessimism pushes them to unjustified lows. When markets are rich (high P/E), future returns are low and when markets are cheap (low P/E), future returns are high.

How do we translate P/E mean reversion into expected annual return? Here we need a simple formula. If long-term average P/E is 15 and current P/E is 10, we estimate

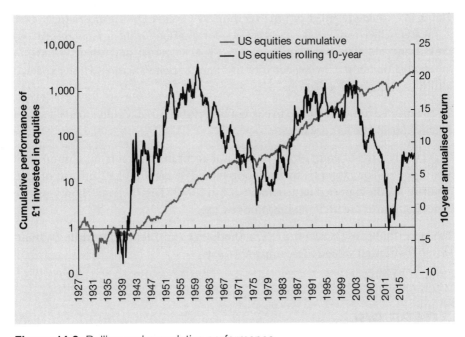

Figure 14.3 Rolling and cumulative performance

Source: Bloomberg. S&P 500 Index. January 1928 to December 2015. Based on monthly total returns, measured in $

the equity market will appreciate by 50% due to P/E mean reversion.[7] To express this 50% as annual average return over the next 10 years we use the formula:

$$r = (P/E_{\text{long-term average}} \div P/E_{\text{current}})^{(1/n)} - 1$$

The annual compounded average return is 4.14% over the next 10 years.[8] It matches a 50% overall return.[9]

The current P/E of the FTSE 100 Index is about 18.0.[10] The index's long-term average P/E is around 15.8. It suggests the index is expensive. P/E reverting back to its long-term average implies a −1.3% annual return over the next decade.[11]

P/E average greatly depends over which time period it is calculated and which P/E is used (based on reported or estimated EPS). Use the longest history available since a last structural change and the same P/E methodology for both current and historic average. Assumptions about P/E can have a big impact on expected returns.

Putting everything together, assuming 4.0% dividend yield, 2.6% trend earnings growth, and −1.3% re-pricing, the total expected return for the FTSE 100 Index is 5.3%.[12] The expected return is above the index's historic 4.9% return since January 1998.

This is an estimated average return over the next 10 years. During most single years, it is going to be wrong. However, it is a good indication for the level of return and the current valuation of the equity market. Expected return and valuation have an inverse relationship. Low expected return implies rich valuation. High expected return implies cheap valuation.

Since expected return is related to current observable variables (dividend yield and P/E) we can update it every month.

Expected returns of equity markets are not accurate; they rely on a number of assumptions. For example, using a long-term average P/E of 12 instead of 15.8 would swing the expected return from 5.3% to 2.6%.[13] This illustrates how sensitive expected returns are to the assumptions we use.

The important thing is keeping the methodology consistent across different markets so they are all valued in a comparable way.

CAPE P/E

One issue with P/E is that it is volatile. It uses one-year reported or estimated earnings. Not only earnings can be manipulated using creative accounting, but also one-year earnings are unstable to provide a good idea of the company's true earnings potential.

Nobel laureate Robert Shiller popularised the use of a **cyclically adjusted price-to-earnings** (CAPE) ratio, often called **Shiller P/E**. CAPE uses 10-year average real earnings (adjusted for inflation to today's value) instead of last reported earnings. CAPE is considered a better valuation ratio for equities than P/E.[14]

Bonds

Bonds' sustainable, long-term expected return is made of three building blocks:

1 Yield to maturity (YTM).

2 Price movement.

3 Cost of default.

YTM is the return you will realise by holding a bond to maturity, assuming it does not default. It incorporates coupons and the positive or negative return you realise when buying a bond at a discount or premium, respectively.

When not holding a bond to maturity, **price movement** is total return's second building block. Price movement is a function of changes in yield. The question is how to estimate whether the yield will move and if yes to which level.

For 10-year government bonds, an estimate for a yield's fair-value level is the economy's year-on-year (YoY) *nominal* GDP growth rate.[15] The 10-year yield reflects expected inflation and expectations of future short-term interest rates, which are linked to economic growth.

For example, if current 10-year gilt yield is 2% and UK nominal GDP growth rate is 4.6%, yield may rise by a whopping 2.6%.[16] If duration of 10-year bonds is 9.5 years, a 2.6% increase in yield means roughly a 24.7% capital loss.[17] This is massive, in particular when the carry from the yield is only 2%. Govies' downside risk can match that of equities.

We do not know when and if yields will normalise, reaching fair level. First, we need to estimate whether trend real GDP growth rate is likely to persist in the future. Second, we do not know whether the inflation rate will hit BOE's 2% target. So the 'normal' level for yields is questionable. And third, we do not know the impact of central banks' unconventional monetary policies on yields. QE distorts markets.

Assuming conservatively that within our 10-year horizon yields are likely to reach a level of 2.5%, price movement is −4.8%.[18]

The total expected return of 10-year gilts is therefore −2.8%.[19] At this yield level govies are expensive. They are expected to generate negative total returns.

Buying gilts may still be sensible if they are held to maturity or if they add benefits of diversification and protection to your portfolio. In case of a flight to quality, yields might drop, not increase. Assuming they are held to maturity, the expected return of 10-year gilts is 2.0% (YTM).

The third building block of bonds' expected return is **cost of default**. Whilst you should not expect the UK, US, German and Japanese Governments to default on their sovereign debt – if it happens, it is a financial Armageddon – corporations and emerging nations might do so. The expected cost of default should be deducted from expected return.

Cost of default (**credit loss rate**) on a diversified bond basket is a function of average credit rating, probability of default (default rate) and average recovery rate. When bonds default, lenders usually recover some of their loans – not all is lost.

The rating agency Moody's publishes reports online with historical statistics on default rates and credit loss rates. Apply the average historic rate to the appropriate credit rating of your bonds. Table 14.1 includes the average credit losses of different credit ratings.

Table 14.1 Credit loss rates by letter rating, 1982–2010

Credit rating	Credit loss rate (%)	Rating description
Aaa	0.00	Highest quality, minimal credit risk.
Aa	0.02	High quality, subject to very low credit risk.
A	0.03	Upper-medium grade, subject to low credit risk.
Baa	0.13	Moderate credit risk, medium grade, may possess certain speculative characteristics.
Ba	0.73	Have speculative elements, subject to substantial credit risk.
B	3.01	Speculative, subject to high credit risk.
Caa to C	13.70	Caa poor standing, subject to very high credit risk. C typically in default, with little prospect for recovery of principal or interest.
Investment grade	0.06	Ratings Aaa to Baa.
Speculative grade	2.78	Ratings Ba to C.
All rated	1.01	Ratings Aaa to C.

Source: Moody's Investors Service, Corporate Default and Recovery Rates, 1920–2010

The UK's credit rating is Aa. A gilt's cost of default is negligible (2 basis points). The cost of default becomes relevant for bonds with a credit rating of Ba and below.

Spread products

The first building block of IG credit, high yield and emerging market debt (spread products) is **YTM**. Spread products offer a spread over rates (yields) of comparable bonds of creditworthy governments as compensation for higher credit risk.[20]

The second building block, **price movement**, is a bit tricky. Assuming spread remains constant, changes in the government bonds' rates affect the spread product's price, adjusted for duration (normally shorter than that of govies).

For example, the 10-year gilt rate is 2% and it is expected to rise to 2.5%. We wish to buy a portfolio of UK corporate bonds with an average duration of 6.7 years (compared to the 9.5-year duration of 10-year gilts).[21] Assuming a constant spread and a parallel shift of the yield curve, the expected drop in price due to increasing rates is −3.4% when considering the corporate bonds' duration.[22]

However, increasing govies' rates usually correspond with improving economic conditions, so spreads should narrow, absorbing some of the rise in rates. Conversely, spreads should widen when underlying rates fall, as the economy may be slowing.

It gets convoluted since, over the short term, increasing rates tend to correlate with narrowing spreads. However, over the long term, higher rates tend to cause spreads to widen. So, to make it simple, we assume the price of spread products moves by half the duration-adjusted yield movement (if for govies we expect rates to rise 0.5% from 2.0% to 2.5%; for credit we expect yields to rise by half of that, so 0.25%).[23]

The third building block is estimated **cost of default**.

This all sounds knotty. An example can simplify. Say you want to formulate an expected return for UK corporate bonds. In a website of an ETF tracking the index, you find its YTM is 3.6%, duration (often called effective or modified duration) is 8.7 years and average credit rating is A.[24,25]

The expected return is YTM 3.6% plus price movement of half yield change times duration of −2.2% minus cost of default for A rating of 0.03% (negligible).[26] The expected total return is 1.4%.[27]

This low expected return echoes the expensiveness of gilts and credit. IG credit still offers better returns than gilts due to higher yield (carry) and shorter duration. Going through this methodology facilitates understanding why different assets offer different projected returns.

Cash

For cash, expected return is simply short-term current rate. If, for example, the base rate is 0.5%, expected return is 0.5%. Add a spread depending on the rate of a money market fund in which you invest or the saving rate on your cash ISA or bank's savings account. A time deposit or a fixed rate ISA can offer higher rates, but you commit your money for the term.[28]

When the BOE increases or decreases its base rate, expected return changes accordingly (immediately for variable rate accounts, with a lag for fixed rate accounts).

Property

Property's sustainable expected return is made of three building blocks:

1 Net rental yield.

2 Trend nominal GDP growth rate.

3 Costs.

Similar to dividend yield for equities and YTM for bonds, **net rental yield** is the income component of property's total return. Since property is a heterogeneous asset class, rental yield depends on each specific property or property fund.

Trend nominal GDP growth rate represents property's expected long-term price appreciation. It should keep up with inflation and economic expansion. Apply this estimate to both residential and commercial property.

Since buying property can be expensive and ongoing costs are high, subtract **costs** from total return.

Some ongoing costs are already deducted to reach net rental yield. One-off charges can be annualised over the time horizon. For example, 5% stamp duty when buying a property is equivalent to 0.49% per year over 10 years.[29]

Putting it all together, assuming a 3.5% net rental yield (after subtracting ongoing costs), 4.6% trend nominal GDP growth rate and 0.49% annual costs due to stamp duty, property's expected return is 7.6%.[30]

Other asset classes

Other asset classes in your portfolio are likely to be listed on the stock exchange. These include REITs, listed infrastructure and listed private equity. The same methodology as that of equities applies to them.

By choosing different indices and data for a relevant country, you can calculate expected return for assets classes across the world. For example, for US equities, use dividend yield and P/Es of the S&P 500 Index and US trend GDP growth rate.

Compare and contrast your expected returns with other sources.[31] It is always advised to have a reality check, ensuring you are not out of whack.

Expected risk

Whilst past returns are not a good forecast of future returns, historic risk levels are useful to indicate assets' sustainable risk level. Simply use annualised volatility of monthly returns as the risk yardstick.

Figure 14.4 shows annualised volatility of US equities during each decade since the 1930s. Whilst volatility changes, since the 1950s it has been range-bound between 12% and 16%. Annualised volatility since the beginning of the 1950s is 14.4%.

To annualise monthly volatility, calculate the standard deviation of monthly returns and multiply it by square root of 12.[32] For example, multiplying a standard

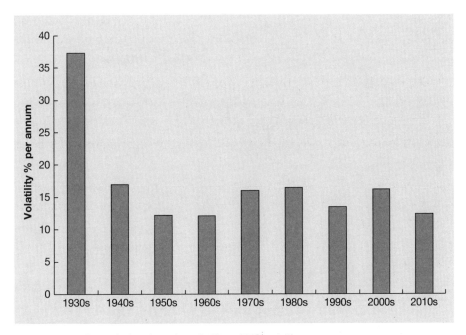

Figure 14.4 Decade by decade volatility of US equities

Source: Bloomberg. S&P 500 Index. January 1928 to December 2015. Based on monthly total returns, measured in $

deviation of monthly returns of 4.3% by a square root of 12 gives an annualised standard deviation of 15%.

Since we aim to formulate CMAs over at least the next decade, use historic monthly returns over the last 10–20 years or longer, if available, since a structural change.

The 1930s and 1940s are examples of structural changes. Following the 1930s Great Depression and the 1940s Second World War, financial markets have been noticeably less volatile. Returns since the end of the War are appropriate to estimate future risk.[33]

Expected correlation

Correlation is the most difficult to estimate since it lacks economic fundamentals predicting it. It can wildly swing from one period to the next. Luckily, the most important CMA is return, then risk and, finally, correlation.

Figure 14.5 shows rolling 36-month correlations between UK equities and global developed equities and between UK equities and emerging market equities (EME). Notice how correlation vividly changes over time.

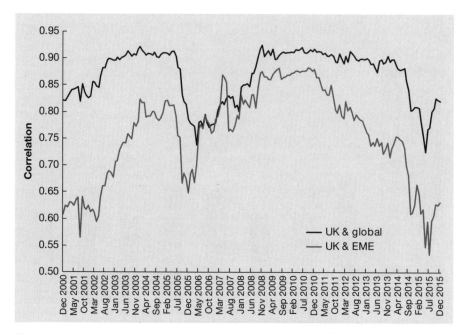

Figure 14.5 Rolling correlation between UK and global equities

Source: Bloomberg. MSCI UK Index, MSCI World ex UK Index, MSCI Emerging Markets Index. January 1998 to December 2015. Based on monthly total returns, measured in £

For example, in December 2015 the correlation between UK equities and EME was 0.63 but, during 2009, when most risk assets fell together, it was close to 0.90. This demonstrates the fluctuating benefits of diversifications.

Use historic correlations between monthly returns. The time horizon should be 10–20 years or the longest available since a structural change.

This method of estimating CMAs is by no means the most sophisticated or exact. It has limitations. However, this is a quick and dirty way to estimate the long-term returns, risks and correlations of asset classes.

A professional financial adviser may do a better job at modelling assets. However, even advisers may not be able to more accurately predict the future. Use this methodology as a second opinion to challenge your adviser.

Data

Tables 14.2 and 14.3 include data for formulating CMAs of major asset classes. The data need updating to keep the CMAs up to date with current market conditions.

Table 14.2 Historic returns, risks and data

	UK equities	Global equities	EME	Gilts	UK IG credit	UK linkers	Global HY	EMD	£ cash[34]	Property[35]
Return pa %	4.9	6.4	7.0	6.0	6.2	7.0	6.3	9.2	3.5	8.5
Risk pa %	14.2	15.2	23.1	5.4	5.0	6.9	9.5	14.1	0.7	4.0
Yield %[36]	4.0	2.6	2.9	2.0	3.3	1.9	5.4	4.8	0.5	5.5
Duration years				9.8	8.7	21	4.0	7.0		
Credit rating				AA	A	AA	BB	BBB		

Source: Bloomberg. FTSE 100 Index, MSCI World Index, MSCI Emerging Markets Index, iBoxx £ Gilts Index, iBoxx £ Non-Gilts Overall Index, Barclays Capital UK Govt Inflation Linked Index, BofA Merrill Lynch Global High Yield Index (measured in $), JPM Emerging Markets Bond Index Plus EMBI+ Composite, UK Cash LIBOR TR 1 Month Index, UK IPD TR All Property Index. January 1998 to December 2015. Based on monthly total returns, measured in £ except when indicated otherwise

Table 14.3 Correlation matrix

	UK equities	Global equities	EME	Gilts	UK IG credit	UK linkers	Global HY	EMD	£ cash	Property
UK equities	1.00	0.90	0.73	−0.15	0.19	0.12	0.58	0.42	−0.07	0.18
Global equities	0.90	1.00	0.80	−0.10	0.14	0.17	0.54	0.58	−0.07	0.14
EME	0.73	0.80	1.00	−0.12	0.12	0.12	0.60	0.61	−0.04	0.09
Gilts	−0.15	−0.10	−0.12	1.00	0.75	0.66	−0.14	0.19	0.08	−0.16
UK IG credit	0.19	0.14	0.12	0.75	1.00	0.61	0.31	0.22	−0.04	0.06
UK linkers	0.12	0.17	0.12	0.66	0.61	1.00	0.24	0.24	−0.01	0.00
Global HY	0.58	0.54	0.60	−0.14	0.31	0.24	1.00	0.30	−0.19	0.15
EMD	0.42	0.58	0.61	0.19	0.22	0.24	0.30	1.00	−0.01	−0.09
£ cash	−0.07	−0.07	−0.04	0.08	−0.04	−0.01	−0.19	−0.01	1.00	−0.13
Property	0.18	0.14	0.09	−0.16	0.06	0.00	0.15	−0.09	−0.13	1.00

Source: Bloomberg. FTSE 100 Index, MSCI World Index, MSCI Emerging Markets Index, iBoxx £ Gilts Index, iBoxx £ Non-Gilts Overall Index, Barclays Capital UK Govt Inflation Linked Index, BofA Merrill Lynch Global High Yield Index (measured in $), JPM Emerging Markets Bond Index Plus EMBI+ Composite, UK Cash LIBOR TR 1 Month Index, UK IPD TR All Property Index. January 1998 to December 2015. Based on monthly total returns, measured in £ except when indicated otherwise

A free data source on indices is websites of ETFs (Exchange Traded Funds). ETFs normally closely track underlying indices and provide their key facts.

Summary

- Capital market assumptions (CMAs) estimate sustainable expected return, risk and correlations of asset classes over the long term (5–10 years).
- CMAs are based on observable market indicators, inferring valuations and expected returns of assets as implied by the market's collective wisdom.
- Formulating expected returns involves breaking down assets' returns into building blocks and estimating each one's expected return.
- Equity's expected return consists of dividend yield, trend earnings growth and P/E mean reversion. Bond's expected return consists of YTM, price movement and cost of default. Property's expected return consists of net rental yield, trend nominal GDP growth rate and costs.
- Expected risk is historic volatility since a structural change.
- Expected correlations are historic correlations since a structural change.

Notes

1 Source: factsheet of FTSE 100 Index at **www.ftserussell.com**. Dividend yields of US indices are available on the market data centre of the *Wall Street Journal* at **markets.wsj.com**.

2 The paper 'Earnings Growth: The Two Percent Dilution' by William Bernstein and Robert Arnott is available for free online. It includes dilution factors for different equity markets. Its data is also available at **www.efficientfrontier.com**, the website of William Bernstein. Visit the website for a wealth of useful information on asset allocation and investing.

3 Source: Office for National Statistics at **www.ons.gov.uk**. Trading Economics at **www.tradingeconomics.com** is a free source of economic and financial data for different countries, including forecasts of economic growth. The Bank of England at **www.bankofengland.co.uk** is a source of historic economic data and forecasts for the UK.

4 2.6% = 2.6% real GDP growth rate, plus 2% inflation, minus 2% dilution. Instead of using Bank of England's target inflation, you can use the breakeven rate of 10-year linkers.

5 Sources for economic forecasts include the Office for Budget Responsibility at **www.budgetresponsibility.org.uk,** the Organisation for Economic Co-operation and Development (OECD) at **www.oecd.org,** the International Monetary Fund (IMF) at **www.imf.org** and Trading Economics at **www.tradingeconomics.com.**

6 **Earnings yield** (E/P) is the ratio of EPS over the last 12 months divided by current price. It is the inverse of P/E. Comparing E/P with bond yields indicates the relative valuation of equities and bonds.

7 $50\% = 15 \div 10 - 1.$

8 $4.14\% = (15 \div 10)^{(1/10)} - 1.$

9 $50\% = (1 + 4.14\%)^{10} - 1.$

10 As of December 2015; based on monthly end-of-month P/Es since May 1993. Ask your financial adviser for long-term average and current P/Es. Current P/Es of equity indices are available on the CNN Money website at **money.cnn.com.** The factsheets of MSCI indices include P/Es. Check the website of MSCI at **www. msci.com.** The average P/E of the S&P 500 Index is 12.0 based on monthly end-of-month P/Es since January 1973.

11 $-1.3\% = (18.0 \div 16.2)^{(1/10)} - 1.$

12 $5.3\% = 4.0\% + 2.6\% - 1.3\%.$

13 $\text{P/E effect} = -4\% = (12 \div 18)^{(1/10)} - 1; 2.6\% = 4.0\% + 2.6\% - 4.0\%.$

14 Visit the website of Robert Shiller at **www.econ.yale.edu/~shiller** for long-term data on the US equity market with calculations of CAPE. The GuruFocus website at **www.gurufocus.com** offers a number of valuations for different equity markets. The two valuation methodologies on the website are market-cap/GDP valuation and Shiller P/E. The website is free and includes detailed explanations of the methodologies.

15 10-year bond yields can deviate from nominal GDP growth rate due to supply and demand for bonds and capital, inflationary pressures and expected returns of substitute investments. These and other factors impact the 'normal' level of yields.

16 Current bond yields are available on Bloomberg's website at **www.bloomberg.com.**

17 $-24.7\% = -9.5 \times (4.6\% - 2\%).$

18 $-4.8\% = -9.5 \times (2.5\% - 2\%).$

19 $-2.8\% = 2\% - 4.8\%.$

20 Credit spread is determined by credit risk, differences in tax treatment between govies and corporate bonds and liquidity (govies are more liquid than credit).

21 The duration of a portfolio is the weighted average duration of its constituencies.

22 $-3.4\% = -6.7 \times (2.5\% - 2\%)$.

23 This is a rough, generalist simplification. The relationship between changes in rates and changes in credit spread depends on many factors, such as economic regime, slope of the yield curve, inflation expectations, duration, credit rating, callability, coupon rate, time horizon, liquidity and forces of supply and demand.

24 For example, check the website of iShares at **www.ishares.com/uk** for iShares Core £ Corporate Bond UCITS ETF, tracking the Markit iBoxx GBP Liquid Corporate Large Cap Index.

25 **Effective duration** considers the embedded options in the bonds. Embedded options typically represent callable bonds.

26 $-2.2\% = -8.7 \times (2.5\% - 2\%) \div 2$.

27 $1.4\% = 3.6\% - 2.2\% - 0.03\%$.

28 For example, now that the base rate is 0.5%, a 5-year fixed rate ISA can offer a rate of 2.5%. A savings bank account for children can offer a 3% rate up to a certain savings amount (£3,000).

29 $0.49\% = (1 + 5\%)^{1/10} - 1$.

30 $7.6\% = 3.5\% + 4.6\% - 0.49\%$.

31 GMO provides free 7-year asset class real return forecasts on its website at **www. gmo.com**. Register on the website for free access. Research Affiliates offers long-term capital market forecasts at **www.researchaffiliates.com**. BNY Mellon offers 10-year capital market assumptions at **www.bnymellon.com**. JP Morgan Asset Management provides long-term capital market assumptions at **am.jpmorgan.com**.

32 Historic returns are available on Google Finance at **www.google.co.uk/finance** and Yahoo! Finance at **uk.finance.yahoo.com**. You can use historic returns of ETFs tracking equity, bond and liquid alternative indices.

33 Two improvements to formulating expected risk are incorporating the asymmetry (fat tails) of returns (as measured by skewness and kurtosis) and unsmoothing appraisal-based returns.

34 YTM is BOE base rate: **www.bankofengland.co.uk**.

35 Property rental yield is available on factsheets of property fund and trusts.

36 Dividend yields are available on factsheets of indices. FTSE 100 Index: **www. ftserussell.com**. MSCI World Index and MSCI Emerging Markets Index: **www. msci.com**. Check **www.bloomberg.com** for 10-year gilt yield. Factsheets of ETFs include data for indices they track, including YTM, duration and credit rating. Check **www.ishares.com/uk** for ETFs and their key facts.

CHAPTER 15
STRATEGIC ASSET ALLOCATION

Aligning your portfolio with your investment objectives

'Have a strategic asset allocation mix that assumes that you don't know what the future is going to hold.'

Ray Dalio

Asset allocation is probably your most important investment decision. It determines somewhere between 50% and 90% of your portfolio's return and risk. It is a critical decision, deserving attention and time.

For example, if your investment strategy is **capital preservation**, you might allocate 20% to equities, 60% to bonds and 20% to cash. This allocation should deliver modest returns with a relative low risk level.

However, if bond yields are low and expected to rise, bonds may suffer capital losses. In a low-yield environment, cash may deliver meagre returns, perhaps lagging inflation. This allocation might fail preserving capital in such settings. It must adapt to current market conditions.

If your strategy is **income and growth**, you might allocate 50% to equities, 40% to bonds and 10% to cash. Equities aim to deliver long-term growth, as well as income (dividends). Bonds aim to deliver income, as well as to diversify equity risk.

Whilst this allocation appears balanced, most of its risk comes from equities. In fact, well over 80% of its risk can come from the 50% equity allocation.

If your strategy is **aggressive growth**, you might allocate 80% to equities, 15% to bonds and 5% to cash. Here, equities should deliver high growth over the long term. The asset allocation is risky with high expected volatility. The role of bonds is mainly diversifying equity risk.

If you do not mind volatility and your time horizon is long, consider investing only in equities. However, you will miss out on an opportunity to reduce some risk through diversification without giving up the same amount of return. In other words, your strategy will not be optimal.

Asset allocation fulfils several roles:

- It allows for formulating an investment strategy that should deliver a level of return and risk in line with your objectives. Once you understand the characteristics of assets and project rational assumptions about their future expected returns, risks and correlations, you can blend them, aligning the mix with your objectives.

- It diversifies your portfolio across different assets to reduce risk. Correlations across different asset classes are normally lower than correlations amongst securities within an asset class. Therefore, multi-asset investing comes with diversification benefits.

- It expands the investment opportunity set, methodologically including a wide range of asset classes in your portfolio. It is a structured way to blend investments.

Asset allocation can be divided into a long-term, static allocation, often called **Strategic Asset Allocation**, and a short to medium term, dynamic asset allocation, often called **Tactical Asset Allocation**. Combine the two since what can spoil a long-term plan is short-term volatility.

Strategic Asset Allocation

Strategic Asset Allocation (SAA) commonly forms a portfolio's long-term, anchor allocation. SAA does not take into account current market views, but rather allocates capital to different assets, based on their long-term characteristics.

SAA is often fixed. You choose your SAA, you allocate your portfolio accordingly and you do not change the allocation. However, forgetting about your allocation is a mistake. Markets change and with them assets' characteristics.

For example, there is a big difference in the expected future behaviour of 10-year gilts when their yield is 2% or 5%. Yield of 2% means low carry and expected capital losses, whilst 5% yield means decent carry and potential capital gains. Whether the base rate is 0.5% or 4% has a huge impact on what cash will deliver.

Making the same SAA decisions regardless of current market conditions is naïve. Review SAA regularly, at least every year or two. But, unless circumstances have indeed changed, you do not need to modify it. Keep your SAA dynamic and relevant, not static and irrelevant.

Optimisation

Once we have formulated the expected returns, risks and correlations of asset classes (capital market assumptions – CMAs), the next step is blending them together into an asset allocation. Optimisation is an iterative quantitative process of generating an asset allocation with the highest expected return for a certain risk level or the lowest risk for a certain return level.

Maximising the ratio between return and risk (Sharpe ratio) means you get the most you can out of your portfolio, given your risk tolerance. An optimal or efficient allocation does just that.

Investment professionals use a computer program based on a mathematical algorithm to produce an optimised allocation. The inputs are expected returns, risks and correlations for asset classes in the portfolio's universe.[1]

The most common optimisation technique is **mean-variance optimisation**. The simplest computer program tries different allocations until it cannot find an allocation with a better return/risk ratio than the last one. Then it stops and the efficient allocation is identified.[2]

Commonly, optimisation tools plot a chart, called the **efficient frontier**, showing a curved line with an efficient allocation for each risk level. The allocations on the frontier offer the maximum expected return available for each risk level. You do not need to construct a frontier. The explanation here is just a jargon booster.

Since we are seeking simple, pragmatic solutions to help you manage your portfolio, you can do it yourself. Instead of sophisticated optimisation, try different mixes of a small number of up to six asset classes by calculating the expected return and risk of each mix. The asset allocation may not be optimal, but it should be close enough, matching your investment objectives.

Anyway, many optimisations are flawed since they are based on historic relationships that may not hold in the future and on numerous assumptions that may turn out incorrect – garbage in garbage out (GIGO).

Asset allocation models

Table 15.1 includes five asset allocation models for different investment objectives. Use these models as guidance for a starting point.

Table 15.2 shows the assumptions used to calculate the expected returns and risks for the allocation models. Update the assumptions using the methodology that we have covered earlier to calculate the current expected returns and risks of the allocation models.

Assumptions

The models use UK equities, although you should diversify globally and include emerging market equity (about 10% of equities).

For bonds, the models assume investing in gilts and holding them to maturity. Therefore, the expected return is current 10-year gilt yield. However, bonds should include spread products (IG credit, global high yield hedged to British pound and EMD, hedged to pound if hard currency).[3]

For alternatives, the models use a mix of 75% listed alternatives, assuming the same characteristics as those of UK equities, and 25% commercial property.

Table 15.1 Asset allocation models

Investment strategy	Capital preservation	Income	Income & growth	Growth	Aggressive growth
Equity	20%	40%	55%	70%	85%
Bonds	60%	40%	30%	15%	5%
Cash	10%	10%	5%	5%	5%
Alternatives	10%	10%	10%	10%	5%
Backtested[4] return pa %	6.4	6.5	6.7	6.7	6.6
Backtested volatility pa %	4.9	7.2	9.3	11.5	13.5
Backtested Sharpe ratio	0.60	0.43	0.35	0.28	0.23
Expected return %	**2.9**	**3.6**	**4.1**	**4.6**	**4.9**
Expected volatility pa %	4.6	6.6	8.6	10.7	12.5

Source: Bloomberg. FTSE 100 Index, iBoxx £ Gilts Index, UK Cash LIBOR TR 1 Month Index, UK IPD TR All Property Index. January 1998 to December 2015. Based on monthly total returns, measured in £

Portfolio volatility using matrix algebra

To calculate a portfolio's volatility, first construct a **covariance matrix**. Each cell in the matrix is the product of the correlation between two assets and their volatilities.[5] Then, the easiest way is using matrix algebra. If w is a vertical vector of portfolio weights (w' is transpose of w) and Σ is the covariance matrix, then portfolio variance is **w'Σw**. If this is too technical, and it is for nearly everyone who is not a professional (and for many professionals), ignore it.

Table 15.2 Assumptions

	Equity	Bonds	Cash	Alternatives
Expected return pa %	5.3	2.0	0.5	5.9[6]
Volatility pa %	14.2	5.4	0.7	10.9[7]
Correlation				
Equity	1.00	−0.15	−0.07	0.80
Bonds	−0.15	1.00	0.08	−0.15
Cash	−0.07	0.08	1.00	−0.08
Alternatives	0.80[8]	−0.15	−0.08	1.00

Source: Bloomberg. FTSE 100 Index, iBoxx £ Gilts Index, UK Cash LIBOR TR 1 Month Index, UK IPD TR All Property Index. January 1998 to December 2015. Based on monthly total returns, measured in £

Expected returns do not include any potential alpha from active management or an allowance for fees and costs. By adding alpha, as well as diversifying across additional asset classes, you can achieve potential higher returns with lower risk. However, being conservative about assuming alpha is prudent, in particular if most of your portfolio is invested in index trackers.

Current expected returns are low because of the low-yield environment. When base rate is higher as well as gilts' yields, the expected returns of the asset allocation models would be higher.

For example, assuming a 1.5% base rate and 3% 10-year gilt yield, the expected return of capital preservation increases by 0.7% from 2.9% to 3.6% (allocation to bonds and cash is large) and that of aggressive growth increases modestly from 4.9% to 5.0% (allocation to bonds and cash is small).

Achieving a 6% total return per year is challenging in current market conditions of not cheap equity markets and low yields. An all equity portfolio, including emerging market equity and assuming alpha, can achieve it. However, risk level would be high. A 6% return is more achievable when equity markets are cheaper and bonds' yields are higher.

Figure 15.1 plots the allocation models on the risk/return plane using their forward-looking returns and risks. The risk/return space is commonly used to illustrate how different assets and allocations compare with each other.

Figure 15.2 shows the backtested cumulative performance of capital preservation and aggressive growth, against an annual 5% investment objective.[9]

This figure illustrates how the two models would have comfortably surpassed the objective. It also shows that during the particular backtesting period, an aggressive strategy only marginally outperformed a conservative one, but with a much higher risk. During the majority of the back-testing period, the aggressive strategy lagged the conservative one.

Be vigilant extrapolating the past into the future. During the specific backtesting period, fixed income investments enjoyed a strong lift, due to falling rates. Do not assume such a decreasing bond yield environment going forwards. Yields are expected to rise over time (eventually).

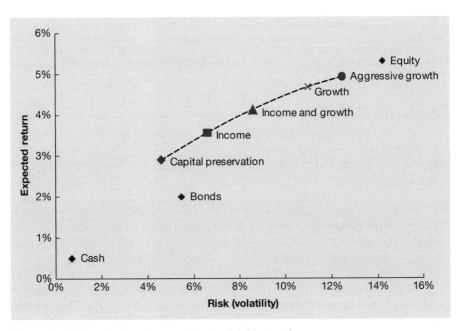

Figure 15.1 Asset allocation models on risk/return plane

Source: Bloomberg. FTSE 100 Index, iBoxx £ Gilts Index, UK Cash LIBOR TR 1 Month Index, UK IPD TR All Property Index. January 1998 to December 2015. Based on monthly total returns, measured in £

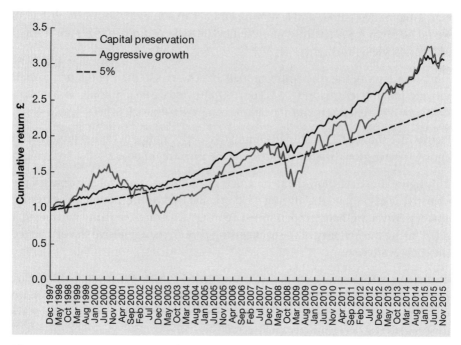

Figure 15.2 Backtesting of asset allocation models

Source: Bloomberg. MSCI World Index, MSCI Emerging Markets Index, iBoxx £ Gilts Index, iBoxx £ Non-Gilts Overall Index, Barclays Capital UK Govt Inflation Linked Index, BofA Merrill Lynch Global High Yield Index (measured in $), JPM Emerging Markets Bond Index Plus EMBI+ Composite, UK Cash LIBOR TR 1 Month Index, UK IPD TR All Property Index. January 1998 to December 2015. Based on monthly total returns, measured in £ except when indicated otherwise

Dynamic SAA

SAA is designed for the long term. However, since our CMAs can be updated regularly and they are linked to current market conditions, you can update your SAA periodically.

For example, when equity markets are expensive, dividend yield is low and P/E is high.[10] Equities' expected return is therefore low. Similarly, when bonds are cheap, their yield is high and so are their expected returns. This is in line with the principle: higher price today means lower returns in the future and vice versa.

With such expected returns, the allocation to equities should be lower and that to bonds should be higher, promoting a healthy discipline of selling high, buying low.

For example, you implement the growth asset allocation model of 70% equity, 15% bonds, 5% cash and 10% alternatives. Given the updated expected returns, you underweight equities to 60% and overweight bonds to 25%.

If your expectations are correct, deviating from SAA can add value. Remember, however, that these are *long-term* expectations. You can lose for years before *potentially* benefiting from deviating from SAA. You might not benefit at all since expectations are expectations, they are not certain. You need perseverance, patience and an ability to handle your **regret risk**.

Regret risk is regretting unprofitable investment decisions. When managing investments, expect to make regretful, wrong decisions. It is part of the game. Learn how to not regret too much when your decisions seem to be losing.

Good things come to those who wait. Sometimes.

One advantage of dynamic SAA is that you do not formulate views about how financial markets are likely to behave over the short term. Dynamic SAA is based on CMAs, which form objective estimates of markets' future long-term returns, reflecting current valuations. CMAs reiterate what financial markets are implying, not our own subjective market views.

Unless you have a special insight about markets, leave predictions to professionals. It is challenging enough for them. They do it, but only occasionally get it right. Nobody owns a crystal ball foretelling the future. Sadly, successful active investing firmly relies on the skill of correctly forecasting the future.

However, adjusting your allocation once every six or twelve months, based on dynamic SAA, can help systematically buying undervalued assets and selling overvalued ones (taking profits). It follows the investing principle of Warren Buffett of long-term value investing.

Identify attractively priced assets, buy them and hold them for the long term. The long time horizon allows low prices to revert back to fair valuations. However, try avoiding **value traps**. Sometimes an asset is cheap since it should be cheap. Rubbish is cheap because it is rubbish, not because it is a bargain.

Setting an investment strategy

The plan is in place. You have articulated your investment objectives and designed an investment strategy with the highest likelihood of achieving them. The next step is implementing a solution – turning your plan into reality.

Implementing a solution includes three main activities: actively changing asset allocation to position your portfolio to current market conditions; choosing investments under each asset class; and constructing and managing a portfolio reflecting the asset allocation and investment choice.

Summary

- SAA aligns your portfolio with your investment objectives. This is probably your most important investment decision.

- Optimisation is a process of generating an asset allocation with the highest expected return for a given risk level. Choose a broadly optimised asset allocation aligned with your objectives.

- Use the asset allocation models as a starting point to formulate your SAA.

- Dynamic SAA updates the asset allocation periodically (every 6–12 months) based on current market conditions with a medium-term view (1–5 years).

Notes

1 The portfolio's universe usually includes only a subset of all available asset classes. The universe may be defined by investment constraints, such as excluding illiquid assets, such as property, due to liquidity constraints.

2 Solver in Microsoft Excel is sufficient to perform simple optimisations with a small number of asset classes. You need to constrain each asset weight between 0% and 100% and the sum of weights to 100%.

3 EMD soft currency should not be hedged to British pound. The hedging costs are too high.

4 Backtested return and risk are based on calculating hypothetical returns assuming the static asset allocation (rebalanced monthly) and using monthly total returns of indices representing the asset classes of each asset allocation model. Backtesting demonstrates how the models would have performed in the past.

5 The value in each cell in the covariance matrix is $\text{Cov}_{i,j} = \rho_{i,j}\sigma_i\sigma_j$. Since in the diagonal of the matrix $i = j$ the values in its cells are the assets' variances.

6 $5.9\% = 75\% \times 5.3\% + 25\% \times 7.6\%$. For property, the assumed expected return is 7.6%, considering a 3.5% net rental yield.

7 $10.9\% =$ square root of $(75\%^2 \times 14.2\%^2 + 25\%^2 \times 4\%^2 + 2 \times 75\% \times 25\% \times 14.2\% \times 4\% \times 0.19)$; where 14.2% is the volatility of UK equities, 4% is the volatility of UK commercial property and 0.19 is the correlation between them.

8 $0.80 = 75\% \times 1.00 + 25\% \times 0.19$. This is the weighted average of correlation of equities with themselves (1.00) and correlation of equities with property (0.19).

9 Capital preservation 18% global developed equity, 2% EME, 42% gilts, 12% IG corporate bonds, 3% global high yield, 3% EMD, 10% cash, 5% commercial property, 2.5% REITs and 2.5% commodities. Aggressive growth 76.5% global developed equity, 8.5% EME, 3.5% gilts, 1.0% IG corporate bonds, 0.3% global high yield, 0.3% EMD, 5% cash, 2.5% commercial property, 1.3% REITs and 1.3% commodities.

10 Dividends at the numerator are more stable than rising prices at the denominator, pushing dividend yield downward. In P/E the price at the numerator rises more rapidly than earnings at the denominator, pushing P/E upward. Prices reflect the expected future rises in earnings.

CHAPTER 16
BEHAVIOURAL FINANCE

Let me introduce you to your investor self

'The investor's chief problem – and even his worst enemy – is likely to be himself.'

Benjamin Graham

Successful investing requires forming objective, emotionless and rational views about assets' future performance. This is a key to correctly formulating an investment strategy matching your investment objectives.

Dynamic Strategic Asset Allocation (SAA) is used to position your portfolio for the long (5–10 years) and medium term (1–5 years). It is grounded on what markets are objectively implying. It does not necessitate you to form subjective views on how markets are likely to behave over the short term (up to 12 months).

However, you may wish to reposition your portfolio due to short-term developments. Geopolitical events, such as an unexpected dissolution of the Eurozone, or economic events, such as the USA suddenly sliding into a recession, could be adequate reasons to act considering the short term. Dynamic SAA might be slow in capturing such events or completely overlook them.

Accounting for short-term situations requires the formation of short-term market views and a swift reaction. **Tactical Asset Allocation** (TAA) addresses this. But, before turning to TAA, we will cover how you are likely to be deceived by the market. And you are not the only one; the market misleads us all. TAA is subjective and bad behavior can lead to bad investment decisions.

We are all humans (at least most of us). We make mistakes. Whilst we aim to rationally forecast the future, we should acknowledge our investor psychology and mental biases affecting our rational decision making.

Behavioural finance explores the effects of psychological, social, cognitive and emotional factors on financial decision making and the impact on markets. Our mind is an amazing machine; however, it is susceptible to limited available information, prejudices, anchoring and illusions. It is easy to play tricks on it.

In this chapter we review some of the common behavioural biases that tend to affect decisions of investors, both amateurs and professionals. Being aware of these biases is unlikely to eliminate them. But, being aware of them, you will, possibly, identify when you are under their influence, take a step back, think rationally and decide with a clearer head.

When you manage your portfolio, your decisions are likely to be affected by behavioural biases. For example, volatility of markets might induce you to sell when markets fall close to the bottom and buy when markets rise close to the top. This behavioural tendency turns otherwise potentially harmless volatility into a wealth-destroying activity.

By understanding the behavioural biases, you may be able to mitigate their impact and control your potentially harmful instincts.

Herding and myopic thinking

'Successful investing is anticipating the anticipation of others.'

John Maynard Keynes

Two of investors' most common behavioural tendencies are herding and myopic thinking.

Herding is people's inclination to think and act in the same way as the majority. Investors often do what everyone else appears to be doing because of a fear of missing out. They use a flawed logic that if everyone is doing something, it must be right. Herding is one cause for unsubstantiated rallies (bubbles) and sell-offs (crashes).

We are conditioned to believe collective wisdom is superior to any one individual's opinion. When seeing people queuing for a new restaurant, we eagerly join the line, assuming it must be fantastic since everyone obviously thinks so.

An example of herding is the 1990s technology bubble. Investors piled up on technology stocks since everybody seemed to be doing so. Their prices far exceeded fundamentals. Companies were valued based on traffic in websites, rather than any foreseeable profitability.

It all ended badly. The bubble exploded in 2000. Herding then went the other way when everyone sold all tech stocks indiscriminately. The higher the peak, the harder the fall.

The issue with herding is that when everybody is buying something, it is probably already overvalued. Try avoiding it by doing your homework. Do not fly on auto-pilot, make a conscious effort to form your own opinion and take time to make decisions. You are managing your private portfolio; it is all right to stand out from the crowd – it is nobody's business but your own.

The second common behaviour tendency is short-termism (**myopic thinking**). It is everywhere: cannot help but eat a fourth piece of delicious pizza, loaded with calories, whilst sabotaging your diet; buying a red Ferrari you cannot afford out of an urge, whilst derailing long-term financial planning; or chasing recent returns, hoping latest success will be replicated.

It is easy to fixate on the market's short-term movements. However, as a saver for retirement, you are here for the long haul. It does not matter what markets do over a week or a month; it is noise. It matters what markets do over 5–10 years.

Not only is it nearly impossible to predict markets over a week or two, and recent winners might be a passing fad, but also swinging your portfolio back and forth generates performance-biting transaction costs.

Investing is a marathon, not a sprint. Do not let news distract you, leading to instinctive but flawed decisions out of fear and greed. Position your portfolio to benefit from market movements over a number of years, not next week. This is one advantage of dynamic SAA. It takes a long-term view based on asset valuations, helping to avoid short-termism.

Prospect theory

Nobel laureate Daniel Kahneman and Amos Tversky developed the **prospect theory**, which describes how people value gains and losses differently. Losses have a larger emotional impact than equivalent gains, leading to risk aversion.

Let's play.

Pick one of two choices:

(A) 50% chance of gaining £1,000 and 50% chance of gaining £0.

(B) 100% chance of gaining £500.

Now, pick again one of two choices:

(C) 50% chance of losing £1,000 and 50% chance of losing £0.

(D) 100% chance of losing £500.

Which ones did you choose?

Most people pick B (certain gain) in the first exercise and C (gamble for a chance of not losing) in the second one.

In both cases, A and B and C and D are equivalent, having the same expected result.[1] The reason for the common choices is loss aversion – the propensity of focusing on minimising the downside. Losing hurts more than gaining pleases.

Prospect theory leads to a number of biases in decision making.

Framing effect means the way a problem is described leads to systematically different decisions. It depends whether the description emphasises the potential profit or loss. It is all in the positioning and marketing.

For example, choose between two investments:

(A) Investment with 5% probability of losing money.

(B) Investment with 95% probability of gaining money.

Which investment do you prefer?

Most people select B, although the risks of A and B are equivalent. The focus in A is on losing and in B is on gaining. The way information is presented sways decisions. This is the skill of salespeople.

Disposition effect explains why some investors hold on to losing investments for too long and sell winning investments too soon. Continuing to hold a loser avoids admitting failure and the hurtful feeling of losing. Impatiently selling a winner generates the joy of success.

Feelings and emotions, rather than cold, objective monetary calculations, drive decisions.

Mental accounting

Mental accounting is people's inclination to arbitrarily categorise economic outcomes, such as winner account and loser account.

For example, you bought two assets:

(A) You paid £100 for A; its price now is £80.

(B) You paid £60 for B; its price now is £80.

You think the price of both is going to plunge. Which asset do you sell or hold?

Most people choose to take profits, selling B – it is in the winner account, and keep holding A, avoiding crystallising a loss – it is in the loser account.

You enjoy winning but want to avoid admitting losing, forgetting the concept of **sunk costs**. Sunk cost has been incurred and cannot be recovered. There is nothing to do about it; no point of throwing good money after bad, trying to salvage it.

Assets A and B should be sold since your prospective view is negative on both. The **reference point** of a purchase price is irrelevant. It doesn't matter whether you're in a profit on one and losing on the other. The past is in the past. Let bygones be bygones. Forward-looking views should drive decisions. But yet, psychologically it is more difficult to sell at a loss than at a profit.

Cognitive biases

Cognitive biases are patterns of deviations in judgement, whereby inferences about people and situations may be drawn in an illogical fashion.

Anchoring is a tendency to rely too heavily on the first piece of information offered when making decisions. An irrelevant value influences the answer.

For example, you are looking to buy a house. You view two identical houses in the same street. On the first one, the asking price was £400,000 but the seller agrees to sell it for only £375,000. On the second house the seller insists you pay the £375,000 asking price.

On which house do you make an offer?

Most people would go with the first house. Its initial asking price was £400,000 and they negotiated it downwards. The opening asking price is an anchor or reference point. They feel delighted getting a good deal, £25,000 less than the asking price.

But the two houses are identical. The second house's price is as good as that of the first. Anchoring is one reason shops offer discounts on the original price. It makes you feel you get a bargain. Sometimes, retailers offer goods at a discount from the onset – they have never asked for the full price. It is a selling gimmick.

Over-confidence and **over-optimism** describe the propensity of people to have too much subjective confidence in their judgement, far above its objective accuracy.

When asking fund managers whether they think they are better than the median manager, everyone would say yes. Statistically, however, half are above and half are below the median.

Most managers would speak with conviction about their views on the future. However, most managers get it wrong.

When a person claims to know the exact truth about anything, it is safe to assume this person is inexact. Subjective certainty is inversely proportional to objective certainty. The more that people are uncertain they are right, the more they feel they need to show proof validating their claims.[2]

Confidence is important, but be realistic where you should be confident and where you should be humble, admitting you can use advice. Financial markets can be humbling after experiencing some disappointments. It is better being uncertain and cautious, than confident and wrong.

Confirmatory bias means people tend to see what they want to see to confirm their view. If you are bullish on stocks, you are inclined to agree with positive analysis, corroborating your view, ignoring negative analysis, contradicting your view. You listen more to those who boost your confidence, not to those disagreeing with you. However, it can be beneficial to listen to others; they may offer perspectives you did not consider. This is one benefit of teamwork.

Hindsight bias is the thinking you knew it all along – the writing was on the wall; it was obvious. It is easy to explain what happened in the past with the benefit of hindsight. The challenge is having foresight, forecasting what will happen in the future.

Often, economists are excellent at articulating the past and present. But, whilst explaining the future with confidence, they are often clueless. When presenting their views with conviction, people tend to believe they know what is going to happen. Rarely, they do.

Self-attribution bias is people's tendency to assign skill to good decisions and luck to bad decisions. If your investments do well, it is because of your skill in selecting the right ones. If your investments do poorly, it is because of bad luck. Self-attribution is a way to boost self-confidence.

Sample size bias is the habit of giving too much significance to conclusions based on small samples.

For example, you toss a fair coin five times, each time getting heads. You conclude the coin always falls on heads. However, you reached a conclusion based on a small sample – it could be a coincidence. Tossing the coin 100 times, getting heads each time, could lead to a reasonable conclusion that it is biased.

You find a correlation between the number of snowy days in Scotland and the performance of the FTSE 100 Index, concluding that when it snows in Scotland, the

UK stock market performs well. However, this is an example of mixing spurious correlation and causality. December and January happen to be strong months for the stock market on average and the depth of winter. It is a coincidence.

Another example is calculating standard deviation or average based on 12 monthly returns. This sample is far too small to reach statistically significant figures. You need at least 36 or 60 monthly observations to do so.

It is rather common for experts to misuse and present statistics in such a way that supports their story. **Representativeness bias** helps them, as people tend to judge by appearances, not likelihoods.

For example, a fund manager boasts the fund has posted positive returns over the last six months, every month in a row. What does it say about the fund?

Not much really. The fund appears to do a good job. But it is over such a short time frame and you do not know how it compares to a benchmark and peer funds. Perhaps markets have rallied and most other funds did much better.

Recency effect is people's propensity to preferentially remember the recent past. For instance, if equity market has gained over recent years, investors tend to be complacent, increasing equity holdings disregarding risks. They focus on recent past, forgetting history.

The opposite tends to occur following a crash. Investors' attention is on the down-side, staying away from the market, due to recent bad experience, although it may be a buying opportunity. Recent experience has a big impact on our emotions.

The **status quo** and **endowment effects** explain why once owning something you may value it more than others, feeling an affinity towards it. When selling an investment, you tend to ask a higher price than that you would pay to buy an equivalent one.

For example, when selling a house, you feel emotionally attached to it. You would probably ask more for it than its fair value because it is yours.

Being aware of the biases affecting your decision making is the first step. Markets drop and your surviving instinct tells you 'sell, run away from danger'. But you are impacted by the mood of doom, gloom and fear.

One way to alleviate the biases is teamwork. When having an urge to sell or buy, run your idea by someone else. It could be your adviser, spouse, a trusted family member or a good friend. Peer review by someone emotionally detached can highlight when your thinking is not entirely rational.

Listening to someone disagreeing with you might be annoying. But it may be more valuable than listening to someone agreeing with you. Do not boost your ego; boost your returns.

Another way to alleviate biases is following a process as mechanical and systematic as possible, leaving emotions aside.

Know yourself

'The time to buy is when there's blood in the streets.'

Baron Rothschild

Know your investor self. You feel depressed or panicky when markets correct or euphoric and overly brave when markets rise. Often, after markets fall, it is a buying opportunity. It is too late to sell anyway just to materialise losses.

After markets rally, they might be overvalued, overbought and crowded. If you are in, consider taking profits – fight your greed for more. If you are out, it might be better to wait for a correction and a better entry point. But do not wait too long and risk missing the rise whilst waiting on the side lines.

This is **contrarian investing**. News is priced in quickly. For markets to continue falling or rising, more bad or good news is needed. When it looks bad or good, the worst or best might be behind us.

Follow a disciplined valuation-based investment process, with an eye on the medium term, fed by different objective inputs to overcome the effects of behavioural finance. Common sense, judgement, clear head, intuition and experience (grey hair) are all required for consistent successful investing.

Investing requires making brave decisions, facing the unknown – we do not know what the future holds. We must make rational decisions with the information we have.

Investing is not an exact science; it is a social science. It is an art as much as it is a science. To succeed, you do not only need to know economics and mathematics, but also crowd psychology. Understand the 'animal spirits' of the masses.[3] To be a good investor, you need independent thinking, scepticism and emotional self-control.

At least by being aware of the biases clouding the markets' judgement we increase our chances of triumph, in particular when making decisions such as tactical asset allocation.

Summary

- Herding and myopic thinking are two behavioural tendencies of investors, often leading to mistakes.

- Prospect theory explains risk aversion. Losing hurts more than gaining pleases. You are likely to take more risk to avoid losing than try to profit.

- Framing effect means the way information is presented can affect decisions, rather than the information itself. We judge books by their covers.

- Mental accounting is the tendency to categorise economic outcomes, such as winners and losers. You are more likely to sell at a profit than at a loss, even when having a negative view on an asset, using the purchase price as a reference instead of focusing on the future.

- Anchoring is the tendency to rely too much on the first piece of information as a reference point for future decisions.

- Overconfidence is putting too much subjective weight in your judgement, surpassing its objective accuracy. Be confident where you have an edge and humble where you need advice.

- Hindsight bias is the propensity to think that what happened was obvious. Explaining the past is easy. Forecasting the future is hard.

- When having an urge to make a decision, use peer review as a sounding board to avoid making emotional, irrational decisions. Stop, clear your head, do your research, think why you are making the decision and ensure it follows common sense.

Notes

1   £500 = 50% × £1,000 + 50% × £0 = 100% × £500; −£500 = 50% × (−£1,000) + 50% × 0 = 100% × (−£500).

2   Inspired by Bertrand Russell.

3   'Animal spirits' is a term John Maynard Keynes used in his 1936 book *The General Theory of Employment, Interest and Money* to describe the instincts and emotions influencing human behaviour.

CHAPTER 17
THE ECONOMIC CYCLE

Round it goes, where it stops nobody knows

'An economist is an expert who will know tomorrow why the things he predicted yesterday didn't happen today.'

Laurence J. Peter

We are going to have a crash course in economics before turning our attention to Tactical Asset Allocation (TAA). In this chapter we will look at the basics of economics since economic conditions are the backdrop for the performance of asset classes.

The economic cycle

TAA aims to identify the current and next stages of the economic cycle to position the portfolio accordingly. The economic cycle (**business cycle**) is the economy's natural fluctuation between growth and contraction of output, jobs, income and spending.

Trend rate of economic growth is average sustainable growth rate over a long time period. It is determined by growth in productive capacity, consistent with low inflation. Actual, short-term growth is quite volatile, drifting away above and below trend growth rate.

This volatility around trend growth is the economic cycle, going through four main stages:

1 Expansion.
2 Slowdown.

3   Recession.

4   Recovery.

Expansion or boom (**growth**) is when national output is rising faster than trend growth rate. Its origins are a virtuous circle amongst the consumer, corporations and the government.

Demand for goods and services companies sell begins with the consumer. Consumption is supported by personal **wealth effect**, fuelled by rising real income, falling unemployment and appreciating house prices.[1] People feel confident and wealthier so they spend money and save less.

Due to rising demand, firms are more profitable. Businesses invest in capital goods (capital expenditure – CAPEX) and hire employees to expand capacity to meet increasing demand. The government collects more taxes, as unemployment falls and corporate earnings rise. The public sector expands, creating more jobs.

As interest rates are low, asset bubbles might inflate in property, stock and bond markets. Individuals and corporations may over-leverage themselves due to positive sentiment, low borrowing costs and complacency. Leverage further inflates asset prices. Valuations become stretched. Imbalances and excesses are created.

Eventually, the economy overheats, running a positive **output gap** (actual output exceeds potential output), leading to inflationary pressures due to demand surpassing supply.

The output gap

Output gap or **GDP gap** measures the difference between the economy's actual and potential output. Potential output is the maximum the economy can produce at full capacity. Positive output gap indicates growth in demand outpaces growth in supply, potentially creating inflation. A negative output gap can create deflation.

The **slowdown (optimism) stage** is when growth decelerates, but GDP is still rising (the *level* of GDP growth is still positive, but *momentum* is declining). That is, the second derivative of growth rate (the pace of growth rate) is decreasing. If the economy slows without falling into a recession, it is called **soft-landing**; otherwise it is **hard-landing**.

A number of factors can cause a slowdown. Inflation that was rising during late expansion stage erodes real income so consumption retreats. Central banks may increase interest rates to tame inflation, causing bursting of asset bubbles and the wealth effect to fade. As rates rise, the currency tends to appreciate, hurting the competitiveness and profitability of exporters, as their produce is more expensive. Now, with rising borrowing costs, leverage starts to bite. Excesses that were built during the expansion cause problems.

People may maintain optimism, hoping the economic expansion will continue. However, with the economy showing signs of weakness, elevated asset prices, rising borrowing costs and inflation, confidence is fragile. The economy can tip over; it is losing steam.

The **recession (despair) stage** is when GDP is contracting. Technically defined, a recession is a fall in real GDP for two consecutive quarters. Often, some systemic shock, such as a large debt default, leads to a recession.

Negative growth leads to increasing unemployment, as corporations face over-capacity and scale down. Real income decreases and with it consumption, corporate profitability, government's tax revenues and spending (austerity). Fiscal deficit rises and the currency depreciates.[2]

A negative wealth effect caused by a dropping stock market, housing market and income leads to gloom and tumbling confidence. Inflation falls because of weak demand for goods and services. Central banks ease monetary policy. Individuals and corporations de-leverage, repairing their balance sheets. Corporations cut costs and become more efficient, leaner and meaner.

A more severe recession is a **depression**: a prolonged and deep recession, leading to a significant fall in GDP and average standard of living. In a depression, real GDP can fall by more than 10%. In the 1930s, the Great Depression hit the USA and the rest of the world.

The **recovery (hope) stage** is when GDP growth rate turns positive from the trough it reached during the recession. Eventually, after the recession has run its course, the economy starts to recover, running a negative output gap (actual output lags potential output). Things start looking normal again.

Mending confidence of individuals and businesses is critical for a turnaround. Confidence leads to increasing consumption, rising corporate profits, hiring, growing government tax collections, public expenditure and investments.

Inefficiencies and leverage of the expansion stage have been addressed. Individuals, corporations and the economy are efficient and de-leveraged. Weak currency helps exporters. Excesses are eliminated and the economy is set for repair, when conditions stabilise.

Often, central banks and governments deliberately attempt to stimulate demand to kick-start a recovery. Central banks use monetary tools, such as cutting interest rates, now that inflation has eased, and quantitative easing (QE) when conventional monetary policy is insufficient.

Governments use **fiscal policy** to influence the economy. Fiscal policy is a government's actions of adjusting revenues (mainly taxes), borrowing and expenditures. In a slowing economy, the government can cut taxes and increase spending to reflate it. National infrastructure projects, for example, can create employment and demand for raw materials. When the economy accelerates and overheats, the government can raise taxes and cut spending to slow it down.

After recovery, the economy normally heads back to expansion. However, it can fall back into a recession, called a **double-dip recession**.

The four economic stages can be described using a four-by-four matrix of GDP growth relative to trend and inflation. In expansion, GDP and inflation are both rising. In slowdown, GDP is slowing, whilst inflation is rising. In recession, both GDP and inflation are falling. In recovery, inflation is falling, whilst GDP is rising.

Other atypical economic stages include deflation and stagflation. **Deflation** means negative inflation. The concern is that consumers postpone spending because prices are expected to fall in the future. A deflationary spiral hit Japan in the 1990s – dubbed 'the lost decade'.

Stagflation means negative growth with high inflation. This is a tricky situation as it is difficult to stimulate the economy. Central banks cannot cut rates as inflation is high.

Goldilocks is when growth is not too hot to generate inflationary pressures and not too cold to enter a recession. This is a perfect regime for most asset classes, across both equities and bonds.

The role of central banks has increasingly taken centre stage since the 2008 crisis. Central banks' primary role is setting **monetary policy** to control money supply to smooth the economic cycle and inflation. They do so by setting short-term interest rates and cash amounts that banks need to keep as reserves.

When inflation is high, central banks can increase borrowing costs, making money more expensive, dampening demand and reducing inflation. Recently, central banks, such as the Bank of England (BOE), the Federal Reserve (Fed), the European Central Bank (ECB) and Bank of Japan (BoJ), have started focusing more on reflating economies, using unconventional monetary policies (QE and forward guidance).[3]

Forward guidance

Forward guidance is an attempt by central banks to influence market expectations of future short-term interest rates with central banks' forecasts. Whilst the central bank sets only short-term rates, through forward guidance it aims to convert short-term rates into long-term rates, which reflect market expectations. The problem with forward guidance is that it is always data dependent and the data will be discovered only in the future.

QE means the central bank effectively 'prints' money by buying financial assets, adding them to its balance sheet to stimulate the economy, creating inflation and demand.

Too accommodative monetary policy can create bubbles in assets, such as property, bonds and equities, since bonds' yields decrease, borrowing is cheap and ample liquidity pushes asset prices upwards. The risk is when bubbles deflate.

During past economic cycles, some claimed, 'this time is different' and the economic cycle is dead. For example, during the expansion at the end of the 1990s, in the build-up of the high-tech bubble, some declared the economic expansion was to last forever, as the world entered a new digital economy. After the 2008 crisis, some asserted the economic cycle was broken due to QE.

However, 'this time is different' are probably the four most expensive words in finance. Each time is indeed different since the specific circumstances are not the same. We have never been here before now. But the economic cycle continues, oscillating amongst its four stages.

The investment clock

Different assets perform differently during different stages of the cycle. Investors can use the economic cycle to rotate amongst asset classes. Imagine a clock with each of the four stages of the cycle at each of its quadrants.

During **expansion** (between 9 o'clock and 12 o'clock), inflation is rising, GDP growth is above trend and sentiment is positive. The assets benefiting the most are commodities and property. Demand and inflation support commodities. Low mortgage rates and inflation support property.

Equities should perform positively, but they are becoming expensive. Government bonds suffer due to rising inflation. High yield should perform well due to carry and steady spreads. Local currency tends to appreciate due to expectations of rising rates, so hedge foreign currency.

During **slowdown** (between 12 o'clock and 3 o'clock) GDP growth falls below trend, inflation is still rising and sentiment begins to vanish. Commodity prices start falling due to weaker demand. Equities struggle since they start pricing in the fears of a looming recession and they are expensive. Volatility intensifies.

Inflation-linked bonds should perform well, as inflation is rising above expectations. IG credit and high yield suffer due to inflation and concerns about corporate profitability.

During **recession** (between 3 o'clock and 6 o'clock) GDP growth falls below trend, inflation is dropping and sentiment is shattered. The assets benefiting the most are government bonds (govies) and cash. Falling inflation and interest rates support govies. Cash outperforms when risk assets lose value.

Equity markets fall. Large cap and growth stocks tend to outperform small cap and value stocks during contractions.[4] Local currency tends to depreciate, depending on how foreign economies are faring. Investing in strong overseas assets and currencies is an opportunity.

During **recovery** (between 6 o'clock and 9 o'clock) GDP growth rate moves above trend, inflation is still low and sentiment turns around. The assets benefiting the most are equities and spread products. Economic growth and improving sentiment support equities, which are attractively priced. Wide spreads of spread products narrow due to improving economic conditions.

Govies lag since they are expensive and the market starts to price in expectations of higher rates.

This is a stylised description of how assets should behave across stages of the cycle. Real life is full of surprises, though. Often, assets misbehave, drifting away from expectations.

Summary

- The economic cycle rotates amongst expansion, slowdown, recession and recovery.

- Correctly identifying the current stage of an economic cycle and predicting the next one is challenging, in particular forecasting inflection points between regimes.

- Different assets behave differently during different stages of the economic cycle. By forecasting to which stage the economy is heading you can rotate your portfolio to better performing assets.

Notes

1   Wealth effect is changes in demand of consumers due to changes in the value of their assets, such as stocks, bonds and property. Increase in the value of assets leads consumers to feel more confident and wealthy, encouraging them to spend more, dampening savings.

2   Fiscal deficit is the difference between a government's expenditures and revenues, excluding borrowings.

3   Central banks can justify focusing on unemployment as part of setting monetary policy. The **Phillips curve** inversely links unemployment rates with inflation rates. Decreased unemployment in the economy tends to correspond with higher inflation rates.

4   The opposite tends to occur over expansions: small cap and value stocks tend to outperform large cap and growth stocks. Since expansions are typically longer than contractions, small cap and value stocks tend to outperform large cap and growth stocks over the entire cycle.

CHAPTER 18
TACTICAL ASSET ALLOCATION

Aligning your portfolio with current market conditions

'Most investors want to do today what they should have done yesterday.'

Larry Summers

Tactical Asset Allocation (TAA) deviates from the weights of SAA in that it attempts to mitigate risks and enhance returns. For example, if you think an asset in your portfolio is likely to lose money, you can sell it or reduce its allocation. Or if you think an asset in or outside (**off benchmark**) your portfolio is likely to perform well, you can buy more of it or include it. Hopefully, you will add value.

Dynamic SAA and TAA differ. Dynamic SAA targets a medium (1–5 years) to long (5–10 years) horizon, whilst TAA targets a short horizon (up to 12 months). Dynamic SAA is not based on subjective market views, whilst TAA is. Together, dynamic SAA and TAA make active (dynamic) asset allocation.

When deviating from SAA, mind the magnitude of the deviations. It might derail your investment strategy's return and risk profile. For example, having a positive view on equities, you decide overweighting them by 20% relative to their 50% SAA weight. Your portfolio's risk level increases considerably. An overweight of only 5% is likely to keep risk level closer to that of SAA. Manage your TAA within some asset allocation ranges (limits) around target SAA weights.

When the overweight is too small, such as 2%, it hardly makes an impact on results. It might be meaningless. If you do something in your portfolio, it should have an impact. Otherwise, it is a waste of efforts.

The difference in time horizons between tactical and strategic allocation is critical. The success of market views is a function of three variables:

1 Direction.

2 Magnitude.

3 Time.

For example, you think the stock market will rise. The questions are whether it is going to go up or down, by how much and when. Direction is whether your view is correct. Magnitude is whether you will make a net profit if you are correct.[1] Time is whether you can wait for your view to materialise. Eventually, the stock market will go up. But can you wait one month, one year or a decade for your view to come to fruition?

TAA is more easily said than done. Forecasting how financial markets will behave is challenging. It is especially difficult to predict tipping points between economic regimes (switching from growth to contraction, from high inflation to low inflation). And this is particularly so over a short term.

To understand why, we will review the groups of main drivers affecting asset performance. The objective is to create a framework to support TAA decisions.

The MVST framework

Asset performance is affected by four groups of drivers:

1 Macroeconomic.

2 Valuation.

3 Sentiment.

4 Technical.

Macroeconomic (M)

Macroeconomic factors relate to the broad economy, the backdrop for assets' performance. They include economic output (GDP), inflation, unemployment, savings, investments, currency, housing market and monetary and fiscal policies.

Macroeconomic factors are used to identify the current stage and future direction of the economic cycle. Correctly identifying the current stage and predicting the inflection points are critical for TAA.

Asset prices are affected by macroeconomic factors. For example, equity price reflects the future prospects of economic growth. Increasing expected GDP means more demand for goods and services that companies sell, higher earnings, dividends and, ultimately, share price.

Economic growth can mean the opposite for govies. When the economy grows, inflation is expected to rise and central banks are expected to raise interest rates to control it. Higher inflation and rates are both bad news for govies. Macroeconomic factors affect assets differently, as was reviewed in the previous chapter on the economic cycle.

Valuation (V)

Valuation refers to current prices of assets relative to their fair value. When current prices are deemed rich, they are expected to fall. When they are deemed cheap, they are expected to rise.

The ways to derive valuations vary. Assess how long it is likely to take for valuation to revert back to a historic mean, or determine whether a structural shift has set a new level for comparison.

Each asset class has a different set of valuation matrices. For equities, common measures are dividend yield, price-to-earnings (P/E or CAPE), price-to-book (P/B) and price-to-cash-flow.[2] For bonds, a standard measure is yield to maturity (YTM). For property, it is rental yield.

Whether we turn valuations into profits depends on several conditions. For example, a stock is traded at a price of £10. Using a dividend discount model the stock's fair value is £20. According to our calculations, the upside potential is 100%.[3]

We buy the stock. However, we do not know whether our calculation is correct since we use assumptions that can turn out to be wrong. Even if our calculation is correct, we do not know how long the price of the stock will take to reach its fair value. It can take a month, a year or, perhaps, more. Are we going to wait that long?

And, even if our calculation is correct today, tomorrow the economy can turn over or the company can hit unexpected difficulties, making our calculation invalid. Plenty of reasons exist for assets not to behave the way investors expect them to.

The important consideration for valuation is applying a consistent methodology across assets to have a fair comparison. This is what capital market assumptions (CMAs) aim to do, as was discussed in Chapter 14 on expected return and risk.

Sentiment (S)

Sentiment refers to investors' overall attitude towards an asset. It is, typically, revealed through activity and price movement or momentum in a market. For example, rising prices indicate a bullish sentiment, whereas falling prices indicate a bearish sentiment.[4]

Sentiment is not usually based on fundamentals but on behavioural forces like fear and greed, affecting supply and demand. Sentiment can drive prices away from fair valuations and, if correctly identified, can present opportunities for dynamic investors to enhance returns or mitigate risks.

Investors' feelings, emotions and attitude are difficult to predict. It is about psychology of the masses, as was described in Chapter 16 on behavioural finance. Many short-term traders and investors follow the news flow, overreacting by selling or buying securities.

In many cases, what matters is news relative to expectations. The economy can slow down but, if it does not slow as much as feared, equity markets can actually rise on better-than-expected news.[5]

Occasionally, good news can be bad news. For example, when investors are concerned about central banks raising rates, news about a strengthening labour market can cause equity markets to sell off. The odds are that an interest rate hike is approaching. In other circumstances, an improving labour market should be good news and a reason for markets to rise, not fall. The context in which news is interpreted is essential.

Sentiment usually comes in waves. During optimistic waves, investors focus on positive news. Seeing the cup half full, they are willing to take risk since they emphasise rewards, pushing asset prices upwards. This was coined 'irrational exuberance' by former Fed chairman Alan Greenspan. Such behaviour can inflate bubbles.

During negative waves, investors focus on negative news. Seeing the cup half empty, they shy away from risk, pushing asset prices downwards. Typically, there are always some reasons for concerns lurking in the shadows: low/high growth, low/high inflation, geopolitical events, and so on.

At the extreme, flight-to-quality means investors sell all risk assets universally, looking for safety in conservative assets. Such behaviour can quickly and surprisingly deflate bubbles, causing crashes or corrections.

Intense negative sentiment can be a buying signal. It may indicate capitulation and that no more marginal sellers are left to push prices further down.

Predicting inflection points between regimes of **risk on** (investors take risk) and **risk off** (investors rush to safety) is nearly impossible. Do not try going against the momentum, catching a falling knife – make the trend your friend. It is more plausible to identify a new regime a couple of days after the inflection point. Nevertheless, generating superior returns often require contrarian investing, which needs skill and guts.

Technical (T)

Technical factors focus on studying historic chart patterns, seasonality and price trends. Whilst these factors should not solely drive decisions, they can help to identify entry and exit points. They should complement or challenge conclusions and output from other drivers.

According to finance theory, technical analysis does not work since security prices reflect all historic data. Looking at performance charts, showing nothing more than past data, should not affect future prices. However, if enough investors use technical analysis and trade based on it, it can be a self-fulfilling prophecy, as trades can move asset prices.[6]

Another set of technical factors include market dynamics and behaviour of large market participants that can move asset prices. For example, cash flows due to changes in regulations, issuance of bonds and buying by central banks.

MVST in TAA

MVST factors impact asset prices over different horizons. Macroeconomic and valuation factors mostly impact prices over the long term, as prices eventually tend to converge to their fundamentals and fair values. Over the short term, however, prices are affected mainly by sentiment and technical factors.

Valuation and technical factors are, typically, more quantitative, whereas macroeconomic and sentiment are, typically, more qualitative (judgemental).

When considering different factors, differentiate between leading and lagging indicators. **Leading indicators** tend to forecast other factors, such as the state of the economy or asset performance. They are used to predict the direction of the economy and assets, but they are not always accurate. Often, they turn out misleading indicators.

Examples of leading indicators include bond yields and the slope of the yield curve, as they reflect expectations about growth rate, inflation and future short-term rates.[7] Another example is results of surveys about new orders of consumer and capital goods and raw materials or initial applications for unemployment.[8]

Lagging indicators represent the past. They are backward looking and can confirm patterns in the economy, but they are not helpful for predictions. Examples of lagging indicators are unemployment, GDP growth rate and consumer confidence. Reflecting on how the economy is doing or has been doing recently, they do not signal where the economy is heading. However, they can impact sentiment and re-calibration of assumptions in valuation models.

As markets are rather efficient, news is immediately reflected in prices. For example, when you hear about the latest GDP figure, inflation or unemployment on, say, the *BBC News at Ten,* financial markets have already reacted. News becomes old news quickly.

Your market views must forecast what will happen in the future. The saying, 'Buy on the rumour, sell on the news' echoes the notion you need to trade on how you think markets are going to behave to certain news, before the news is out. Once it is out, it is too late. You snooze you lose.

Since the price of equities, bonds and currencies is driven mainly by sentiment and technical factors over the near term, and it is difficult to predict sentiment, TAA is a formidable task. Unless you have a strong view or an insight, you are probably better leaving TAA for professionals.

Acting on a high-conviction tip from your hairdresser is bad. When everyone across internet forums says equities are a must buy, bonds are a disaster or the US dollar is going through the roof, these may be **crowded trades**. It means many investors already hold these positions.

If you join the trade now, you need **marginal** buyers or sellers to join in after you to move prices. These marginal buyers and sellers may not be around any more. You may be one of the last ones in. You do not want to be at the bottom of a pyramid in a **Ponzi scheme**.

TAA, like any other active investment activity, needs commitment and research, as well as skill. If you are dedicated and you think you possess a skill to call markets correctly, then go ahead and use TAA. However, if you do not commit, avoid active investment management altogether and stick with dynamic SAA.

MVST in action

An example can illustrate how the MVST framework works in practice. To simplify, we will analyse UK equity, gilts and IG credit. However, MVST should be applied to a broader universe. The UK economy depends on international trade and the fortunes of other countries, in particular the USA, Europe and emerging markets (China). They should be analysed as well.

Beginning with macroeconomics, UK real GDP expanded by 1.9% in the last quarter of 2015, whilst its long-term average growth rate is about 2.6%.[9] The **level** is below trend growth and the **dynamic** is negative, as GDP has slowed over the last few quarters (always consider level and dynamic). The question is whether the slowing trend is likely to continue.

The unemployment rate fell to 5.1% in the last quarter of 2015, below its 7.2% long-term average.[10] The level of unemployment is positive, while the dynamic is stable, as unemployment has remained the same over the last six months.

The inflation rate was close to nil over the last four months, moving higher from negative territory.[11] However, breakeven inflation rates imply expectations of increasing inflation to a level of 2.4% over the next several years.[12]

Monetary policy remains accommodative with the base rate at 0.50%.[13] Liquidity is ample and money is cheap. Low inflation allows the BOE to keep low rates until the economy stands on solid ground. However, the US Fed has raised its rate and the BOE is likely to follow eventually, normalising rates depending on data and economic conditions. In the next recession, the base rate should be higher than the current level for the BOE to have monetary ammunition.

It seems the UK economy is in a late expansion or early slowdown stage of the economic cycle. However, the BOE appears to be behind the curve in tightening monetary policy. This macroeconomic environment should be marginally positive for equities and negative for gilts.

Inflation and rates are expected to rise. These are headwinds to bonds. Corporate bonds should do better than gilts, as decent economic backdrop should support corporate earnings, keeping spreads tight.

Next is valuation. Current P/E of the FTSE 100 Index is about 18.0 whilst its long-term average is 15.8. Equities are slightly expensive relative to their history.

The 10-year gilt yield is 2% – low relative to historic levels. Taking nominal GDP growth rate as a fair-value yardstick for gilts (2.6% real GDP plus 2.4% expected inflation), gilts are overvalued, as well as corporate bonds. Equities are cheap relative to gilts. Equities offer a 4.0% dividend yield, higher than bond yields.

As for sentiment, over recent months, momentum has been negative. Investors were concerned about slowing China, falling oil price and the first hike of the Fed rate. However, China does not seem hard landing, falling oil price is an oversupply issue, rather than a sign of weak demand, and the Fed will be data dependent, likely to rise rates at a measured pace. Sentiment is turning around from negative to more positive.[14]

Technically, equities have been falling lately and now they seem to be in oversold territory.[15] With turning sentiment and recent weakness, this could be a buying opportunity, but caution is warranted.

M, V, S and T are all positive for equities relative to bonds. Based on the MVST analysis, taking a medium-term outlook, equities should be overweight relative to bonds. Within bonds, duration should be short and corporate bonds should be overweight relative to gilts.

As always, there are risks to this view, but that is life. This view is a snapshot, relevant to when it was formulated. A number of weeks or months in financial markets can make a huge difference and short-term views should be updated.

Example

Table 18.1 shows an example of an SAA of a capital preservation strategy with illustrative TAA. Similar to the rule that each asset in your portfolio should have a role, every active allocation position should have a rationale – a reason for having it and a story behind it.

Table 18.1 SAA and TAA

	SAA weight %	TAA weight %	Rationale
Global equities	18	18	Neutral on global equities
European equities	0	5	Recovery in Europe, QE of ECB
Emerging market equity	2	2	Neutral on global EME
Emerging Asia	0	5	Low oil price benefits China and India
Total equity	**20**	**30**	**Equities more attractive than bonds**
Gilts	42	28	Gilts are expensive, yields are low
IG corporate bonds	12	12	Neutral on IG credit
Global high yield	3	5	Search for yield supports high yield
EMD	3	5	Search for yield supports EMD
Total bonds	**60**	**50**	**Bonds are expensive**
Cash	**10**	**5**	**Low cash rate**
Property	5	10	Low rates and improving economy
REITs	2.5	3.5	Low borrowing costs
Commodities	2.5	1.5	Weak demand from China, oversupply
Total alternatives	**10**	**15**	**Overweight through property**
Total	100	100	No leverage

Article 18.1

Saving for retirement is the new cool

By Sophia Grene

Financial Times, 18 May 2014

Towards the end of the last century, an Irish advertising campaign for a pensions provider attempted to make it cool for the under-thirties to save for retirement. On the radio ad, a lust-filled young woman's voice, set against a background of party hubbub, would say, "That's Vince, he's a [breathy pause] . . . pensioner".

Given that we are all pensioners now, in the sense that we must pretty much universally take responsibility for making our own provision for retirement, my juniors should probably not dismiss such appeals out of hand, as I did.

That everyone needs to save for retirement is an oft-repeated and rarely questioned mantra of the 21st century, but as countries all over the world develop retirement savings systems based on individuals saving, a little bit of questioning would not go amiss. Getting it wrong at this stage risks generations of retirees discovering that despite doing everything by the book, they still end up in poverty at the end of their lives.

Ignoring the less financially conventional methods of securing wellbeing in old age, such as relying on a large family to look after granny, or buying a house, secure in the knowledge that house prices can only ever go up, we should look closely at the tax-advantaged savings vehicle that is the pension.

In recent years, investment risk has been shifted from plan sponsors to individuals, people unlikely to be qualified to understand the investment decisions they are making.

This problem has not gone unnoticed and there are a number of ways to mitigate it. In the US, employers are turning to target-date funds, which adjust the asset allocation in accordance with the theory that as investors approach retirement, they should shift into lower-volatility assets, implying lower risk. The concept is catching on in other countries, under different monikers, such as life cycle funds or life-styling.

However, this fails to address the main issue facing the pensions sector: many people are simply not saving enough to maintain the lifestyle they expect to have in retirement. Although Australia and Chile have gone down the route of making a certain level of savings mandatory, this is not a popular option in most countries.

The standard method of guiding savers in deciding how much to contribute to a pension plan is not particularly helpful here. Traditionally, advisers (whether in person or in some paper form such as decision trees) have focused on risk appetite, where risk is defined as volatility, and investment decisions are based on a combination of risk aversion and years from retirement.

This seems intuitively reasonable until you start to apply it to the real world. Do you really care what happens to your pension pot along the way, provided it is big enough to secure you a sufficient retirement income? If the outcome is your priority, would putting a risk-averse saver in a low-volatility fund not mean a higher risk that they will not meet their objective?

US investment manager GMO has recently brought out a paper* identifying this problem and suggesting a framework that focuses on minimising the expected wealth shortfall (where wealth is the amount needed at retirement for the desired post-retirement income).

This change from maximising risk-related return is similar to the kind of liability-driven investing that old-school defined benefit pension schemes are increasingly turning to as accounting regulations require them to be clearer about the risk of not being able to meet their liabilities.

This makes it more obvious what the risk-averse saver should do: save more, like the company that realises it needs to put more money into its pension fund.

The paper goes on to view the investment decision process through the lens of "expected returns" as they vary over time. That is to say, valuation, which is the drum GMO has been banging ever since it lost clients ahead of the dotcom crash in 2000 for pointing out that many internet start-ups were overvalued.

Although the authors agree most target-date "glide paths" (the predetermined process of rotating from stocks to bonds as retirement approaches) are reasonable, all things being equal, the problem is that "all things are rarely equal".

GMO's solution is dynamic asset allocation, which is reset each year according to how far above or below historic average valuations the stock market (and other assets) trade at.

Although this might be simple enough for GMO to implement, as it is not dissimilar to many of its existing strategies, other investment managers might struggle to change their mindsets sufficiently.

However, if the investment management industry is not to fail the many millions who are relying on it to help them retire in comfort, or at least security, it has to consider these problems and come up with some sort of solution. GMO's suggestion may not be the best response but at least it is out there for discussion.

*Investing for Retirement: The Defined Contribution Challenge, by Ben Inker and Martin Tarlie

Summary

- TAA deviates from the weights of SAA to enhance returns and reduce risks based on your views about future performance of assets.

- Limit deviations of active allocation (dynamic SAA and TAA) from SAA so your portfolio's risk profile does not change dramatically.

- The MVST framework groups the drivers explaining asset performance into macroeconomic, valuation, sentiment and technical (MVST). They influence asset price movements over the long term (M & V) and short term (S & T).

- News is immediately priced into security prices. For TAA to be successful, you need to forecast future news. Like in chess, think a number of moves ahead.

- Successful active asset allocation needs dedication and skill. Without them, stick with dynamic SAA.

Notes

1 If trading costs are 0.5% and the market rises by 0.3%, being correct is not sufficient to make a profit net of costs.

2 Book value is the value of an asset on the balance sheet. Book value usually does not include mark-to-market adjustments due to price movements since the asset was purchased.

3 $100\% = 20 \div 10 - 1$.

4 Some sentiment indicators include asset flows with respect of risky funds (such as high yield, EMD and EME), average pairwise correlations amongst securities (correlations tend to rise when sentiment is bad) and put/call ratio (measuring the amount of protection relative to speculation investors hold through listed options).

5 A helpful gauge to whether economic activity is above or below expectations is the Citi Economic Surprise Index.

6 Two simple technical tools are channel (movement between highs and lows constituting a trend) and RSI (Relative Strength Index), which compares recent gains and losses, attempting to indicate oversold and overbought signals.

7 An upward sloping yield curve indicates economic acceleration whilst an inverted yield curve indicates economic deceleration and potential recession.

8 The Purchasing Managers Index (PMI) published by the Institute for Supply Management (ISM) is a common leading indicator for economic activity.

9 Source: Trading Economics at **www.tradingeconomics.com**, as reported by the Office for National Statistics at **www.ons.gov.uk**.

10 Ibid.

11 Ibid.

12 Source: Bank of England at **www.bankofengland.co.uk**.

13 Ibid.

14 Seeking Alpha at **seekingalpha.com** provides daily news about markets. CNN Money at **money.cnn.com** offers news and a Fear & Greed Index, gauging investor sentiment in the USA. Follow performance of markets and news on Bloomberg at **www.bloomberg.com**.

15 Google finance offers charts and technical analysis of indices at **www.google. co.uk/finance**.

CHAPTER 19
CHOOSING INVESTMENTS

Investment selection

'Only buy something that you'd be perfectly happy to hold if the market shut down for 10 years.'

Warren Buffett

So far, our focus has been on top-down asset allocation. It is probably the most important investment decision you will make, determining the preponderance of your portfolio's return and risk. However, choosing bottom-up investments makes a big difference.

After setting your asset allocation, the next step is selecting investments under each asset class. Choices are sometimes bewildering. For example, you decide to allocate 20% of your portfolio to UK equities. You can choose individual UK stocks, a passive index tracker or an ETF, an active fund or blend a number of the above. Each choice has different consequences in terms of return, risk, fees and efforts.

Investment selection can make the difference between success and failure in achieving your financial goals. Do not neglect it.

This chapter is dedicated to selecting investments. We review some choices between passive, active and hybrid funds and propose a framework for selecting actively managed funds. In the next chapter we will go over various investment vehicles and their costs. Understand what you buy and why you buy it.

Funds versus individual securities

When selecting investments, first choose between individual securities and funds.

A fund (**collective investment scheme** – CIS) is an arrangement enabling numerous investors to pool their assets so they are invested and managed by an independent fund manager on their behalf. By pooling assets, investors benefit from economies of scale and professional management.

For example, you have £500 to invest. When selecting individual stocks, you can buy a limited number of stocks since each stock's price ranges from about £1 to £75. So, your diversification is narrow.

Some brokers charge £100 or more per year for holding securities on your behalf in addition to a fee when buying securities. Some charge a percentage of the value of traded securities, but with a certain minimum. Others do not charge for holding securities once you have paid a dealing commission.

Say your dealing commission is 1% or a £20 minimum. Had you traded £10,000, you would have paid £100, which is 1%. But, since you trade £500 you pay £20, which is a massive 4%.[1]

And you need to pick the stocks yourself as £500 is not enough to pay for professional advice.

If, however, you invest your £500 in a fund together with other investors, it can buy many stocks, diversifying its holdings. All investors share transaction costs, making them a much lower proportion of each investment.[2] And a professional fund manager, picking stocks for everyone, manages the fund.

The Financial Conduct Authority (FCA) in the UK regulates certain funds. Regulated funds include authorised UK schemes and recognised offshore schemes. Unregulated funds are subject to restrictions on marketing and are not usually open to investment by retail customers. Your platform is likely to include authorised funds. Managers of authorised funds must follow strict rules about risk management and disclosures.

Most long-term savers use funds. Some buy individual securities. However, unless you are committed to researching individual securities and you think you have a skill to select the right ones, investing through funds is the recommended approach.

Active funds might be more expensive than securities, due to fees, but you get better diversification and professional fund management. Index trackers offer diversification at a reasonable price.

Instead of choosing individual securities, spend most of your time saving in ISAs and pensions, dealing with property, formulating an appropriate investment strategy, thinking about asset allocation and investing via funds.

Active versus passive

Your next investment selection choice is between active and passive funds. As always, each choice has advantages and disadvantages.

Active funds

Active funds aim to generate alpha in excess of their benchmark. Fund managers select investments, constructing a portfolio different from the benchmark.

Active management's first advantage is *potential alpha*. Alpha is precious. Adding some return to your portfolio can have a large impact, in particular over the long term.

Active management's second advantage is *risk management*. Professional fund managers can control risks, especially in risky asset classes such as high yield, emerging market debt (EMD) and emerging market equity (EME).

For example, managers can avoid buying bonds with high chances of default and stocks of companies in financial distress. The caveat is that if these bonds do not default and these companies make it through, their securities' price can rally.

Active management's third advantage is *unconstrained investing*. In funds allowing managers flexibility, such as some multi-asset funds, managers can enhance returns and mitigate risks, benefiting from a wide investment opportunity set. Managers are not tied to a benchmark, which dictates a large portion of performance.

Skilled managers can add value when given freedom. An added benefit is that you can learn from your multi-asset fund managers, using their insights to manage your portfolio. Most active funds, however, are tied to a benchmark through tracking errors and limits.

Nevertheless, like everything with investing, every decision has its pros and cons.

Active management comes with a number of disadvantages; the first one being *fees*. Active funds are generally more expensive than passive index trackers.

Management fees can range between 0.50% and over 1% per year. It depends on the asset class and fund manager's style and reputation. However, investing in an expensive star fund manager, who delivers, can be money worth spending.

High *costs* could be another disadvantage, depending on portfolio turnover. **Portfolio turnover** measures the frequency of buying and selling investments.[3] A 100% portfolio turnover or more does not necessarily mean all securities were changed, but it is a high turnover strategy. A low turnover of about 20% to 30% indicates a buy-and-hold strategy.

Active management involves trading securities. Ever changing markets and market views lead managers to reposition their portfolios. A manager with a short investment horizon might buy and sell securities frequently, generating transaction costs. A manager with a long investment horizon, buying and then holding securities for a long time, may have a low turnover.

You might not even see the trading costs. Unlike fees, that should be disclosed, transaction costs are netted from performance.

Given fees and costs, active managers face a high hurdle to pass to generate net alpha. Most of the time, the average manager underperforms the benchmark (manager risk) because of fee and costs, as well as due to bad investment decisions.[4]

The probability of success of aggregated active management does not solely rely on manager skill. Skill is a prerequisite, but the specific time period, general market conditions and the type of asset class influence the chances of success.

To outperform a benchmark, managers need divergence in performance of individual securities (high **cross sectional volatility** and low average correlation amongst securities).[5] If all securities move in a similar way, it is difficult to pick any that outperform the general market.

For instance, when markets rally strongly, like they did at the end of the 1990s, across different sectors and securities, managers are more likely to lag the benchmark. However, when markets move sideways or downwards, performance of securities tends to diverge, increasing the chances of managers' success.

Another dimension of success is **market leadership**. Narrow leadership means a small number of securities drive the entire market's performance. The odds are lower for managers to select the right ones. For example, when Apple and other IT stocks perform strongly, they can take the entire US equity market with them. Many managers underweight Apple just because of its sheer weight in the index. When it outperforms, their relative performance may suffer.

Broad leadership means a large number of securities outperform the market, increasing the likelihood of managers picking the right ones. In the FTSE 100 Index, for example, about 40% of the total index's weight is concentrated in the largest 10 mega-cap stocks. When they lag the benchmark, managers can select from the other 90 smaller stocks, having a better chance of outperforming.

Managers' probability of success depends on the characteristics of each asset class. Efficient markets are deeply researched. It is harder to locate mispriced securities. For example, the US large cap equity market is highly efficient, making it tough for active management.

Inefficient markets are less researched. More securities may be mispriced. For example, the EMD and EME markets are not as efficient as their developed peers. However, managers need extensive resources researching securities in these markets since transparency and disclosure standards might be weak.

Managers need markets to be neither completely efficient nor completely inefficient. If a market is too efficient, security prices do not diverge from value, so investment opportunities are rare. If a market is too inefficient, security prices do not converge with value, so investment opportunities are rare as well. It needs to be not too hot and not too cold.

Market **breadth** measures the number of securities in the market. A small number of securities offers limited opportunities for security selection. For example, the UK gilt market is a narrow market, including about only 40 bonds. On the contrary, the global IG credit market spans thousands of securities. Breadth offers choice. Choice presents managers with more levers to pull to add value.

The **Fundamental Law of Active Management** validates the importance of breadth.[6] According to the law, information ratio is a function of **information coefficient** (skill or correlation between decisions and successful results) and breadth. Breadth is the number of independent investment decisions per time period. You need not only to make more good decisions than bad ones, but also to make many decisions.

The secret for successful investing in active funds is a skill to select outperforming managers. Whilst many investors rely on past performance to select winners, it can be inconsistent. Past winners might be future losers and vice versa. Manager selection should differentiate between repeatable skill and unrepeatable luck.

Select active funds only if you think a fund is likely to generate alpha, justifying its fees, and you have the skill to select funds that are likely to deliver. Alpha is valuable and can make a difference. It can be worthwhile to make the effort to research active funds. But if you cannot commit or do not believe you can select successful funds, go with passive index trackers.

Passive index trackers

'I'd compare stock pickers to astrologers, but I don't want to bad-mouth the astrologers.'

Eugene Fama

Passive index trackers aim to track the index's performance. They are called passive, since they do not use active management trying to beat the index. Rather, they use different methods to replicate the index's performance. Do not expect them to outperform or underperform. Doing a good job, they should perform in line with the index.

Trackers offer a number of advantages. Using trackers to implement your asset allocation is simple and diversified. They replicate the performance of broad markets, without concentration in a small number of securities. Active funds, on the other hand, are usually concentrated in a portfolio of 30–40 holdings.

Trackers have modest tracking errors relative to indices used in SAA. A portfolio of trackers should match the SAA more closely than a portfolio of active funds.

Trackers eliminate manager risk. Human error is not a severe risk when the index tracker's provider is experienced and reputable.

Trackers are less expensive than active funds. The turnover of trackers may be lower. They have some turnover, however, as securities are added to and deleted from indices (index rebalancing).

Fund size is not a concern. Active funds becoming too big may close to new investors – too much money chasing too few opportunities. Large amounts might move the market when traded (**market impact**). Trackers have bigger capacity than active funds.

Market impact

Market impact is the effect market participants can have on prices of securities when buying and selling them. Closely connected to liquidity, market impact measures how market prices move against the trader; prices moving up when buying and down when selling.

Often, trackers offer better liquidity than active funds due to their size. Implementing short-term views using trackers may be superior to active funds since active managers need time to generate alpha.

Finally, trackers' net performance can be better than that of the average active manager during some time periods, when active management struggles.

Trackers also have disadvantages – nothing is perfect. You need to understand the **replication methodology**. Trackers using derivatives, such as swaps, can have counterparty risk.[7] However, providers use a number of techniques to reduce counterparty risk (such as diversifying counterparties, over-collateralisation and covenants).

Some trackers use **securities lending**.[8] Check the risks of securities lending and whether a share of its revenues is reflected in performance.

Trackers, by definition, underperform the index because of fees, albeit small. Securities lending can improve performance.

Some trackers might have a tracking error with the index. It depends on the replication methodology, fees, costs and the provider's experience.

So what should you choose?

Your choice between active and passive focuses on three main factors:

1 Your skill in selecting active managers and the effort you are willing to spend on selection – having skill means active is an option; if lacking skill, go passive.

2 Your fee budget – the fee you are willing to spend on active funds.

3 Some asset classes should prefer active management (such as high yield and EMD) or they cannot be tracked (such as direct property).

Using active funds requires a commitment. You need to research, select and monitor them. Trackers also require commitment, but it is far less than that needed for active funds.

The choice of active funds in your ISAs and pension is another dimension. If you can access only unattractive active funds, then passive funds may be your only option.

Importantly, trackers usually track market-capitalisation indices that have some shortcomings. One solution is smart beta strategies.

Smart beta

Most indices (such as FTSE 100, S&P 500) follow a market-capitalisation (market-cap) weighting scheme. The weight of each security is the product of the number of outstanding securities and its price.

For example, company A has one million outstanding stocks with a price of £10. Its market capitalisation is £10 million. Company B has two million outstanding stocks with a price of £15. Its market capitalisation is £30 million. A market-cap index with stocks A and B as its constituents has a 25% weight in stock A and 75% in stock B.[9]

Market-cap indices suffer from a number of weaknesses. Large cap companies have material weights in the index, which might have a concentration in the largest stocks. For example, the weight of the top 10 stocks in the FTSE 100 Index is nearly

40%. Whilst the index seems to be well diversified across 100 stocks, the top 10 drive a large portion of its overall risk and return.

Furthermore, the FTSE 100 Index has high concentration in a number of sectors, such as oil & gas and banks. A banking crisis or a drop in global commodity and energy prices, for instance, can especially hurt the UK equity market.[10]

IG credit indices are concentrated in financials and utilities. For example, before the 2008 credit crunch, tracking a corporate bond index heavily exposed investors to financials, which plummeted in the crisis.

Tracking market-cap indices seems like a good way to diversify. However, concentrations might be lurking underneath.

The exposure of market-cap indices to sectors changes over time. Indices can amass an increasing exposure to sectors whose value undergoes rapid appreciation. Commonly, it happens during the build-up of bubbles, just before they explode. For example, before the 2000 high-tech bubble burst, the IT sector's weight surpassed 30% of the S&P 500 Index. It ended in tears as technology stocks crashed.

Market-cap indices are exposed to unrewarded risks. One risk factor attracting a risk premium is small caps, not large caps. Growth stocks have a large weight in indices since their price has appreciated recently and so has their weight. However, value stocks tend to outperform growth stocks.

IG credit market-cap indices tend to have a large exposure to the most indebted companies, since they issue a large amount of debt. However, leveraged companies can also be the riskiest.

Smart beta strategies aim to address the shortcomings of market-cap indices by following a different weighting methodology and systematically exposing the portfolio to rewarded risks, normally by following a rule-based strategy.[11]

Whilst **discretionary management** is based on fund managers' decisions, **rule-based** strategies follow a set of rules that can be systematically implemented in portfolios. For example, a rule could be reducing exposure to the IT sector when its weight reaches 15% by selling proportionally all the securities in it.

Smart beta strategies sit between active and passive. They are not active as they do not aim to add value through discretionary security selection. And they are not passive since they do not blindly track market-cap indices. Their fees should be lower than those of active, but higher than those of passive.

Some smart beta strategies aim to control risks through diversifying and avoiding concentrated exposures. For example, some strategies diversify the portfolio equally across sectors or equally across securities (**equally weighted**). Such an index may have large exposure to small cap securities. Others aim to enhance returns by tilting the portfolio to rewarded risks, such as quality, size, momentum, value and low-beta stocks.[12]

Credit smart beta strategies can reduce transaction costs by following a **buy and maintain** philosophy – purchasing securities and holding them to maturity without good reasons to sell them, such as imminent default.

Selecting smart beta strategies requires due diligence. They have become popular. The choice is plentiful and diverse in terms of construction and philosophies. Some strategies are better than others. Some are completely quantitative, based on past trends and market behaviours that might not continue into the future. Not everything labelled smart beta is necessarily smart.

FWI, minimum variance and risk parity

Fundamentally Weighted Index (FWI) uses metrics such as revenues, dividends, earnings, cash flows or book value to weight securities. **Minimum variance** strategies follow an optimised portfolio with the minimum standard deviation on the efficient frontier.

Risk parity is a type of strategy, arguably also falling under smart beta, where weighting is equal across each security's contribution to portfolio's risk. The strategy offers a better spread of risks. However, its main flaw is that it normally needs leverage, due to high weighting of securities with relatively low expected return (such as govies).

The investment spectrum

The investment spectrum describes the array of different strategies, ranging from passive index trackers, through enhanced indexing and smart beta strategies (hybrids), to active funds.[13]

In **enhanced indexing** strategies, fund managers take a relatively low tracking error, aiming to add a relatively small alpha. Usually, it should come with lower fees relative to full-blown active funds. Fee level should be proportional to the level of expected alpha.

By blending investments from across the investment spectrum, control your portfolio's overall fee, diversify different management styles and align your investments with your investment strategy.

Relative versus absolute return strategies

Relative funds aim to beat an index. Its performance determines a significant portion of their performance. The fund manager aims to add alpha, usually with a tracking error constraint against the benchmark. When paying for these funds, you are paying for both beta and alpha. However, you can get beta return cheaper through index tracking.

Absolute return funds are normally benchmark-agnostic. They target a return irrelevant to any index. These strategies can target investment objectives that better fit yours. Increasingly popular, they offer lowly correlated returns with equity and bond markets, which make the majority of most portfolios.

Whilst they may offer more alpha than beta, many funds still rely on beta returns. However, most, absolute return strategies' performance should depend more on manager's skill than on market returns.

When a fund does not follow a benchmark, classifying it in your portfolio is challenging. For example, a market neutral long/short equity fund may have a distinctly different return from that of the equity market. Putting such a fund under equities in line with your SAA may be mismatching. You are investing in a manager's skill, not in the equity market.

Managers of relative and absolute strategies have different perspectives on risk. Stating the obvious, relative managers focus on relative risk, whilst absolute managers focus on absolute risk.

For example, when expecting an equity market crash, relative managers may hold more cash (usually up to a 10% maximum in long-only funds) and invest in defensive stocks. But they will not increase tracking error with the index beyond their limit. They aim to outperform the index when it falls, not avoid the fall.

Absolute managers, on the other hand, may move big portions of the portfolio to cash and bonds to protect the downside, as well as buy downside risk protection instruments, such as put options. They do not have a tracking error, limiting them when aiming to manage downside risk. They want to avoid or mitigate the fall. But this means that if they get it wrong, they might lag the equity market.

Absolute versus target return

Absolute return often refers to strategies aiming to generate a positive return every year, independent of market conditions. For example, even when the FTSE 100 Index falls by 10% in a year, an absolute return strategy still targets a positive return.

This sounds wonderful. However, such absolute return strategies depend entirely on a fund manager's skill, they are typically expensive and they might not achieve their goals.

A target (total) return strategy usually aims to deliver a certain return but over a number of years, such as three to five years, typically reflecting a full economic cycle. Such a strategy does not aim to deliver a positive return every year.

The two types of strategies require a different mindset from managers. Absolute return typically uses derivatives, leverage to amplify small profits and high frequency trading. Based mostly on relative (pair) trades, it uses long/short positions to neutralise some of the beta exposure to market movements.

Target return typically uses physical investments (not solely derivatives), leverage is less common, and its trading frequency is not as high as that of absolute return. It can have more exposure to market returns.

Do it yourself or multi-asset funds

Another choice is between single asset class funds, investing in equities, bonds or alternatives, and multi-asset funds, investing in a blend of asset classes.

A substitute to designing your own investment strategy or changing it based on different phases of your life cycle, is investing in Diversified Growth Funds (DGFs) or target date funds (TDFs). You outsource your portfolio's management to an external fund manager.

Most DGFs are dynamic multi-asset funds, targeting a return broadly in line with your investment objectives, such as cash +4%. They can come with different names than DGF, but the principle is similar. You can control the DGF's return and risk by blending it with cash, bonds and equities.

For example, reduce the return and risk of a DGF with an objective of cash +5% to cash +3% by allocating 60% to the DGF and 40% to cash. The expected return of the mix is cash +3%.[14]

Blend a number of DGFs to control their overall return and fees, as well as diversifying manager risk.

DGFs could be a viable choice. Nevertheless, even when using DGFs, plan for your retirement and dynamically control the blend of DGFs according to your changing investment needs.

Mostly common in the USA, **target date funds (lifestyle funds)** basically aim to do the dynamic investment strategy for you throughout the different phases of your journey to retirement.[15]

Each set of funds has a target retirement year. You should invest in a fund whose target date is close to your retirement. Most funds invest in growth assets during the growth stage. Then, they gradually and automatically move to a mix of gilts, inflation-linked gilts and cash, assuming investors buy an annuity and take a 25% cash lump sum when retiring. Effectively, you outsource managing your glide path to the fund.

With pension freedom, lifestyle funds need adapting, as more people are likely to retire in stages, continuing to invest after retirement.

The main advantage is simplicity. You do not need to do anything; a professional manager is doing everything for you. You buy a single fund and that is it.

The main disadvantages are that the fund may not match your particular needs; the fund lacks flexibility and it does not adapt to changes in your circumstances (such as deciding to postpone retirement); the glide path is automatic (without considering market conditions); fees may be toppy; and manager risk – you hand over your financial future to a single manager. If you invest in TDFs, diversify across a number of funds from different providers.

Information on funds

After deciding which types of funds to use (active, trackers and so forth), the next step is gathering information to select funds within chosen types.

Two online sources with free information on funds are:

1   The Investment Association (IA) at **www.theinvestmentassociation.org**.
2   Morningstar at **www.morningstar.co.uk**.

The IA categorises funds in **IA Sectors**, principally according to the assets in which each fund invests, as well as geographic focus. Some sectors emphasise investment strategies. The sectors are helpful to compare funds. For example, you can screen funds by UK Smaller Companies, Global Emerging Markets Bond or Mixed Investment 40–85% Shares.

Morningstar lets you search funds according to criteria, including asset class (Broad Category), IA Sector, Morningstar Rating and Morningstar Analyst Rating.[16,17] For each fund you can view a report, showing performance, key stats and a basic Morningstar analyst report. Register for free for access.

These online resources make it easier to analyse and select funds. In addition, you can readily download each fund's factsheet, which summarises key information on the fund.

Fund selection based on past performance

When selecting funds, selectors often tend to focus solely on past performance, choosing funds with good recent results. This approach has two concerns.

First, understand the performance. Differentiate between the underlying index's performance (manager's style) and the manager's added value. Check whether relative performance was due to security selection or the manager's style being in or out of favour.

For example, a manager with a value style tilt can show strong performance when value outperforms, not because of skill in selecting securities. The manager might have been lucky, not smart.

The second concern of basing selection on past performance is that performance is in the past. You buy a fund today because you believe it will outperform in the future. Past performance is not, necessarily, indicative of future results.

Grounding decisions on past returns is backward looking, not forward looking.

When selecting managers, try to qualitatively understand how they manage money to ascertain whether past performance is likely be repeated in the future. This is not a simple task.

Being pragmatic, it is more undemanding to focus on past performance when selecting funds than to conduct a full-blown manager due diligence. It is relatively easy and does not require extensive research.

When selecting a fund, it should have:

1   A long-term record of outperforming the benchmark (over 3 and 5 years).
2   A recent short-term record of outperformance (last 12 months).
3   An incumbent manager who has been managing it for a number of years.
4   A top-quality Morningstar rating of 4/5 stars and gold/silver/bronze.

A fund meeting these criteria is most likely a good, best-of-breed fund. Plan to hold it for the long term (5–10 years), allowing its manager time to generate superior returns.

Due diligence process – 6P

When choosing active funds, the 6P due diligence process ensures you consider all relevant angles. Some Ps are also relevant when choosing trackers.

The process goes over all the qualitative and quantitative factors to consider, namely:

1 Platform.

2 People.

3 Philosophy.

4 Process.

5 Portfolio.

6 Performance.

Platform

Platform refers to the organisation (asset management firm) offering the fund. It considers the reputation of the organisation, its size, track record, domicile, resources, depth and breadth of experience (investment teams and operational staff), compensation structure and client base.

Since you are not a full-time manager selector, limit your choice to well-known trustworthy firms. Identifying niche players, which may have interesting potential, is demanding, requiring considerable research. It is safer to select top-tier, renewed asset managers. Check their website for information, including assets under management (AUM). Firms managing over £100 billion are quite large. Consider their funds' performance. If they offer a range of funds across different asset classes with good performance, it indicates the firm is successful.

People

People are the fund managers and support teams. When entrusting your money to people, you need to trust them. Every fund, whether it is based on a fundamental judgemental or a quantitative process, depends on people.

Search for good or bad news concerning fund managers. Choosing seasoned fund managers with a proven track record and reputation is prudent when having limited capacity to research the team. A risk with a star fund manager is a key person risk. If the star leaves, the fund is in jeopardy.

Ensure the fund manager has been managing the fund for a while. Unless it is a truly team-based process, confirm the fund's track record belongs to the current manager.

Philosophy

Philosophy is the manager's beliefs on how value is added. Do you buy into the philosophy?

Managers have different approaches to adding value. Some believe in **fundamental analysis**, calculating the intrinsic value of securities and buying or selling when value deviates substantially from price. These managers invest in research, analyse financial reports and industry trends and meet managements of companies.

Believing markets are not entirely efficient, they think they can take advantage of mispriced securities. Often, they use judgement, intuition and subjective gut feeling.

Some 'fundamental' managers base their 'research' on tips from brokers and relative valuations, such as P/Es – hardly fundamental and hardly research.

Some managers use **technical analysis**. Typically, it is used in conjunction with other philosophies, mostly to time trades, rather than as the sole rationale for decisions.

Others use **quantitative analysis** aiming to identify market trends, arbitrage opportunities or mispriced securities relative to valuation models. These managers do not meet companies' management. They use computer programs, algorithms and technology to analyse data (increasingly **big data**) to generate trades.

If a quant model works, it is marvellous. However, one weakness is that quant models rely on historical patterns. They may fail to forecast changes in behaviours or inflection points.

Some managers believe in top-down asset or sector allocation, whilst others believe in bottom-up security selection. Some focus on the short term, frequently changing their portfolios, whilst others adhere to long-term buy-and-hold. Some believe in value, whilst others believe in growth or momentum. Some believe in cost-cutting passive management, whilst others believe in active management.

There is no right or wrong philosophy. The question is whether the manager can consistently add value by using it.

What is your philosophy?

Process

Process is the framework and steps of managing the fund. A good process helps delivering repeatable and predictable results. Normally, process goes through the following broad stages:

1   Establishing investment objectives.

2   Setting a philosophy and an investment strategy to achieve the objectives.

3   Implementing the strategy by selecting investments and constructing a portfolio.

4   Ongoing monitoring of risk and performance.

Not being a full-time manager selector, you will not meet managers, questioning their philosophy and process. The process' highlights may be available in the fund's marketing materials (fact sheet, brochures). However, it would be difficult for you to scrutinise it.

Portfolio

Portfolio is the fund's characteristics.

The fund's holdings should match the manager's philosophy and process. Most funds publish at least their top 10 holdings. Assess whether the fund holds what it is supposed to.

Consider fund size. Small funds with AUM below £100 million might be too small and doubtful as a viable, ongoing business. Huge funds with AUM above a number of billions may run into capacity issues. The fund should be not too small and not too big.

Portfolio also covers product characteristics, such as investment vehicle, fees and costs. These topics will be covered in depth in the next chapter.

Performance

Whilst you should not base your selection solely on performance, it is essential. You want managers who demonstrated they could add value.

Bad recent performance of a manager with a long good track record may be a buying opportunity. Perhaps going through a bad patch, the manager can recover.

Try to understand the reasons for performance and whether it matches the philosophy and process. Professional manager selectors comprehensively analyse performance. They have tools to break it down to its drivers, checking whether it is in line with the manager's style.

For example, performance can be due to continuous excess risk taking, enhancing performance as long as markets perform well (**fair-weather investing**). This is not skill. It is luck that will run out when markets turn around.

If performance of a manager who claims to be a bottom-up security selector is explained by top-down sector rotation, for instance, then it does not match the manager's claims. It is not enough that performance is good or bad. How it was generated is critical.

De-selection

De-selection is the process of selling funds you own.

Fund due diligence is not only an initial step, but also it is ongoing. After selecting a fund, monitor its performance and other factors, ensuring it delivers and no material changes warrant a review. The time may come to deselect or switch funds.

Observe fund performance. However, do not be trigger happy, switching funds lightly. It may involve costs (transaction costs, switching costs) as well as time and effort choosing new funds.

A disappointing performance over a couple of months should not be a sole reason to switch a fund, unless it is an abrupt, severe underperformance without an explanation. Performance should be evaluated over the medium term (1–5 years). If it is consistently bad, consider switching.

Material changes, such as a manager leaving, might be an argument to contemplate de-selection. Use judgement and common sense to ascertain if the changes compromise your conviction in the fund's ability to perform in the future.

Monitor market conditions, ensuring they still support your fund selection. For example, if you chose a defensive fund since your market view was negative, you may want to switch to an aggressive fund if market dynamics improve.

If in serious doubt about a fund, sell it. Do not let behavioural biases, such as affinity to funds you own, deter you from selling for good reasons. They are not your funds. You hold them to make money – have no emotional attachment.

Summary

- Funds have several advantages over individual securities. Unless you are willing to make the effort and skilful in selecting securities, use funds. Funds charge fees, but you gain diversification, lower transaction costs and professional fund management.

- Active funds can add alpha. However, they are more expensive than trackers and they come with manager risk. Consider active if you commit to select and monitor and possess selection skills. Trackers are cheaper than active and manager risk is low. However, they do not add alpha.

- The investment spectrum includes funds ranging from passive, through enhanced indexing and smart beta, to active. Use funds from across the spectrum.

- Past performance is important but it is in the past and may not repeat in the future. The key is selecting funds that are likely to perform going forward.

Qualitatively assess funds and managers, following the 6P due diligence process – platform, people, philosophy, process, portfolio and performance.

- Deselecting funds should be based on long bad performance and/or by qualitative rationale, such as a fund manager leaving the firm.

Notes

1 4% = £20 ÷ £500.

2 If the minimum dealing charge still applies, consider accumulating larger sums before investing to reduce the number of transactions.

3 Portfolio turnover is calculated by dividing the lesser of values of purchases and sales by the fund's net asset value (NAV), typically over one year. The ratio loosely indicates the percentage of the portfolio's holdings that have been changed. Portfolio turnover can generate taxes. Stamp duty can be charged when buying securities and CGT can be charged when selling securities at a profit.

4 A number of academics claim that, on average, active managers underperform. See Burton Malkiel (1973), Charles Ellis (1975) and William Sharpe (1991).

5 Cross sectional volatility measures the variation or dispersion across returns of securities at one specific time. Standard deviation, on the other hand, measures volatility of returns over time. $\sigma_{CS} = \sqrt{\left[\Sigma(r_i - r_m)^2 \div n\right]}$ where r_i is return of all n assets i at time t and r_m is average market return at time t.

6 The Fundamental Law of Active Management was developed by Richard Grinold. $IR = IC\sqrt{BR}$; where IR is information ratio, IC is information coefficient and $\sqrt{BR}$ is square root of breadth.

7 Counterparty risk is the risk of each party to a contract that the other party – the counterparty – will breach the contract. Swaps are over-the-counter (OTC) derivatives, which are contracts between parties. Counterparty risk is similar to default risk.

8 Securities lending involves loaning securities to other investors or firms for a fee. The borrower posts collateral with the lender to reduce the risk of not returning the securities and paying the fee. Securities lending is important for short selling.

9 25% = £10 million ÷ (£10 million + £30 million); 75% = £30 million ÷ (£10 million + £30 million). A price-weighted index will have 40% in stock A and 60% in stock B. An equally weighted index will have 50% in stock A and 50% in stock B.

10 The top sector weights in the FTSE 100 Index are banks 14%, oil & gas 14%, personal & household goods 11%, healthcare 9%, basic resources 7%, insurance 7% and industrial goods & services 6%.

11 The definitions of smart beta vary. Some define smart beta as a weighting scheme different from market-cap. They exclude exposure to rewarded risks from smart beta. Systematic exposure to rewarded risks often is called alternative beta or risk premia.

12 The tendency of low-beta stocks to outperform is an anomaly since, according to finance theory, high-beta stocks should outperform.

13 Enhanced indexing and smart beta strategies are called hybrids since they mix the characteristics of passive index trackers and active funds.

14 Cash + 3% = 60% (Cash + 5%) + 40% (Cash).

15 Some workplace pension schemes use lifestyle funds or a mix of DGFs and TDFs as the default choice – you might be invested in one without knowing it.

16 Morningstar's star rating assigns one to five stars to funds. It measures how well a fund has balanced risk and reward relative to its peers. Keep in mind that fund star ratings are strictly returns-based and do not take into account fund fundamentals, such as manager changes.

17 Morningstar's analyst rating assigns gold, silver, bronze, neutral and negative rating to funds. It is a qualitative, independent view on funds, considering five key areas for each fund: People, Parent, Process, Price and Performance.

CHAPTER 20
INVESTMENT VEHICLES
Platform and funds

'If I had asked people what they wanted, they would have said faster horses.'

Henry Ford

Investment vehicles are the actual investment products that you buy for your portfolio. When choosing funds, the different acronyms are not always clear – OEIC, ICVC, CIS, NAV, ACD, UCITS, NURS, SICAV, ETF, CEF, KIID. It all sounds a perplexing gibberish. However, the choice of investment vehicle can impact results.

We will try to clarify it all.

Your platform

The universe of investment products from which you can select is part of the platform that you use. Your ISAs and pensions may be part of a platform.

A **fund platform** is an online service, allowing financial advisers to manage their customers' investment portfolios. Customers can directly use some platforms. They often offer ISAs, SIPPs, life insurance products, funds, securities and financial instruments. You can manage your entire portfolio, including personal pension and ISAs, using a platform.

Some platforms offer tools for investment profiling and planning, as well as model portfolios or a **guided architecture** service. The latter directs advisers and customers to funds managed by chosen managers, allowing access to a limited, albeit sometimes large, number of funds, rather than the whole of the market.

Open architecture allows advisers and customers to buy funds managed by different fund managers on a single platform. It can give access to the entire range of funds on the market.

There are two types of platforms. **Whole of market** platforms (sometimes called **wraps**) offer access to a wide range of investments, potentially covering all the funds offered in the UK. Financial advisers commonly use them.

The second type of platform is a **fund supermarket**, offering a narrower range of products than a wrap. Fund supermarkets usually offer a simple, online access and are commonly used directly by customers.

Compare charges, features and choices of different platforms. Use a SIPP to actively manage your portfolio. If you are not active, a simpler, potentially cheaper choice, such as a stakeholder pension, can suffice. However, not all SIPPs are necessarily more expensive than stakeholder pensions.

Platform fee (often called **service fee**) is about 0.25% per year. Check switching charges levied on changing funds. Some platforms offer unlimited switching, others give you a free annual allowance (such as five switches) and charge you on switching funds above it.

The platform is your system to manage your portfolio. The look and feel of its website should fit your style and needs. Have a trial run before choosing. It is like test-driving a car before buying it.

Investment vehicles

OEICs

In plain English, an OEIC is a UK fund. You buy shares in the fund, which has many shareholders. It invests their money collectively in securities and investments. Your shares represent your proportional claim to the fund's assets. When their value appreciates, share price rises accordingly. It falls when fund's assets depreciate.

In not-so-plain English, an **open-ended investment company** (OEIC) or **investment company with variable capital** (ICVC) is an open-ended collective investment scheme (CIS) incorporated in the UK.

The fund is equitably divided into shares whose price varies in direct proportion with the value of the fund's **net asset value** (NAV).[1] OEICs normally have one director (manager of the fund), which is an authorised company, referred to as the **Authorised Corporate Director** (ACD). The ACD appoints the investment manager.

An **open-ended fund** means the OEIC creates new shares when money is invested and redeems shares when money is divested. Investors buy shares from the fund and sell shares to it, rather than trading with other shareholders. The supply and demand of shares does not affect share price, which reflects the NAV. Open-ended funds are normally priced once a day.

OEICs have a single price for buying and selling shares (no bid-ask spread).

UCITS

UCITS stands for **Undertakings for the Collective Investment of Transferable Securities**. It's a directive of the European Union, aiming to allow funds to operate freely throughout the EU on the basis of a single authorisation from one member state (passporting).

For example, a French authorised fund complying with UCITS regulations can be marketed to retail investors across member states in the EU, such as the UK and Germany, without full authorisation in each state.

UCITS restricts compliant funds on the types of permitted investments they can hold (such as no direct property and commodities), on concentrations (ensuring diversification) and on leverage and transparency.

NURS

Non-UCITS Retail Scheme (NURS) is a UK fund that is not compliant with UCITS regulations. NURS funds comply with FCA's rules and regulations. NURS can invest in a wider range of eligible investments and has more flexibility than UCITS.

It should not matter to you whether you buy UCITS or NURS funds. Both are regulated.

Offshore funds (SICAV)

Offshore funds are incorporated outside the UK. One common type is a SICAV, which, in French, stands for an investment company with variable capital (similar to an OEIC). Often, offshore funds are incorporated in Luxembourg or Ireland.

Reporting fund status

When investing in offshore funds outside of a tax-efficient wrapper (pension and ISAs), check whether they have successfully applied to HMRC for **reporting fund status**. It should be stated on the fund's fact sheet.

For UK resident-investors, disposal of such investments is treated as a capital gain, subject to a 20% maximum tax rate. Disposal of non-reporting funds might be taxable as income, subject to a 45% maximum tax rate.

Reporting fund status can be critical from a tax perspective. However, when investing in funds in a pension or ISA, you are exempt from tax anyway.

ETFs

An **exchange-traded fund** (ETF) is traded on a stock exchange. Most ETFs aim to track the performance of an underlying index. ETFs use different methods to replicate the index's performance, such as full replication, statistical stratified sampling replication and synthetic replication. Each technique has benefits and risks.

One risk of ETFs is tracking error with respect of the index. **Full replication** (holding all securities in the index) minimises tracking error, but might be costly. **Statistical replication** (holding a subset of securities in the index) balances tracking error and transaction cost reduction. Costs and fees are an important factor and one of the potential appeals of ETFs over other investments.[2]

ETFs come with a number of advantages since they are traded on the exchange. They are priced and traded throughout the day and you can short them. They behave like listed securities. However, this flexibility comes with a cost. Unless you are a day trader, you are unlikely to take advantage of these features.[3]

Index tracker funds (such as OEICs) price once a day and you cannot short them. However, if your investment horizon is longer than a few weeks, index-tracking funds may be cheaper than ETFs. Nevertheless, the fees of some core ETFs (such as those tracking the S&P 500 Index and FTSE 100 Index) have come down materially over recent years, making them more attractive.

Unit trusts

A unit trust is an open-ended fund constituted under a trust deed. Units in a unit trust have different purchase (**ask**) and sell (**bid**) price. This difference is called **bid-ask spread**. It varies depending on the liquidity of assets in which the unit trust invests.

The trend in recent years is to move from unit trusts to OEICs. OEICs are a simpler structure that can be sold across Europe when UCITS compliant.

Investment trusts

An investment trust is a closed-end fund, common mostly in the UK, incorporated as a company and normally listed on a stock exchange.

A **closed-end fund** (CEF) issues a fixed number of shares through an IPO. No new shares are created to meet investors' demand. Rather, shares are traded in the market between buyers and sellers. Therefore, unlike open-ended funds, supply and demand impact share price, which can diverge from NAV.

When share price is above NAV, it is traded at a **premium**. When it is below NAV, it is traded at a **discount**. The premium and discount can be a source of volatility in share price.

Check the liquidity of investment trusts (average value of shares traded per day). Lacking demand for their shares, price can plunge, as a discount to NAV can be created or can widen. Buying an investment trust at discount may appear a bargain. However, poor demand can drive a discount to further expand.

Pay attention to the bid-ask spread. For example, when buying an investment trust, the bid price could be £105 – that is what you pay for every share. The ask price could be £100 – that is what you get when selling shares. In this case, when buying and selling, you lose 5%.

Be careful when buying CEFs. They can exhibit equity-like volatility as they are priced throughout the day and listed on the exchange. When they are traded at a premium, you can lose if the premium shrinks. Many investment trusts use leverage, augmenting volatility.

Investment trusts often have higher fees than OEICs and their fee structure is more opaque.

One advantage of investment trusts for their managers is that they can benefit from a long investment horizon. The money remains in the investment trust, as managers do not need to redeem shares. This could be advantageous when investing in illiquid assets, such as property, private equity and infrastructure.

Unit-linked funds

Unit-linked funds (insured funds) are linked to plans issued by insurance companies (such as investment bonds and endowment policies), allowing policyholders to invest in funds. Similar to OEICs, policyholders buy units in funds and their price depends on NAV.[4]

KIID

Key Investor Information Document (KIID) is a short document with key facts and figures about a fund. It has a standard layout describing what the fund does, its investment risks, charges and performance. Regulations require every investor to receive a KIID before investing in a fund in an ISA, for example, but not in a pension.[5]

Fees and costs

Welcome to the magnificent world of fees and costs. Often, fees and costs are misleading, due to jargon, inclusion and exclusion of some costs and hidden fees.

AMC

Annual Management Charge (AMC) is the management fee the fund manager charges. The AMC's level depends on the asset class (higher for equities, lower for bonds), the management style (higher for active, lower for passive) and the asset management firm's reputation. AMC normally ranges between 0.40% and 0.75%, but can be lower or higher.

AMC is an ongoing charge.[6] It is an annual per cent deducted from the assets you invest in the fund. For example, an AMC of 0.50% means every year 0.50% is deducted from the fund's performance. It is taken from income that the fund generates or from its capital (assets).

AMC compensates the manager for professional asset management services, including expertise, research and daily fund management. It is charged at the same rate, whether the fund performed well or poorly.

TER

Total Expense Ratio (TER) supposedly measures the fund's total costs.[7] It includes AMC and additional costs, such as custodian fees, legal fees, auditor fees and other operational expenses.

TER does not include transaction costs, due to trading securities and financial instruments. Transaction costs average about 0.40% per year for an active fund and

0.10% for an index tracker, depending on asset class and investment style.[8] Transaction costs come out of performance.

When investing in funds, look at TER, not AMC. TER better represents how much you will pay for the fund each year. For example, a fund with an AMC of 0.55% and TER of 0.75% means your net performance will be lower by about 0.75% than gross performance.

When investing in an ETF with a 0.50% TER, for example, expect it to lag the index by 0.50% per year. This number can be higher or lower due to the ETF's tracking error and potential benefits from securities lending.

OCF

Ongoing Charge Figure (OCF) is close to TER. Its name better describes what it represents than TER – recurring charges.

One-off charges

Initial charges (**front load**) are deducted when investing in a fund. The majority of an initial charge is paid to cover administrative and marketing costs, such as commission to the adviser who sells the fund. Your adviser may refund some or all of the initial charge as a rebate.

This means, for example, that when investing £1,000 in a fund with an initial charge of 5%, you are left with only £950 invested in the fund. You immediately 'lost' 5%. Avoid investing in funds with a high initial charge.

When shopping around for pensions and ISAs, check there are no front loads. It is silly to 'lose' 5% before you start investing.

Some funds have an exit charge (**back load**). Avoid investing in funds with back load. It is the same principle as front load – instead of ripping you off when entering; you are ripped off when exiting.

An **exit penalty** is a charge levied when redeeming a fund within a certain time since buying it. This could make sense to protect the interests of the fund manager and other investors when funds invest in illiquid investments or to deter short-term investors from buying and selling funds repeatedly, disrupting performance.

Dilution levy

Dilution levy (or the similar **swing pricing**) is an adjustment made to the fund's share price, reflecting transaction costs resulting from inflows and outflows. It is intended to protect existing shareholders against the adverse performance impact of new or leaving investors. The dilution levy's magnitude depends on the asset class, fund's AUM and size of inflow or outflow.

For example, when buying shares in a fund investing in high yield bonds, the manager needs to spend the cash to buy securities. This involves transaction costs. The dilution levy reflects the transaction costs in the share price of the new investor, who is the only one bearing them, without unfairly affecting other shareholders.

As a relatively small investor, when investing in large funds (with AUM above £100 million), your dilution levy should be minor. This is one reason to invest in funds with decent AUM – size matters.

Performance fees

Performance fees reward fund managers for superior returns. They are normally charged on performance in excess of a benchmark or a hurdle.

For example, hedge funds historically followed a model of 2 and 20, meaning 2% ongoing charge on assets and 20% performance fee. Say the benchmark is Libor +4% and the fund returned 6% when Libor was 1%. Outperformance is 1%, so you pay 0.20% performance fee, leaving 0.80% net outperformance.[9] Ongoing charge is 2%, leaving an overall net return of 3.8%.[10] That is 2.2% below the 6% gross return. A 2.2% fee is expensive on a 6% return.

The performance fees' objective is better aligning interests of managers with those of investors. With an ongoing charge on assets, managers are financially incentivised to accumulate assets. With a performance fee, managers are incentivised to maximise returns.

However, a performance fee might cause conflict of interest and managers to take excessive risks or low risks. This is known as a **principal-agent problem**.

When underperforming the benchmark, a performance fee is unlikely and managers might lose their job. They might take disproportionate risks. If materially enhancing returns, they may still be awarded a performance fee and save their job. If failing, they were doomed to fail anyway.

When having good performance before year-end, managers might de-risk the fund. With low risk they will lock in the performance fee. If taking risk and underperforming, they might lose the performance fee. Why risk it?

Managers (the agents) in these cases do not keep the interests of investors (the principals). The principal wants the agent to continue taking a risk level as per the mandate and market conditions, without changing it due to compensation. Agents exploit their information advantage as it is challenging for principals – especially small ones, to monitor the agents' actions and motives.[11]

High water mark is often used to ensure managers are not rewarded a performance fee for poor performance. They are paid a performance fee only if the fund's value is above its highest peak. Some funds do not have a high water mark. Their managers can earn a performance fee even when not surpassing previous highs.

For example, say NAV is £120 at the beginning of the year. The fund lost £20 in the first year, reaching £100. In the second year, the fund gains £10, reaching £110. The manager does not get a performance fee for the second year, even though performance was positive. The fund is still below its peak. Only after the fund exceeds £120 again – the high water mark – can the performance fee kick in.

Stamp duty

When buying shares you pay a 0.50% stamp duty (called **stamp duty reserve tax** – SDRT). It applies to buying UK stocks, ETFs, REITs and investment trusts, as they are all traded on the stock exchange.

Buying OEICs and unit trusts is exempt from stamp duty.

Total costs and regulatory pressure on costs

On average, for an active fund you pay a 0.25% platform fee, 0.75% TER and 0.40% transaction costs. That is 1.40% in total. It means an active fund needs to generate a return of 1.40% just to perform in line with a passive index. This does not include switching fees, one-off charges and a performance fee.

And it used to be even worse.

The **Retail Distribution Review** (RDR) is a set of UK rules aimed at introducing more transparency and fairness to the investment industry. The most significant change is that financial advisers are no longer permitted to earn trail commissions and rebates from fund companies in return for selling or recommending their investment products. Instead, customers now have to agree fees with advisers upfront.

Some of these commissions used to be implicit costs, meaning they were not disclosed to customers. Post RDR, platform and adviser's fees are explicit and must be disclosed.[12] Ask for a full breakdown of all charges when buying funds – everything including everything.

New regulations put a charge cap on default funds in DC schemes.[13] Such regulations, the intense competition in the fund management industry and the scrutiny on costs continue to put downward pressure on charges. This is good news, as long as it does not compromise quality.

Take advantage of these developments; shop around, comparing platforms before opening ISAs and pensions. If you have a large portfolio, you can negotiate your fees. Save precious money.

Share classes

Funds typically come with a number of share classes. Different classes have different features, such as fees, currency and distribution of income.

Check fund factsheets for fees of each share class. Pay close attention to front load, back load and TER/OCF.

Two typical types of share classes are **accumulation** (Acc), where income is reinvested without a reinvesting charge, and **income** (Inc), where income is paid to shareholders. Choose Acc, unless you need income from your portfolio (such as after retirement).

Different share classes can be denominated in different currencies, where currency risk is not mitigated, or **hedged** to a currency (called hedged or currency-hedged) where currency risk is mitigated.[14] When buying a fund investing in overseas assets, pay attention to whether the share class is hedged or unhedged.

Summary

- Investment vehicles are the actual investment products or funds that you buy in your portfolio.
- Understand what charges and costs include and exclude and try to avoid a pension and ISA platform charging entry and exit fees on funds.

Notes

1 The fund's assets or pool of investments are known as the scheme property.

2 Counterparty risk is another risk of ETFs when synthetic replication uses OTC derivatives.

3 Shorting ETFs is not always easy since you need to borrow them to short them. Going short is much easier using futures contracts.

4 **With-profits** funds are a type of CIS offered by insurance companies. Whilst they were popular in the past, they fell out of favour due to poor performance, exit penalties and opaque charges.

5 Each regulated fund produces a **prospectus** that needs to be filed with the regulator. The prospectus contains information about the fund and is normally available online.

6 All regulated funds in states in the European Economic Area disclose ongoing charges, which include the **Fund Management Fee** (FMF). FMF covers investment management, accounting, valuation and management costs; trustee/depositary fees and expenses; audit, custodian, regulator and registrar fees; and payments to legal and professional advisers.

7 TER is calculated by dividing the total costs by the NAV. TER = Total fund costs $\div$ NAV.

8 Simple average of funds in the UK All Companies sector of the Investment Association (IA). The precise averages are 0.39% for active funds and 0.09% for trackers. IA publishes papers on fund management charges, investment costs and performance. Check **www.theinvestmentassociation.org**.

9 $0.20\% = 20\% \times 1\%$.

10 $3.8\% = 6\% - 2\%$ ongoing charge $- 0.20\%$ performance fee.

11 In contract law and economics, information asymmetry is when one party has more or better information than the other. This creates an imbalance of power in transactions.

12 **Bundled share classes** include in their price fund manager rebates, supporting platform cost and adviser's commission. **Unbundled** or **clean share classes** are designed to have a more transparent pricing. Their AMC is lower since they do not include platform cost and adviser's commission.

13 The government introduced a cap on member charges of 0.75% on default funds available in DC pension schemes to comply with the automatic enrolment legislation.

14 Institutional share classes are labelled as I. They have larger minimums and lower fees compared to retail classes and they are designed for large investors. Retail share classes are labelled as R. They have lower minimums and higher fees than I shares.

CHAPTER 21
MANAGING YOUR PORTFOLIO
Putting it all together

'There is a difference between knowing the path and walking the path.'

Morpheus

Top-down you have allocated your assets and, from the bottom up, you have selected the underlying investments for your portfolio. Now you need to marry these two opposite perspectives together into a coherent portfolio.

Portfolio construction does that. It involves deciding how much to allocate to each underlying investment, ensuring your portfolio is efficiently aligned with your investment strategy.

In this chapter we review portfolio construction and implementation. We cover the steps to transfer your investment strategy and fund selection from a theoretical exercise into an actual portfolio and its ongoing maintenance.

Three budgets

When managing your portfolio consider three budgets and how much to spend on each:

1   Risk budget.
2   Fee budget.
3   Governance budget.

Your decision impacts your investment outcome and the amount of time and money you will spend managing your portfolio.

Risk budget

Risk budget is your portfolio's maximum risk level. It is a function of your risk tolerance, dynamic investment strategy and market conditions.

Absolute risk derives a portfolio's absolute return. The risk level should match your risk tolerance and the required return for achieving your objectives. As your risk tolerance and investment strategy change throughout the phases of your life cycle, so does your portfolio's absolute risk level.

Absolute risk is also a function of market conditions. When you are concerned that markets are fragile, reduce it. When believing markets will rise, increase it.

Relative risk refers to deviations between returns of funds and their passive benchmarks. On a portfolio's aggregated level, relative risk measures the deviations between portfolio returns and SAA.

From the SAA, construct a **composite benchmark**. It blends indices representing each asset class with SAA weights. For example, the composite benchmark of a 60% UK equity and 40% bond SAA could be 60% FTSE 100 Index and 40% FTSE Actuaries UK Conventional Gilts All Stocks Index.

Your portfolio's performance is expected to deviate from that of SAA because of active asset allocation, security selection, costs and other discrepancies between a theoretical SAA and actual portfolio.

Control relative risk through magnitude of active asset allocation positions and fund selection. Larger deviations between SAA weights and those in your portfolio increase relative risk. Using more active funds, each with a relative risk with respect of its benchmark, also increases relative risk. Minimising deviations between SAA weights and active asset allocation and using more index trackers instead of active funds reduce your portfolio's relative risk.

Strike a balance between keeping close to your SAA and investment strategy, from one side, and aiming to add alpha through active asset allocation and security selection, from the other side. Deviating too much, you can end up with a mismatch between your portfolio and investment strategy. Not deviating, you can miss alpha opportunities.

Fee budget

Fee budget is how much money you are spending on your portfolio. Normally, you pay a fixed fee to your pension and ISA providers. Investments have different price tags based on their type.

Active funds are more expensive, but they can add excess return above benchmark. However, active funds can also underperform. Trackers are cheaper, but they add no alpha and market-cap indices can have some deficiencies.

Set your fee budget based on your platform's investment choices (availability of attractive funds may warrant a higher fee), your conviction in active funds' potential alpha and your required net of fee returns.

For example, assume your investment strategy is 50% equity and 50% bonds. Your equity expected return is 8% and that of bonds is 2%. This expected return is for asset classes, not considering costs and alpha. Your portfolio's *gross* expected return is 5%.[1]

Say you can choose:

(A) Active equity fund with 2% target alpha net of fees and 1% OCF.

(B) Equity tracker with 0.50% OCF.

(C) Active bond fund with 1% target alpha net of fees and 0.50% OCF.

(D) Bond tracker with 0.20% OCF.

If you have a high conviction that the active funds are likely to meet their return objectives, paying extra fees is worthwhile. The potential alpha is 1.5% for a 0.75% OCF.[2] Anyway, you must pay a 0.35% OCF for trackers, so you pay an incremental 0.40% for a potential 1.5% alpha.[3]

If you lack conviction in the ability of the funds to meet their target returns and you are concerned that alpha might be negative, go with trackers, paying 0.35% OCF.

If you do not want to spend more than 0.60% on fees, select your higher-conviction active fund and one tracker.

Governance budget

Time is money. Time is one of our scarcest resources. Governance budget is the amount of time you spend governing your portfolio. You may enjoy investing – spending your leisure time with your portfolio could be a pleasure. However, most people want to spend as little time as possible with their pension, in particular because you cannot use the money until retirement.

To minimise your governance budget, keep it as simple as possible. Leonardo da Vinci said that, 'Simplicity is the ultimate sophistication.' Simplicity does not necessarily mean you settle for a lower quality.

An extremely simple portfolio includes a single holding of a global or UK equity tracker. This 'buy and forget' investment strategy requires minimal monitoring.

However, it is not for the faint-hearted. It is volatile and lacks an active manager overlooking risks.

Buy-and-hold strategy involves formulating an asset allocation, buying investments and holding them statically. It needs planning and setting up at the onset. However, once the portfolio is in place, it is low maintenance. It requires a review every couple of years and when you switch phases in your life cycle, but not much more. It is light on governance.

Some savers dynamically change their asset allocation and often switch active funds. Such strategy is demanding on governance.

However, dynamic management is not always profitable. Changing your portfolio generates transaction costs and bad investment decisions can hurt performance.

The more sophisticated and opaque your portfolio, the more governance is needed. Unless you blindly trust fund managers to do a good job for you, monitor your investments. Saving for your financial future is too important to leave unmonitored.

Simple, governance-light, buy-and-hold strategies are appropriate for you if you are not actively managing your portfolio. Dynamic, governance-heavy strategies are appropriate if you are actively managing your portfolio.

Portfolio construction

We are looking to construct a portfolio as simply as possible. The objective is to minimise the demand on the three budgets of risk, fees and governance. One efficient portfolio construction methodology is core-satellite.

Core-satellite

A **core-satellite** divides your portfolio into core and satellite – no surprises there. The core is around 50% to 80% of the portfolio (depending on how much alpha you seek from active management), made of trackers aligned with the asset classes in your SAA. Some assets can be accessed only through active management even when they are part of the core, such as direct property.

For example, your SAA is 50% equity, 40% bonds and 10% cash. For the core you allocate 40% to equity trackers, 32% to bond trackers and 10% to cash.[4] Cash does not follow a core-satellite approach.

The core's relative risk is low since tracking error with the SAA composite benchmark is minimal. Fees of trackers are relatively cheap. The demand on governance is light, because you do not select and monitor active funds or sophisticated investments. The core has modest demands on the three budgets.

As for the satellite (10% equity and 8% bonds), make it punchy. Use high-conviction active funds, aiming to add alpha. These funds are riskier than trackers, more expensive and require selection and monitoring. They are demanding on the three budgets. However, they make less than 20% of the overall portfolio so risk, fees and governance are under control.

Implementation

The objectives of implementation are aligning as closely and efficiently as possible your actual portfolio with your target portfolio, minimising tracking error and transaction costs. The portfolio should reflect your target asset allocation (SAA and active allocation), as well as size allocations to your chosen funds.

A SIPP is the most flexible pension for implementation. It offers the widest selection of investments. However, since the menu on some DC platforms is limited, use your stocks and shares ISA to complement it. The choice of funds and ETFs in your ISA can be wider than that in your pension.

ETFs

When implementing TAA views, ETFs offer a number of advantages compared with actively managed funds. Typically, TAA expresses short-term views. Therefore, ETFs minimise transaction costs of buying and then selling funds. Trading ETFs is normally cheaper than trading active funds, since ETFs are more liquid.

When investing in active funds, plan to hold them for the long term, allowing fund managers sufficient time to generate alpha. Using active funds for TAA purposes does not make sense.

Constructing a portfolio

Table 21.1 shows an example of portfolio construction. The portfolio spans a pension and ISAs, it is divided between core and satellite and TAA is implemented using ETFs.

Your actual portfolio will not perfectly match your target portfolio. There are constraints, such as the amounts you can hold in your pension and ISAs, the choice of investments, minimum investment amounts and timing of cash flows. The best you can do is try to keep it as aligned as possible. It will not be perfect.

The number of active funds for each asset class depends on its allocation's size and styles of funds. Large allocation warrants manager and style diversification. If active UK equities are 20% of your portfolio, for example, consider splitting the allocation amongst two or three managers, ideally with complementary styles.

Table 21.1 Implementation

	Allocation %	Selection %	Implementation
Global equities	18	15	Core, tracker, in pension
		3	Satellite, active fund, in pension
European equities	5	5	TAA, ETF, in ISA
Emerging market equity	2	2	Core, tracker, in pension
Emerging Asia	5	5	TAA, ETF, in ISA
Total equity	**30**	**30**	
Gilts	28	22	Core, tracker, in pension
		6	Satellite, active fund, in pension
IG credit	12	10	Core, tracker, in pension
		2	Satellite, active fund, in pension
Global high yield	5	3	Active fund, in pension
		2	TAA, ETF, in ISA
EMD	5	3	Active fund, in pension
		2	TAA, ETF, in ISA
Total bonds	**50**	**50**	
Cash	**5**	**5**	**Cash ISA**
Property	10	5	Core, active fund, in pension
		5	TAA, active fund, in ISA
REITs	2.5	2.5	Core, tracker, in pension
Commodities	2.5	2.5	Core, tracker, in pension
Total alternatives	**15**	**15**	
Total	100	100	

Complementary styles mean investment approaches with different characteristics that should perform differently during different market conditions. For example: value/growth (50% value, 50% growth), large/SMID (small and mid) cap (80% large, 20% SMID) and aggressive/defensive.

Rotate the style allocation based on your views. For example, overweight value and SMID cap, as they tend to outperform growth and large cap over a full economic cycle. Split aggressive and defensive based on market conditions.

If the allocation to an asset class is low (such as up to 5%), use a single, high-conviction core manager. Core managers usually do not have a bias to any particular investment style, such as neither value nor growth.

Trade orders

When trading funds and financial instruments, you can use several types of orders. **Market order** instructs the broker to buy or sell at the best currently available price. **Limit order** is conditional. It is used to buy or sell at a specific price or better. Use market order when you want to fill the order at whatever price. Use limit order when price is more important than filling the order.

Stop loss order is triggered only when a specified price has been reached. Use it to limit the downside of positions (or to take profits) by automatically selling them at a predetermined price. The downside is that if price drops and then recovers you might miss the rebound.

Derivatives

Derivatives are not *financial weapons of mass destruction.* They might be notorious since they have been involved in some financial scandals, but it is not the derivatives' fault, but that of those who abuse them.[5]

Derivatives are a helpful financial tool, instrumental in efficiently managing portfolios. They are not for everyone. You need an intermediate or advanced knowledge in investments and portfolio management to use them.

The two fundamental derivatives are forward contracts (futures in their standardised form) and options. By combining them, sophisticated, complicated derivatives are created, often called **exotic**. However, our focus is on standard **plain vanilla** listed futures and options on indices.

Futures

Futures contract is an agreement between two parties to buy or sell an asset (underlying) for a price agreed today (futures price) but with payment and delivery at a future date (delivery date or contract maturity). Underlying assets include stocks, bonds, commodities and currencies. Maturities are often one or three months.[6]

Forward contracts were originally developed for hedging. For example, you are a farmer growing wheat. The harvest is next year. You can either wait until the harvest to sell the wheat at whatever the prevailing price or sell a forward contract obliging you to sell it next year for an agreed fixed price. With the forward, you lock in a price. If the wheat price falls, you do not lose. However, if the price jumps, you do not benefit. You hedged it. A farmer should focus on growing wheat, not gambling on its price.

Futures contracts are standardised forward contracts, traded on an exchange. When buying (going long) or selling (going short) a futures contract, each contract is written on a defined number of the underlying's units.

For example, you want to go long the FTSE 100 Index.[7] The futures contract written on the index has a £10 multiplier (unit of trading), meaning each contract is for £10 of the underlying index price (index point). The current FTSE 100 Index's price is 6,500.

The futures economic exposure $= n \times m \times p$.

Where n is the number of futures contracts, m is the multiplier and p is the underlying asset's price (spot price). In this case, each futures contract gives an exposure of £65,000 to the FTSE 100 Index.[8]

Futures are **unfunded**, meaning when buying or selling futures, you do not need to commit all the exposure. Rather, you deposit a margin with the exchange to mitigate counterparty risk.[9] The futures contract is marked-to-market daily. You add money to the margin when the futures position loses and receive money back when it gains.

In this example, the initial margin is 25%. You deposit £16,250.[10] Effectively, it is a synthetic leveraged position on the FTSE 100 Index – investing £16,250 to get a £65,000 exposure. If, the next day, the index falls 1%, you add £650 to the margin facility. If the index gains 1%, you receive back £650. The futures price moves almost in the same way as the spot price (without optionality, called **delta one**).

Futures price converges with the spot price as the contract approaches its expiry date. When the contract is close to expiry, you can either let it expire and cash settle it or roll it over to the next futures contract (closing or winding down the existing futures and buying a new one with a later maturity).[11]

When the futures curve is downward sloping (**backwardation**), the closer futures price is higher than next futures price. Rolling costs are positive – you close more expensive futures than the one you roll into. When the futures curve is upward sloping (**contango**), the closer futures price is lower than the next futures price. Rolling costs are negative – you close cheaper futures than the one you roll into.

Over recent years, futures trading and rolling costs have increased.[12] The annualised rolling costs of some futures on equity indices have soared from single digit basis points to 30 to 50 basis points. It is often cheaper to use ETFs. Whilst ETFs charge a TER and they are funded, they have no rolling costs.

Whether to use futures or ETFs depends on your holding period. Futures may be better for a short time (small number of rolls), whilst ETFs may be better for a longer time.

The advantages of futures are that it is easy to short them and they are liquid, unfunded and cost efficient. Also, since profit and loss are based on the underlying's price changes in local currency, your position has no currency exposure (although most futures are based on price return, not total return, so they returns exclude dividends).[13]

Options

Options give the right but not the obligation to buy (call option) or sell (put option) an asset for an agreed price (strike price) at (European option) or before (American option) a maturity date.

When buying an option, you pay a premium. If, at maturity, the option is '**in the money**' your profit is the option's **payoff** minus the premium.[14,15] If, at maturity, the option is '**out of the money**', it expires worthless, and you lose the premium.

The basic uses for options are bullish long call and bearish (protective) long put.

For example, the FTSE 100 Index is at a level of 6,500. You think it may rally above 7,000, but you are unsure and concerned it might fall. You buy a one-month call option on the FTSE 100 Index with a strike of 7,000 for a £200 premium.

If, indeed, the index rallies to 7,300, your payoff is £300 and your profit is £100.[16] If the index ends at a level of 6,900 after a month, your option expires worthless, and you lose the premium (your downside is limited to the premium).

Once again, the FTSE 100 Index is at 6,500. You hold equities in your portfolio and you are concerned the index might crash. You buy a one-month put option with a strike of 6,000 for £200. If the index falls to 5,500, your payoff is £500 and your profit is £300.[17] You insured some of your portfolio's downside.

The advantages of options are optionality, risking only the premium, leveraging your position by spending only the premium and going long volatility (option price depends on volatility so, when volatility rises, the option price rises as well).[18] The disadvantage is if an option expires worthless you can lose your entire premium.

This was only a high-level taste of derivatives.

Currency management

Global investing includes exposure to fluctuations in exchange rates between your home currency and foreign currencies. They can have a huge impact on returns measured in your base currency.

For example, you invest in an S&P 500 Index tracker. The index rises 10%. However, the British pound appreciates by 5% versus the US dollar. When translating the return from US dollars to pounds, it is about 5%, instead of 10%.[19]

Over the long term, currencies tend to oscillate around a certain level. When holding foreign investments for a long run, currency impact could wash out. However, currency movements can notably impact returns over the short and medium term.

When investing in equities or other risk assets, consider three options:

1   Keeping the foreign currency exposure.
2   Buying funds' hedged share classes.
3   Hedging the currency exposure.

Whether hedging the currency or not, foreign equity investments are volatile. Therefore, you can keep the currency exposure, bearing in mind that you will experience times of disappointing performance when your base currency appreciates. A strong British pound is good when you travel abroad – everything is cheaper. However, it is bad for your un-hedged foreign investments.

The second option is buying funds' currency-hedged share classes. Pay careful attention to whether the share is measured in pound or hedged to pound.

A share denominated in pound means returns are translated into pound. However, you are exposed to the foreign currencies of the fund's assets. A hedged share means the currency exposure of the fund's assets is hedged to the share class' currency, mitigating currency risk.

A perfect hedging means your return equals the return in local currency. In the example of the S&P 500 Index tracker moving up 10% and the pound appreciating 5%, a perfectly hedged return is 10%. The effects of currency fluctuations are removed.

However, in the real world, hedging is not perfect. There are transaction costs and the hedging ratio is not 100%.[20]

One cost or benefit of hedging is differences in short-term interest rates between the home and foreign currencies. For example, if the US dollar short-term rate is 0.5% and that on the British pound is 1%, hedging US dollar back to pound generates a return of 0.5%.

Hedging the dollar is like borrowing in dollars and lending in pounds. Effectively, you offset your long US dollar position with a short position (borrowing in dollars), paying a 0.5% interest rate. You offset your short dollar position with a long position (lending in pounds), collecting a 1% interest rate.

The third option to hedge currency is doing it yourself. You can use derivatives, such as currency forward or futures contracts. This may be unavailable in your pension or ISAs. Another way is borrowing and lending in the respective currencies to offset your currency exposures. But this could be complex to implement and time-consuming to monitor.

When investing in emerging market assets, the cost of hedging might be high and it might be overly complicated, due to a large number of currencies. When investing in emerging market equity and emerging market debt (EMD), accepting currency risk may be a necessity. EMD in hard currency can be easily hedged.

Choosing between hedging and not hedging risk assets should depend on your view on currencies. Thinking your base currency is likely to appreciate, hedge some or all of the foreign currency (all if your conviction is high, half if it is not high). If you think your base currency is likely to depreciate, do not hedge.

When investing in bonds or conservative assets, the rule of thumb is to always hedge their currency exposure. Conservative assets' volatility can more than double with currency risk. The asset can lose its intended role in your portfolio, turning from a conservative to a risk asset. If you are unable to hedge the currency risk, you should probably not invest in foreign conservative assets.

Currency valuation

How could you form a view on currencies?

Evaluating currencies is difficult. Exchange rates should be set by fundamentals (carry, valuation). However, in practice, sentiment and trading patterns (momentum) drive currencies' prices.

Purchasing Power Parity (PPP) is an economic model used to determine currencies' relative values. According to PPP, in the long run, a basket of identical goods and services should cost the same across countries (law of one price). Therefore, exchange rates should move to a rate equalising this basket's price.[21]

For example, according to the **Big Mac Index**, a McDonald's Big Mac should cost the same in London and New York City.[22] If it costs £2.89 in London and $4.79 in NYC, it implies an exchange rate of 1.66 £/$ (one British pound equals 1.66 US dollars).[23]

In practice, goods and services have different prices across countries because of differences in quality, barriers to trade and departures from free competition. Yet, PPP should provide a fair-value, long-term yardstick for currencies.

Another economic model used to estimate future exchange rates is **Covered Interest Rate Parity** (CIRP). CIRP claims that interest rate differential between two currencies equals the differential between the future exchange rate and spot exchange rate.

$$(1 + r_£) = (1 + r_f) F \div S$$

Where $r_£$ is interest rate of local currency, r_f is interest rate of foreign currency, S is spot exchange rate and F is future exchange rate.

For example, say the interest rate of the British pound is 0.50%, that of the US dollar is 0.25% and the spot exchange rate is 1.55. According to CIRP, the future exchange rate is 1.554.[24] This means a currency with a higher interest rate is expected to appreciate versus one with a lower rate (more dollars are needed to buy each pound).

Empirical evidence supports CIRP. Investors are attracted to currencies with higher rates, creating demand and pushing their price upwards. However, like other financial theories, exchange rates can deviate from levels that CIRP and PPP predict for long time periods; sometimes years.

Trading currencies involves costs. Even when your bank does not charge a dealing commission, costs can be embedded in the bid-ask spread. Carefully check the quoted exchange rates for buying and selling currencies.

Rebalancing

Portfolio rebalancing is realigning the portfolio's weights with the target asset allocation weights. Different assets perform differently. Over time, weights of strongly performing assets increase, whilst those of lagging assets decrease.

Once in a while – every 3, 6 or 12 months, depending on asset movements – realign the portfolio by selling strongly performing assets and buying weakly performing ones. Alternatively, instead of selling assets, generating transaction costs, use cash inflows to buy only lagging assets, increasing their relative weights. After retirement, use cash outflows to reduce weights of strongly performing assets.

This ensures the portfolio's asset allocation matches your investment strategy. Otherwise, you might end up with a portfolio drifted from the risk and return profile matching your objectives.

For example, you start with a 50% equity and 50% bond portfolio. In a year, equities returned 18% whilst bonds fell 4%. Your portfolio now has 55% in equities and 45% in bonds.[25] Its risk level is higher than intended, due to higher allocation to equities. Selling 5% equities and buying 5% bonds aligns the portfolio with its 50/50 target allocation.

Rebalancing introduces a healthy discipline of taking profits on winners and buying cheap recent losers. However, use discretion. If you believe bonds are likely to continue dropping, for instance, consider keeping the weights as they are or selling equities and buying cash instead of bonds.

Asset allocation should be adaptive to your current market views when rebalancing your portfolio.

Cash flow management

During the accumulation phase, cash flow management for pension investing normally means you have a standing order to allocate monthly contributions across your choice of funds. Investing on a monthly basis leads to a dollar-cost averaging, avoiding buying at market's peak. Instead, you buy your investments at an average monthly price.

Invest cash quickly; otherwise your portfolio can suffer a **cash drag**. Uninvested cash does not participate in markets, lacking upside or downside. When markets rise, cash drags performance down. When markets fall, cash can help performance. However, before celebrating, it is not a deliberate allocation to cash so it should be avoided unless intended. This is especially relevant when topping up your pension or adding lump sums to ISAs.

During the de-accumulation phase, the direction of cash flows reverses. Cash flow management should focus on minimising taxes and costs.

Normally, you can take a tax-free lump sum of 25% of your pension upon retirement. Following that, you may have to pay income tax on pension drawdowns.

You can take out as much as you want when you want. But spread it over separate tax years to minimise income tax. For example, if every year you take only £10,000, it is tax free within your personal allowance.

Use cash outflows to gradually change your portfolio's strategy. If, for example, you wish to de-risk your portfolio over time, sell more risk assets than conservative assets when raising cash. As your time horizon shrinks, you can gradually increase your portfolio's liquidity by selling some illiquid assets every time cash is raised to generate a cash outflow.

If you live for a couple of years from the tax-free lump sum, or have other sources to finance your living, consider taking about £10,000 tax-free each year out of your pension, adding it to your ISA. Then, after accumulating money in your ISA for a number of years, draw the money without paying income tax.

Drawing capital in volatile markets requires a plan. Limit withdrawals and minimise income, aiming to delay drawing capital at depressed prices. Try drawing investment income instead of capital. Build up a cash buffer, trying to hold one or two years' income, allowing you to sit tight and wait for a recovery.

Summary

- When managing your portfolio, consider the risk, fee and governance budgets.
- A core-satellite portfolio construction considers the three budgets. The core is aligned with SAA (minimising risk), consisting of mainly trackers (minimising fees) and keeping it simple (minimising governance). The satellite aims to add alpha.

- Implementation is translating your investment strategy and fund choices into an actual portfolio. Use ETFs for efficiently implementing short-term views. Use stocks and shares ISAs to complement your pension, if needed.

- Currency fluctuations can have a big impact on results. Either hedge or do not hedge currency of risk assets. Always hedge currency of conservative assets. Buying funds' hedged share classes is the easiest way to hedge currency. Ensure the share class is hedged, not just denominated in British pound.

- Rebalancing is realigning your portfolio with its target weights to correct drifting weights, due to market movements. Use cash flows to rebalance to reduce transaction costs. Rebalance to an allocation adapted to current market views.

- Cash inflows into your pension are normally invested on a monthly basis across your choice of funds. This is dollar-cost averaging. When retiring, spread drawdowns to minimise income tax.

Notes

1 5% = 50% × 8% + 50% × 2%.

2 1.5% = 50% × 2% + 50% × 1%; 0.75% = 50% × 1% + 50% × 0.50%.

3 0.35% = 50% × 0.50% + 50% × 0.20%.

4 40% = 80% × 50%; 32% = 80% × 40%.

5 The main risks of derivatives are **basis risk** (the derivative's return differs from that of the underlying), counterparty risk (for OTC derivatives), complexity, leverage and short selling.

6 Most contracts expire in less than a year. A number of contracts last longer, sometimes more than two years. Many contracts expire quarterly – in March, June, September and December.

7 Go online to check the factsheet of a futures contract or the website of the exchange for details.

8 If you want an exposure of £100,000 to the FTSE 100 Index, either choose one contract for an exposure of £65,000 or two contracts for an exposure of £130,000. You cannot get precisely £100,000.

9 One advantage of futures over forward contracts is that your counterparty is the exchange, effectively eliminating counterparty risk.

10 £16,250 = 25% × £65,000.

11 Cash settlement is settling the futures contract by cash rather than by physical delivery of the underlying asset.

12 The **roll yield** is the yield holders of futures capture when a futures contract converges with the spot price. It is positive when the futures curve is in backwardation and negative when the curve is in contango.

13 A **contract for differences** (CFD) is a derivative agreement between a buyer and seller, whereby the seller pays the buyer the difference between the current price of an asset and its price in the future. If the difference is negative, the buyer pays the difference to the seller.

14 The strike price is above spot price for a call option or the strike price is below the spot price for a put option.

15 Payoff of a call option is strike price (X) minus spot price (S). Payoff of a put option is spot price minus strike price. $C = Max (0,X - S)$ and $P = Max (0,S - X)$. Where C and P are payoffs of call (C) and put (P) options.

16 £300 = £7,300 − £7,000; £100 = £300 − £200.

17 £5,00 = £6,000 − £5,500; £300 = £500 − £200.

18 Some option strategies risk more than the premium, such a naked put or call writing (selling). Uncovered put or call is selling options without shorting or holding the underlying for coverage.

19 More precisely, the return is $4.76\% = (1 + 10\%) \div (1 + 5\%) - 1$.

20 Hedging ratio is the ratio between the market values of the hedging instruments and hedged assets. For example, when holding $1 million US stocks and to hedge the currency using a forward contract with a market value of $950,000, the hedge ratio is 95%. The hedge ratio changes because the values of the hedged assets and hedging instrument are not perfectly correlated. This is called **basis risk**.

21 The Organisation for Economic Co-operation and Development (OECD) and the International Monetary Fund (IMF) publish PPP statistics and implied exchange rates at **www.oecd.org** and **www.imf.org**.

22 *The Economist* invented the Big Mac Index in 1986. Check **www.economist.com/content/big-mac-index** for an interactive currency comparison tool.

23 $1.66 = \$4.79 \div £2.89$.

24 $1.554 = (1 + 0.50\%) \div (1 + 0.25\%) 1.55$.

25 The starting allocation is £50 equity and £50 bonds for every £100. After a year, the value of equities is £59 = £50 × (1 + 18%), of bonds is £48 = £50 × (1 − 4%) and that of each £100 is £107 = £59 + £48. New equity weight is 55.1% = £59 ÷ £107 and bond weight is 44.9% = £48 ÷ £107.

CHAPTER 22
MANAGING RISKS
Controlling risks along the journey

'There are old pilots, and there are bold pilots, but there are no old, bold pilots.'

E. Hamilton Lee

The core of investing is bearing and managing risks. You need risk to generate returns. But you need to control it to limit losses. In particular, you must mitigate the risk of ruin – losing so much that recovering the losses is unlikely, for example, because of insufficient time.

Managing risks involves two separate activities: risk measurement and risk management. Risk measurement quantifies risks. Risk management is deciding which risks to take, which risks to mitigate and how to do so.

In this chapter we review some risk measurement and management techniques. We keep it simple, assuming you do not have access to sophisticated risk management tools.

Risk measurement

Volatility

The easiest risk measurement is calculating portfolio volatility. Use your risk capital market assumptions (CMAs), applying them to your SAA (using SAA weights and indices representing asset classes), as long as your portfolio does not deviate significantly from it. To be precise, use the portfolio's weights to funds, their volatilities and your correlation CMAs amongst assets to calculate portfolio volatility.

However, sourcing all required data might be difficult. Some online platforms calculate your portfolio volatility.

Translate volatility to downside risk, linking it with your risk tolerance. Assume that in 19 of 20 years return will not be worse than two standard deviations below the mean, in particular when holding a multi-asset, well diversified portfolio.

Stress testing

Stress testing is a simulation technique measuring how a portfolio should perform under different situations.

Historic stress testing takes the returns of assets during a crisis (such as the 2000 technology bubble burst or the 2008 crisis), applies them to your asset allocation and calculates its hypothetical performance.

The advantages of historic stress testing are that it considers actual historic events (no need to imagine anything), it accounts for correlations amongst assets and it is simple. The disadvantage is that it assumes history repeats itself.

Instead of historic stress testing, you can hypothetically push assets, calculating how asset allocation would react (such as pushing equities down 20%). However, you need to assume how other assets in your portfolio, such as gilts, would perform, considering correlations amongst assets.[1]

For example, your asset allocation is 50% UK equities, 40% gilts and 10% cash. You want to understand how it would have performed during some crises. Table 22.1 shows the results.

Table 22.1 Historic and hypothetical stress testing

Stress test (returns %)	UK equity	Gilts	Cash	Asset allocation
1998: May 1998 to Sep 1998	−13.5	9.0	3.2	−4.2
2000: Jan 2000 to Jan 2003	−43.6	24.3	16.7	−14.7
2008: Nov 2007 to Feb 2009	−39.4	13.0	6.9	−17.8
2011: May 2011 to Sep 2011	−14.0	9.6	0.3	−4.5
Hypothetical I	−20.0	10.0	0.5	−8.0
Hypothetical II	8.0	2.0	1.0	5.7

Source: Bloomberg, FTSE 100 Index, iBoxx £ Gilts Index, UK Cash LIBOR TR 1 Month Index. Based on monthly total returns, measured in £

Scenario analysis

Scenario analysis imagines a number of potential alternative futures with different outcomes. Each scenario estimates asset returns. Assign probabilities to scenarios (base case, upside surprise and downside surprise) trying to position your portfolio to perform reasonably well under different possible events, not a single one.

The trick is you need creativity when thinking about scenarios.

Risk management

There are four risk management techniques:

1 Diversification.
2 Hedging.
3 Insurance.
4 Active management.

Diversification is a proven way to reduce idiosyncratic risk, leaving your portfolio with market risk. It needs to be done properly, ensuring you diversify across imperfectly correlated assets. It should be dynamic since assets' characteristics and correlations change over time.

Hedging is reducing risk of an asset by taking an opposite position in a similar or highly correlated asset. When the first asset falls, the hedging position should appreciate, offsetting some losses.

Hedging is normally done when you do not want to sell the hedged asset due to transaction costs, you are unable to sell it, you do not want to sell it because risks are short-lived or you want to remove exposure to an unrewarded or specific risk.

For example, you hold a global equity fund, with a large exposure to the US dollar (the US equity market makes about 50% of global equities). You think the British pound is likely to appreciate against the dollar. You hedge by buying a hedged share class or by selling dollars and buying pounds with a currency forward.

Insurance is a financial instrument that should generate a payoff when other assets fall. Insurance costs a fee (premium). If the other assets do not fall, you still pay it. If the assets fall, you gain.

For example, put options on equity indices is a type of insurance. You pay a premium. If equity markets fall, the value of your options can appreciate. If equity markets do not fall, the premium is lost. However, with equity exposure elsewhere, the portfolio can still generate positive returns.

Insurance's objective is limiting the downside, not enhancing returns. You buy fire insurance on your house, hoping never to use it. When buying insurance, prepare a budget of how much you are willing to spend on insuring your portfolio. Insurance costs can haemorrhage performance – keep an eye on spendings.

Options cost more when volatility is high and less when it is low. Try buying options when volatility is low, when demand for insurance is weak, as markets are calm. However, when markets are nervous, insurance cost rises. You need to buy insurance before the event, not during or after it.

Buying long-duration govies is also a way to insure your portfolio. When equity markets crash and there is a flight to quality, investors may rush into the safety of govies. They should perform well, offsetting some of equities' poor performance.

Active management is taking dynamic decisions to manage risks. It usually should precede the risky event. Otherwise, taking action after the fact might be too late.

For example, you have a 50% equity and 50% bond portfolio. Yields of 10-year gilts are at a 2% level. You think they might rise to above 3% since the UK economy accelerates. You can reduce your gilt exposure to 30% and increase your equity allocation or allocate some to cash to reduce risk.

If you did not take any action and yields have, indeed, risen to 3% then you need to decide whether to take action or if it is too late. You have already lost on your gilts. This is sunk cost. The question is whether you think yields are likely to move higher from here or fall back lower – look ahead, not backward.

If you still think they are likely to move higher, sell some gilts. If you think they are likely to fall back, keep holding your position or buy more gilts because their price is more attractive now.

Risk management is a continuous activity. Always think about what can go wrong.

Implementing a solution

We have almost reached the end of the investment management process. After formulating objectives, designing a plan and implementing it, it is now time to review. Are you on track to achieve your goals? Is the plan working? Do you need to change and adapt anything?

Answering such questions is the role of reviewing.

Summary

- Risk measurement is quantifying your portfolio's risk.

- Volatility is the simplest way to measure risk. However, downside risk is the true risk of investing.

- Stress test your portfolio to understand how it would have performed during different situations.

- Risk management is actions and techniques to control portfolio risks. The four types of risk management techniques are: (1) diversification; (2) hedging; (3) insurance; and (4) active management.

Note

1 Monte Carlo simulation is often used for stress testing. The simulator generates random returns of assets, considering parameters such as their return distributions and correlations. Repeating the process many times produces a simulated distribution of the portfolio's returns.

CHAPTER 23
REVIEWING

Are you on track to achieve your objectives?

'True genius resides in the capacity for evaluation of uncertain, hazardous and conflicting information.'

Winston Churchill

We are at the final stage of the investment management process: reviewing. After setting objectives, formulating an investment strategy and implementing a solution, it is time to review everything. Assess how the portfolio is doing and whether anything needs altering.

The first objective of reviewing your portfolio's performance is checking whether you are on track to achieve your objectives. Given performance, decide whether you need to adjust your strategy or objectives.

If performance is ahead of objectives and you have accumulated more than planned up to this point, consider either reducing risk since you require lower returns going forward, or increasing risk because you are able to absorb higher losses.

If performance lags objectives, consider either increasing risk because you need higher returns to achieve your goals, or settle for more modest objectives. Differentiate between required and desired goals when deciding.

This is **path-dependent** dynamic risk budgeting. Think about changing the target value of your portfolio at retirement – higher if results are better than planned, lower if worse. The decision depends on the remaining time to retirement. A long time allows to raise risk, while a short time probably means adjusting expectations downward.

Reviewing's second objective is to understand where performance is coming from. Is it SAA, active asset allocation or security selection in your active funds?

Adapt your philosophy and strategy, based on results. If you consistently add value through active asset allocation, perhaps you are skilled and should continue doing it. If you consistently destroy value, perhaps stop doing it. If your selection of active funds adds value, consider continuing to use active funds. If they underperform, consider switching to trackers.

Reaching conclusions requires time. A couple of years of good or bad performance are not sufficient to draw any meaningful conclusions about your talents and track record. Performance should, ideally, be assessed over a full economic cycle.

When comparing funds' performance, ensure it is measured over the same time period. Some DC platforms show fund performance, but it is measured since you bought each fund, not over the same period. Compare likes with likes.

High frequency reviewing is appraising performance often (such as daily or weekly). It can cause undue stress, leading to rush decisions. For example, you might decide to sell a fund just because it underperformed recently. However, managers need time to deliver performance. Judging performance over a short time can be counterproductive.

On the other hand, review performance periodically. Reviewing your portfolio once a quarter is a good frequency for an overview. But it is too short to make decisions on buying and selling funds.

Benchmarks and benchmarking

Benchmarking is measuring performance against some standard. For example, is a return of +10% good or bad? Well, it depends. Against a benchmark of +5% it is good, but against a benchmark of +20% it is bad.

When managing your portfolio, use three benchmarks. The first is the most important: your investment objectives. Compare return against your return objective, as well as risk against your risk objective.

The second benchmark is your SAA composite benchmark. It measures your SAA's performance without active asset allocation or security selection. It helps to measure whether your actual portfolio performs in line with strategy. It shows whether your actions, like TAA and fund selection, add value.

The third benchmark is comparing each fund you select with its benchmark. This allows monitoring whether the funds you are using deliver. Each benchmark should fit each fund's style (for example, a value equity fund should be compared to a value equity index).

Peer group benchmarking

Often, active funds' performance is compared to that of peer groups – the median or average performance of all funds in a category. Whilst peer comparison is helpful to rank managers, your default choice is trackers. Consider active funds only if they are likely to outperform index trackers. The appropriate benchmark for active funds is trackers, not passive indices. The latter are not directly investable.

For example, you are contemplating buying a UK equity fund. The peer group median return is 5%. A fund you consider returned 10%, putting it in the top quartile amongst peers. However, an ETF tracking the FTSE 100 Index returned 15%. The fund is good compared to other active funds, but, during the specific time period, most active funds underperformed the passive index. You are paying extra fees for an active fund to do better than trackers, not to do better than peers.

Nevertheless, peer group comparison can help to identify managers with potential skill. Perhaps, during specific times, all managers struggle to outperform the index. However, in other times, good managers can outperform.

Morningstar publishes an active/passive barometer. It can help you to understand during which time periods and for which asset classes active managers generally do better or worse.

Summary

- The first objective of reviewing performance is confirming whether you are on track to achieve your objectives.
- Path-dependent risk budgeting means changing risk level based on results.
- Reviewing is used to understand performance's drivers to adjust your strategy accordingly. Focus on what you are doing well – buy-and-hold SAA, active asset allocation or selection of active funds.
- Do not rush to reach conclusions based on results – ideally, assess results over a full economic cycle.
- Benchmarking puts performance in context.
- Peer group benchmarking helps you to spot potentially skilful managers. However, you pay a fee for active funds to outperform index trackers, not to outperform other active funds.

CHAPTER 24
YOUR FINANCIAL LIFE PLAN

A step-by-step financial plan for your life

'Know from where you have come and to where you are heading.'

Pirkei Avot

First, congratulations for reaching this chapter! If you have read the entire book, in particular the section on taxes, well done!

Second, this is it.

Now, after reading the whole book, you should know what you need to know and what you need to do. Take the actions to financially secure your retirement.

In this chapter, we will go through a list of general points to remember and then through each decade of your life, suggesting what you should consider. Whatever your age is, read what you should have done and try to catch up.

Main takeaways

It is difficult to summarise the main key points, but here are the top dozen.

1 **Plan, start early and be efficient.** Formulate a plan, visioning your desired outcome (accumulating assets that can generate real income for the rest of your post-retirement life) and how to achieve it. The plan is likely to change but at least it pushes you to take action and move in the direction of your target. Start saving early in a pension. Maximise tax reliefs. Minimise taxes, charges and costs. Learn and educate yourself.

2 **Use ISAs.** Supplement your pension with ISAs. Whilst they do not benefit from tax relief, they give you flexibility, choice and a tax shelter.

3 **Diversify your income.** Aim to diversify your sources of income when retiring, such as annuity, income-generating investments and properties to let.

4 **Buy your home.** Own your house. Aim to pay off the mortgage by retirement. You need a place to live and an owned house is a source of wealth.

5 **Invest, take investment risk and diversify.** Take investment risk to generate investment returns. Not taking sufficient risk is a risk you might regret. The biggest risks are outliving your assets and not having enough assets to live comfortably after retirement. Aim to generate investment returns in line with your risk tolerance, increasing the chances of reaching your planned financial goals. Diversify your investments to reduce risk.

6 **If you are up to it, use active management.** If you are committed and skilled, use dynamic SAA, TAA and active funds to add precious alpha. Every little helps over the long run, empowered by compounding. If you are not committed and skilled, keep it simple. Stick with SAA, using mostly trackers. Choosing in which asset classes to invest (asset allocation) has more impact than which securities or funds you choose.

7 **It is a long journey, so break it up.** Break up your journey into separate phases: accumulation, consolidation and de-accumulation. Set up clear investment objectives and constraints for each phase, with an investment strategy and an anchor SAA. Stick with your long-term plan.

8 **Maximise contributions.** Your contributions should be about 10% to 20% of income. Maximise your employer's contributions. Aim to take advantage of your full annual allowances. Carry forward unused annual allowances from the previous three years. More money in means more money out.

9 **Reverse-engineer your target return.** Think about the target amount to save by the end of the consolidation stage. Aim for an amount to generate at least half of your current salary to maintain your current standard of living. Use annuity rate to calculate the income. Given time and contributions, work out the target return and risk level needed to achieve your goal.

10 **Use a glide path in the consolidation phase.** The consolidation phase needs a dynamic investment strategy, managing the glide path from current to target asset allocation. Apply discretion, avoiding selling just after a market crash. Prepare up to 25% in cash for a tax-free lump sum. Consider an annuity to deliver minimum required income and address some longevity risk. Invest in long-term bonds to hedge annuity price. Invest the rest of the portfolio to generate income and inflation-linked growth, whilst allowing flexibility to tap the assets.

11 **Continue investing post-retirement.** The de-accumulation phase emphasises income and capital preservation, ensuring you are left with sufficient money, even if you live longer than expected. Pace your drawdowns to minimise income tax and to ensure you do not deplete your assets.

12 **Manage your wealth to achieve different goals.** Separate your wealth into three buckets: (1) safe bucket to maintain a minimum standard of living and reserves for emergencies (cash, annuity, insured owned house); (2) market bucket with a diversified exposure to capital markets, matching your investment objectives in a tax-efficient wrapper, to maintain your current standard of living; and (3) speculative bucket to generate high returns (open a business, invest in a private company, buy-to-let property), trying to improve your standard of living.

Decade by decade

We now review the main points to consider at each decade of your life.

Your 20s

In your 20s you may finish higher education, travel, get your first full-time job with a decent salary and enjoy your youth. This is one of the best decades in your life – make the most of it.

Retirement is so far away you do not think about it. Anyway, there are other pressing financial priorities. You are at the beginning of your early accumulation phase. It is never too early to start your financial planning.

Sort out your debt. If you earn more than your living expenses, repay personal loans, overdrafts and credit card debt. These loans come with relatively high interest rates. The longer they are outstanding, the more interest you pay. It is a waste.

Open your first ISAs. Aim to save as much as possible in ISAs. Not using your maximum saving amounts every tax year is losing them.

Experiment with investing. Within your ISAs, start investing some money. You are gaining invaluable experience. Learning how to invest is a long process. Experiment with buying individual securities and funds. Mistakes cost money and you are going to lose along the way. Being humbled by markets, feeling the pain of losing are life lessons. 'One who can't endure the bad won't live to see the good.' With experience, find your unique investing style. Read a book or two on investing, read the economic sections in newspapers.

Join a workplace pension. If your employer offers a workplace pension scheme, join it. If your employer contributes to it, take this benefit. You do not need to start contributing to your pension at this early stage. However, if your budget allows it, contribute. The earlier you start, the better. Acquire the habit of pension savings.

Your 30s

In your 30s you may get married, start a family, purchase a house with a mortgage, buy a family car and progress at your work. You are likely to have increasing responsibilities, income and expenses. Life is getting serious.

During this decade you may move from early to late accumulation phase, depending on your planned retirement age. Most likely, however, you do not know yet when you are likely to retire. It depends on your career and aspirations.

Consider taking professional advice. HMRC rules are not simple and they keep changing.

Prepare a budget. Consider your earnings and expenses. You may start a family and have dependents, such as young children. Keep some cash reserve for contingencies.

Decide whether to buy a house. Buying your house with a mortgage is an investment for the future and a disciplined way for long-term saving. Save for a deposit. Shop around for a suitable mortgage. Ensure your budget accommodates the mortgage payments. Buying a small house is better than not buying your dream house. Jump on the property ladder as soon as possible.

Sort out your debt. Finish repaying any expensive short-term debt. Consider increasing the mortgage on your house to pay off other debt since the interest rate is probably lower. Consolidate your debt to simplify.

Start your pension saving. If your employer offers a workplace pension, join it. Your employer's contributions are, effectively, a pay rise. Consider supplementing your workplace pension with a personal pension. SIPP is the most flexible.

Formulate your investment strategy. Most workplace pension schemes put you in a default fund. However, it may not fit your financial needs. Usually, the default fund is a multi-asset diversified fund. However, your time horizon is long. You should probably invest more in equities if it matches your risk tolerance – potentially 100% in equities. Blend equities with the default fund or do it yourself. SIPP and stocks and shares ISAs provide choice.

Maximise ISA savings. Aim to maximise savings in ISAs. If you do not want to invest, use cash ISAs not to lose the allowances. If you need to choose between saving in ISAs and contributing to your pension, pension is probably more tax-efficient because of tax relief. However, ISAs have more flexibility because you can access your savings at any time.

Your 40s

Life is getting more serious. The children are possibly a bit older. Whilst you are past nappies and waking up in the middle of the night, they bring new experiences. Bigger children mean bigger challenges. You may be a late starter with children or have another last baby.

Hopefully, you have progressed at work. You may reach the peak of your earning power. Midlife crisis may strike.

You are moving from early accumulation to late accumulation. You may move to the consolidation phase, depending on your target retirement age.

Take retirement saving seriously. Retirement is not around the corner, but it is on the horizon. If you have not started pension saving, it is not too late. However, start now. If you do not have a workplace pension, start a personal one. Carry over unused annual allowances from the previous three years to maximise contributions. Use bonuses and pay rises to boost pension savings. Escalate proportional contributions as your salary rises. Continue building your ISAs. Use the maximum annual allowances and maximise savings into ISAs.

Plan for retirement. Think when you want to retire and the quality of life you would like. Calculate your required annual income, assuming it is at least half your current income. Think about your changing income needs throughout retirement, not just at its beginning. Imagine how dependent you are going to be on income from your savings, considering other income sources. Work out the target value of your portfolio at retirement, taking annuity rates as a conservative assumption about income. Separate return objectives between required and desired. Work out the risk level you need, assuming a 0.50 Sharpe ratio, with the current risk-free cash rate.

Investment strategy. Formulate a strategy based on your goals. Considering your contributions, calculate your target rate of returns to achieve your required and desired target portfolios' values. Set a strategy to maximise the probability of achieving your required value. If risk tolerance allows, aim for a strategy that can achieve the desired target as well.

Design a glide path. When entering the consolidation phase, design a glide path to the target asset allocation. The glide path should start about 10 years before retirement. Use discretion, not a completely mechanical approach. If equity markets crash or correct, do not sell unless you must. Stay invested for recovery. If gilt yields are low, invest in investment grade credit and other fixed income investments. Push forward and back decisions, trying to better time changes. However, try using dollar-cost averaging to buy and sell at average prices across years. De-risk your portfolio as you approach retirement. You cannot risk a large drawdown just before you need the money.

Consider starting to build a buy-to-let portfolio. If your budget permits it and it matches your personality, consider buy-to-let. Save for a deposit. Ensure you do not over-leverage yourself. If you take a variable mortgage, run scenarios on what happens if rates rise.

Start saving for your children. Use Junior ISAs to save for your children. They will need the money for university, wedding and deposit on a house. You might end up helping them anyway, so start saving for it in tax-sheltered ISAs. Open a pension for your children, benefiting from a base rate tax relief.

Your 50s

Now, get really serious about your pension. This is probably the most important decade for retirement planning. The children may not need your financial support, but elderly parents might do. You are likely to reach the peak of your earning power in this decade.

Decide broadly when you wish to retire and plan accordingly. Think about the income level you would like to generate from your portfolio after retirement. Decide whether your goal is achievable. Amend it if it is not. Separate your goals between required and desired objectives.

You may reach retirement in this decade when you are 55. It depends on your life style, career and how much you have saved. If you saved enough to support your desired standard of living, you have an option. If you have not saved enough, you need to keep working, saving more. Another 10 years of saving to the age of 65 can make a big difference.

Analyse your situation. Take a holistic count of your current portfolio, including investments, pensions (including State Pension, DB and DC) and property for both you and your partner. Ensure asset allocation matches your risk tolerance. Liquidity should match plans of using money. Diversify across assets and within assets, ensuring you invest in assets that perform differently, not just lowly correlated with each other.

De-risk your portfolio and begin the glide path. Once you decide on the income level and investment strategy post-retirement, start positioning your portfolio accordingly. Consider buying an annuity with some of your portfolio to address longevity risk and provide guaranteed income. Deferred annuity can generate a higher income later in life when other assets are depleted. Phase out volatility from a portion of your portfolio, moving it gradually into long-term bonds to hedge the price of an annuity. Formulate a flexible income and capital preservation investment strategy pegged to inflation post-retirement. Shift your portfolio over time to the target asset allocation. Move away from some equities into more conservative assets, reducing the impact of an equity market dip just before accessing the money.

Use a SIPP. Consider using a SIPP to have more control over your investments. Choose a platform considering investment choice, charges and online service, matching your style and needs.

Maximise contributions. Your earnings from work should be decent. Your living expenses should come down. You may have finished paying your mortgage and the children may be more independent. Whilst they may still need financial support, balance between that and ensuring you save enough to support yourself after retirement, which could last long (longevity). This is also for the benefit of the children since you do not want to be a financial burden on them. Maximise your pension contributions, especially if you are a higher-rate or additional-rate taxpayer. It is now or never.

Your 60s

You are now in or close to retirement. You need to make important decisions about how your pension is going to generate income during your retirement and whether to stay invested.

Take professional advice. Some of your decisions are final and irrevocable. For example, purchasing an annuity with some of your money – you will have the flexibility to change this decision only when a secondary annuity market is introduced. It is important to take professional advice from an Independent Financial Adviser (IFA) for a fee before taking action. Do not rely on advice from your drinking buddy or mates at work. Shop around for the most competitive annuity rate across different providers.

Flexible pension drawdowns. With flexibility and pension freedom, instead of buying an annuity, keep some of your pension pot and drawdown on it when you wish. This allows for greater control over income. Phase drawdowns over tax years, minimising tax. Maintain access to money in the pension if you need a lump sum. Blend annuity's guaranteed income and unsecured pension's flexibility. Plan how to drawdown income during volatile markets.

Sort out your debt. Hopefully, you are close to paying off your mortgage on your home or you have paid it. Consider using the tax-free lump sum from your pension to settle remaining debt. Your children could be a liability if they are financially dependent on you. Discuss all these obligations with your IFA before committing to an annuity.

Keep working. Many people in their 60s are still able, willing and interested in continuing to work. The government is set to prohibit employers from forcing staff to retire at 65. Choose whether to continue working, delaying withdrawing pension benefits and even topping up your pension pot.

Your 70s and beyond

Hopefully, after planning for many years for retirement, saving and taking the right investment decisions, you can enjoy your golden age with financial security.

At some point, you may need to spend more on healthcare. You may require professional care or accommodation.

Simplify. Plan for simple income generation at the late stage of your life because your financial decision making might be impaired. Use a deferred annuity to kick in at an older age. De-risk your portfolio to a simple asset allocation using trackers. If you own properties to let, engage a reliable property management company.

Think about estate planning. Your financial planning can shift to leaving an inheritance to your beneficiaries and mitigating IHT through estate planning. Discuss it with your IFA and solicitor. Pensions are not subject to IHT. Ensure you fill in a nomination form. Your ISAs can be transferred to your spouse tax-free, keeping the tax shelter. Draft a will, naming your spouse as the heir of your ISAs. Annuities cannot be passed on to your children. The flexibility to pass on your pension and ISAs is an incentive to keep investing all your life to preserve and, perhaps, grow your capital.

Enjoy. Enjoy your retirement. Financial security allows you to spend time with your loved ones, travel, invest in hobbies, learn and write a book.

Good health, good wealth and good luck.

INDEX